ECONOMIC ISSUES, PROBLEMS AND PERSPECTIVES

PUBLIC DEBT

IMPACT, MANAGEMENT AND CHALLENGES

Economic Issues, Problems and Perspectives

Additional books and e-books in this series can be found on Nova's website under the Series tab.

ECONOMIC ISSUES, PROBLEMS AND PERSPECTIVES

PUBLIC DEBT

IMPACT, MANAGEMENT AND CHALLENGES

ANTOINE BÉLANGER

EDITOR

nova
science publishers
New York

Library of Congress Cataloging-in-Publication Data

Names: Bélanger, Antoine, editor.
Title: Public debt : impact, management and challenges / edited by Antoine Bélanger.
Description: Hauppauge : Nova Science Publishers, 2021. | Series: Economic issues, problems and perspectives | Includes bibliographical references and index. |
Identifiers: LCCN 2021008281 (print) | LCCN 2021008282 (ebook) | ISBN 9781536193268 (paperback) | ISBN 9781536193749 (adobe pdf)
Subjects: LCSH: Debts, Public. | Monetary policy. | Taylor's rule. | Expenditures, Public.
Classification: LCC HJ8015 .P8223 2021 (print) | LCC HJ8015 (ebook) | DDC 336.3/4--dc23
LC record available at https://lccn.loc.gov/2021008281
LC ebook record available at https://lccn.loc.gov/2021008282

Published by Nova Science Publishers, Inc. † New York

CONTENTS

Preface		**vii**
Chapter 1	Monetary Policy and Width of Public Debt Externalities in a Monetary Union *Séverine Menguy*	**1**
Chapter 2	Is There a Level of Public Debt that Impairs Economic Growth? In Search of a Theory *Roberto Tamborini and Matteo Tomaselli*	**65**
Chapter 3	Are There Limits to Public Debt in Neo-Classical Growth Models with Involuntary Unemployment? *Karl Farmer*	**115**
Chapter 4	Do Central Banks Engage in Public Debt Management? The Case of Emerging Markets Inflation Targeters With Floating Exchange Rates *Joanna Mackiewicz-Łyziak and Dagmara Mycielska*	**163**
Index		**189**

PREFACE

This book comprises four chapters, each of which examines public debt from a specific economic perspective. Chapter 1 studies potential fiscal externalities of the public debt in the framework of a monetary union. Chapter 2 examines the theoretical literature concerning how and if public debt impairs economic growth and finds no univocal and straightforward answer. Chapter 3 discusses the economic impact of the SARS-CoV-2 virus and addresses the question of whether limits to public debt ought to be respected or disregarded in the face of huge unemployment, collapsing tax revenues, and generous public expenditure programs. Lastly, Chapter 4 analyzes the response of central banks in emerging inflation targeting countries with floating exchange rates to changes in public debt.

Chapter 1 - This chapter studies potential fiscal externalities of the public debt in the framework of a monetary union. The common monetary policy of the central bank is contractionary (increase of the nominal interest rate) in case of symmetric positive demand shocks, and expansionary (monetary accommodation) in case of shocks on the average public debt to GDP ratio in the monetary union. However, the monetary policy of an institutionally very independent central bank, and/or which could commit regarding its future monetary policy, would be less active, which would increase macro-economic fluctuations in case of demand shocks. On the contrary, monetary policy is more active if the central bank is subject to budgetary pressures, and if stabilizing the global indebtedness in the monetary union is a secondary goal of this central bank. Such a less independent monetary policy reduces the consequences of demand shocks on economic activity and on the labor market. Nevertheless, the monetary reaction function of a more dependent central bank introduces new fluctuations in case of shocks on the average public debt of the member countries. In the same way, a central bank which would be concerned with the situation of each member country, beyond average variables in the monetary union, would limit macro-economic fluctuations in a country affected by an asymmetric national demand shock; but this would introduce new fluctuations in case of an asymmetric shock on the public debt of a given country.

Chapter 2 - Beyond inconclusive empirical research, this chapter examines the theoretical literature concerning public debt and economic growth finding no univocal and straightforward answer. No meaningful assessment of debt and its effect on growth at any point in time is possible without reference to the whole debt trajectory and the specific state of the economy along the trajectory. An orderly and consistent analysis may be developed along two coordinates of debt assessment: sustainability/ unsustainability, and efficiency/inefficiency. In the authors' view, research should concentrate on the study of specific conditions and cases, and abandon the pursuit of a general law.

Chapter 3 - Governments in advanced countries are currently striving to combat the disastrous economic effects of SARS-CoV-2 related lockdowns by providing generous public expenditure programs. Simultaneously, tax revenues are collapsing due to the dramatic rise in unemployment, failing business earnings and tax deferrals. As a result, the deficits of federal and state governments are exploding. Unemployment rates in all advanced countries have risen to heights not seen since the Great Depression. Thus, the question arises as to whether, in the face of huge unemployment, limits to public debt can and/or ought to be respected, or simply disregarded. Limits to public debt are a standard feature of neo-classical growth models. To the best of the present author's knowledge,

Rankin and Roffia (2003) were the first to detect such limits to government debt in their Diamond-type overlapping-generations (OLG) model with internal public debt. However, as their model assumes full employment, it contrasts starkly with current lockdown-conditions involving high levels of involuntary unemployment. Thus, use is made here of a neo-classical growth model with involuntary unemployment, à la Farmer and Kuplen (2018), in order to investigate whether limits to public debt exist under involuntary unemployment and under full employment. The basic model version with exogenous growth reveals that absolute limits to public debt do exist and that they occur where the unemployment rate becomes zero. While this may be of some theoretical interest, from an empirical perspective it has become more important to investigate the possible connection between public debt and output growth. Does rising debt lead to diminished growth? By extending the basic model version so as to incorporate human capital accumulation and the crowding out of aggregate investment by private and public savings, a debt threshold can indeed be detected. In fact, the numerical values and the growth impact revealed by the extended model, are found to be close to World Bank estimates.

Chapter 4 - In this chapter, the authors analyze the response of central banks in emerging inflation targeting countries with floating exchange rates to changes in public debt. Using panel data the authors estimate Taylor-rule type central banks' reaction functions including government debt as one of the determinants of the policy interest rates. The authors argue that, on the one hand, the central bank observing increasing public debt may try to discipline fiscal authorities by increasing interest rates. On the other hand, increasing public debt may threaten macroeconomic stability and high interest rates translate into higher interest payments that in turn increase public debt further. In this situation, the central bank, trying to prevent the accumulation of debt, may react by lowering interest rates. However, this dilemma is complicated further if a significant proportion of the public debt is denominated in foreign currency as it is often the case of emerging market economies. The authors' findings suggest that central banks in emerging economies tend to lower interest rates in response to increase in government debt denominated in domestic currency and to increase interest rates in response to an increase in government debt denominated in foreign currency. This reaction may suggest a fiscal dominance regime.

In: Public Debt
Editor: Antoine Bélanger
ISBN: 978-1-53619-326-8

Chapter 1

MONETARY POLICY AND WIDTH OF PUBLIC DEBT EXTERNALITIES IN A MONETARY UNION

Séverine Menguy*
Université de Paris, Paris, France

ABSTRACT

This chapter studies potential fiscal externalities of the public debt in the framework of a monetary union. The common monetary policy of the central bank is contractionary (increase of the nominal interest rate) in case of symmetric positive demand shocks, and expansionary (monetary accommodation) in case of shocks on the average public debt to GDP ratio in the monetary union. However, the monetary policy of an institutionally very independent central bank, and/or which could commit regarding its future monetary policy, would be less active, which would increase macro-economic fluctuations in case of demand shocks. On the contrary, monetary policy is more active if the central bank is subject to budgetary pressures, and if stabilizing the global indebtedness in the

* Corresponding Author's E-mail: severine.menguy@orange.fr.

monetary union is a secondary goal of this central bank. Such a less independent monetary policy reduces the consequences of demand shocks on economic activity and on the labor market. Nevertheless, the monetary reaction function of a more dependent central bank introduces new fluctuations in case of shocks on the average public debt of the member countries. In the same way, a central bank which would be concerned with the situation of each member country, beyond average variables in the monetary union, would limit macro-economic fluctuations in a country affected by an asymmetric national demand shock; but this would introduce new fluctuations in case of an asymmetric shock on the public debt of a given country.

Keywords: demand shocks, public debt shocks, monetary policy, fiscal policy, monetary union

1. Introduction

Monetary unification implies large and new externalities between the member countries of a monetary union: between populations (migration), for goods and services (commercial externalities), for financial markets, social protection (social dumping) but also budgetary and fiscal externalities (tax competition, public debt externalities). They have been widely studied in the economic literature. In the European framework, it is then often underlined that the Common Market has favored the mobility of goods and services, whereas the European Economic and Monetary Union (EMU) has, perhaps, not sufficiently taken into account the wide fiscal implications of monetary unification.

Indeed, in case of flexible exchange rates, an expansionary budgetary policy can increase demand and the interest rate in the national country, which implies an appreciation of the national currency. The increase of net exports of the foreign countries can then increase their demand and imply positive fiscal externalities for the partner countries. On the contrary, in case of fixed exchange rates, an expansionary budgetary policy and/or a higher public debt level in a given member country increases the common interest rate for all the monetary union. So, despite the rise in net exports, this can be contractionary for global demand (private consumption replaced by saving, and weaker investment) in the foreign countries, and imply negative fiscal externalities for the partner countries in the monetary union. Therefore, the incentive for an individual member country to conduct an excessively expansionary budgetary policy harmful to its partners is a fear usually mentioned in the literature on monetary unification. Indeed, in a monetary union, a fiscal expansion doesn't imply anymore risk of exchange rate variation. Besides, even with 'no bail-out clauses', countries may expect the assistance of partner countries if they suffer a public debt crisis; or at least, the financial weight of the increase of the common interest rate is shared with other partner countries.

The goal of the current chapter is to study more precisely public debt externalities in the context of a monetary union, particularly those passing through the monetary policy of the common central bank. In the framework of a monetary union, the public debt level cannot remain only a purely national concern. Indeed, in the context of the European Economic and Monetary Union, for example, we have observed a clear convergence and increased correlation between interest rates on governments' bonds of the national countries. So, the weak risk premiums don't seem to reflect anymore the width of the differentials associated with the more or less sane fiscal situations of the European countries; new and strong fiscal and public debt externalities undoubtedly emerge between the member countries of a monetary union. But does monetary unification automatically imply higher negative externalities of a higher budgetary deficit or public debt for the other member countries of the monetary union? The answer is not obvious.

A high public debt makes government solvency very dependent on the interest rate, which significantly impacts the fiscal balance, and therefore, on the monetary policy. In the extreme situation of excessive public debt levels, it becomes even impossible to achieve simultaneously fiscal solvency (respect of the budgetary constraint) and to avoid an out-bidding of the inflation rate (respect of price stability). Therefore, a high public debt level increases the probability of fiscal dominance in the future, of a situation where monetary policy loses part of its independence and efficiency. In an extreme theoretical framework, the Fiscal Theory of the Price Level assesses that when debt sustainability becomes questionable, increases of nominal interest rates for a long period would be dangerous, as they could force the debtor either to default, or to inflate the debt away, in contradiction to the price stability goal. So, the only solution seems to avoid excessive nominal interest rates for highly indebted countries, even if risk premiums would require to do so. Therefore, debt management and monetary policy should necessarily be integrated, if countries are highly indebted and in a situation of fiscal distress. However, if the goal of price stability of the common central bank is strongly anchored, we can also expect that high public debt levels do not imply higher inflation rates, but mainly higher risk premiums and spreads on the interest rates of bonds of the countries in situation of fiscal difficulty. So, there seems to be multiple equilibria.

Chari and Kehoe (2008) show that in monetary unions, a time inconsistency problem in monetary policy implies a novel type of free-rider problem, which leads union members to pursue lax non-monetary policies that benefit themselves individually, but that induce the monetary authority to pursue policies that generate high inflation for the whole monetary union (monetary accommodation). The source of this free riding problem is the behavior of private agents. When commitment is not possible, this problem can only be mitigated by imposing constraints on non-monetary policies. In the same way, because of a commitment problem of the central bank, Cooper et al. (2010,a) show the possibility of multiple equilibria, according to the perceptions of agents regarding the manner in which the debt obligations will be met. In the 'Ricardian equilibrium', the future obligations are met with taxation by a regional government while on the contrary, in the 'Monetization equilibrium', the central bank is induced to print money to finance the region's obligations, with inflationary consequences. Cooper et al. (2010,b) also show that when capital markets are integrated, the fiscal policy of one country influences equilibrium wages and interest rates in the other countries of the monetary union, without possibility of insulation from budgetary spill-overs. Depending on the type of rule adopted by the monetary authority, monetary policy then affects the magnitude and nature of the spillover from regional fiscal policy.

In this context, the current chapter studies potential fiscal externalities of the public debt in the framework of a monetary union. We show that the common monetary policy of the central bank is contractionary (increase of the nominal interest rate) after symmetric positive demand shocks, and expansionary (monetary accommodation) in case of shocks on the average public debt to GDP ratio in the monetary union. However, the monetary policy of an institutionally very independent central bank, and/or which could commit regarding its future monetary policy, would be less active, which would increase macro-economic fluctuations in case of demand shocks. On the contrary, monetary policy is more active if the central bank is subject to budgetary pressures, and if stabilizing the global indebtedness in the monetary union is a secondary goal of this central bank. Such a less independent monetary policy reduces the consequences of demand shocks on economic activity and on the labor market. Nevertheless, the monetary reaction function of a more dependent central bank introduces new fluctuations in case of shocks on the public debt of the member countries.

The rest of the chapter is organized as follows. The second section provides a review of economic literature regarding public debt externalities in the framework of a monetary union. The third section describes a simple analytical modelling of a monetary union with a common central bank, but national governments conducting autonomous budgetary policies. The fourth section studies public debt externalities in the framework of a monetary union, according to the degree of independence or of sensibility to budgetary pressures of the common central bank. The fifth section studies some institutional factors strongly influencing these externalities: the independence or the potential commitment of the central bank, or the possibility for the latter to be concerned with the situation of each specific country in the monetary union. Finally, the sixth section concludes the chapter.

2. Review of Economic Literature

Public debt levels remain, to a certain extent, a national responsibility even in the framework of a monetary union. Risk premiums should and they can still distinguish between the public debts of the various member countries, in order to discipline their budgetary policies. However, monetary unification implies new fiscal externalities, and it increases the interdependencies between the public debts of the member countries of a monetary union. For example, Bernoth et al. (2004) study bond yield differentials among EU Eurobonds issued between 1991 and 2002. They show that interest rate differentials between bonds issued by EU countries and Germany or the USA contain risk premiums which increase with the national debt, deficit and debt-service ratio (default risk premium). This disciplining effect of the fiscal situation of the member countries appears to remain high in the EU. However, the authors also show that EMU membership reduces the effect of own-country deficits and debt accumulation on interest rates, a result they view as being consistent with markets anticipating fiscal support for EMU countries in financial distress.

Indeed, theoretically, monetary unification can reduce fiscal discipline for many reasons. First of all, a higher public indebtedness level increases the common nominal interest rate; the consequences of fiscal laxity are then not fully internalized by appropriate risk premiums. So, budgetary laxity is favored, as negative consequences of a higher interest rate are partially shifted to the other member countries. The lack of commitment and of coordination of national budgetary policies are at the origin of this fear of negative externalities on the partner countries [Aguiar et al. (2014)]. So, there is a financial market channel of transmission of the level of the public debt on the other member countries of a monetary union: excessive borrowing in a given country can increase the risk-premium of government debt in all member countries. Indeed, even a written 'no bail-out rule' may not be fully credible, and then, financial markets may anticipate that all member countries of a monetary union are to some extent liable for the sovereign debt of all other countries. Or at least, risk premiums may increase in all countries because of a risk of financial contagion and of weakened financial intermediation. So, even in absence of monetary accommodation, the existence of implicit or explicit bailout provisions can lead to debt spillovers. Indeed, the interest rate demanded by lenders mainly reflects the ability to pay of the other governments in the monetary union that are likely to provide the bailout. That is, the risk premium incorporated by the market in bond yields of borrowing governments strongly depends on the average public debt level of the whole monetary union.

During the recent public debt crisis: between September 2008 and January 2012, in particular, Constancio (2012) underlines the empirical evidence of contagion in the European Union; contagion from Greece, Ireland and Portugal explains a significant share of Italian and Spanish government bond yields. However, spreads increased between European countries after 2008, governments' bonds interest rates remaining much smaller in France and mainly in Germany. So, investors remain dubious regarding potential bail-out and solidarity between European countries. Broner et al. (2014) also show that creditor discrimination arises because, in turbulent times, sovereign debt offers a higher expected return to domestic creditors than to foreign ones. This provides incentives for domestic purchases of debt. Crowding-out effects arise because private borrowing is limited by financial frictions. With increasing spreads on the national public debt, national creditors buy more public and less private debt, increasing borrowing costs for consumers and firms; so, domestic debt purchases reduce productive investment. The model shows that these purchases reduce growth and welfare, and may lead to self-fulfilling crises (among multiple eventual equilibria), which can be transmitted to other countries in the Euro zone.

In the same way, with an Overlapping Generations model, Chang (1990) shows that in a world with international capital mobility, the fiscal deficit of any single government affects world interest rates and influences intertemporal resource allocation in all countries. So, these negative international externalities (temptation for fiscal laxity as the negative consequences are shared among many countries) may result in inefficiently large fiscal deficits, high real interest rates, and low welfare levels in absence of international policy coordination. Furthermore, Gande and Parsley (2005) find that a sovereign credit rating change by Standard & Poor's in one country has a significant effect on the sovereign credit spreads of other countries from 1991 to 2000. This effect is asymmetric: positive ratings events abroad have no discernable impact on sovereign spreads, whereas negative ratings events imply an increase in spreads. Furthermore, the transmission channel for spillovers would be stronger through capital than through trade flow linkages.

Moreover, Beetsma and Vermeylen (2007) mention that the adoption of a common monetary policy makes the risk-return characteristics of the participating countries' public debts more similar. Using an overlapping generations' model, they show that the implied reduction in the scope for risk diversification (more correlation between the risks of the public debts) raises the average expected real return and real interest rate paid on the debt, which then exceeds its pre-unification level. Also, the share of the union-wide debt (in relative terms) issued by relatively myopic governments (high preference for current situation in comparison with future expected public debt level) or by countries that initially have a relatively dependent central bank increases after unification. This may put the political sustainability of the union under pressure, as high debt countries exert a non-negligible negative externality on the public debt of more disciplined countries.

Besides, national budgetary policies can be constrained to be more active in order to stabilize negative asymmetric shocks in the framework of a monetary union, as the common monetary policy is then only able to stabilize symmetric shocks. Then, the fear of fiscal laxity implies that fiscal criteria have been mentioned in the institutions of the European Economic and Monetary Union since the Maastricht Treaty (1993). The Stability and Growth Pact (1997), and afterwards the Fiscal Compact (2013), mention that the budgetary deficit of the member countries should not exceed 3% of GDP; countries must have a cyclically adjusted budget 'close to balance or in surplus'. Besides, the Fiscal Compact has detailed the condition to comply with regarding the public debt level: the latter should not exceed 60% of GDP, or should sufficiently converge towards this ratio. More precisely, countries running a higher than 60% of GDP public debt ratio will be under an Excessive Deficit Procedure (EDP) if this debt ratio does not fall by 1/20th per year of the gap between the effective debt and the 60% reference value (on average over 3 years).

Landon and Smith (2007) also mention another channel of public debt interdependencies in a monetary union: revenue interdependence. Interdependent revenues exist to the extent that the economies of the members of a federation are interconnected—as a result of trade and financial flows, for example. Excess debt accumulation that causes a fiscal crisis in one jurisdiction then may adversely affect output and incomes in other jurisdictions. This would decrease the tax revenues generated in the affected jurisdictions and inhibit the ability of the governments of these jurisdictions to meet their debt service obligations. For example, using a structural VAR analysis for the period 1970-1998, Giuliordori and Beetsma (2004) study the cross-border spill-overs of fiscal shocks via the trade channel. Fiscal expansions in Germany, France and Italy lead to significant increases in imports from a number of European countries, positive externalities which are even slightly strengthen on average if the authors mimic a situation of potential monetary unification during the period.

Regarding the width of public debt externalities in the framework of a monetary union, what is the importance of the strategic position of the common central bank, of its independence regarding potential budgetary pressures? Debt spillovers may arise if there is a risk of monetary accommodation, implicit or explicit inter-jurisdictional bailout provisions, or interdependent revenues. So, Landon and Smith (2007) analyze empirically two channels through which debt spillovers may affect bond yields, in the case of Canadian provincial bonds for the period 1983-2005: currency depreciation risk and default risk. They find a significant impact of central government debt on provincial government bond yields, but aggregate provincial government debt accumulation is not found to have a statistically significant effect on the yields of the bonds issued by individual provinces. The major source of debt spillovers is the perceived risk of monetary accommodation. As a consequence, in a monetary union, if the market believes that the central bank is independent and will not be pressured by governments with large debts to inflate, yields may be less likely to rise with central government debt accumulation.

However, does monetary unification affect the strategic position of the central bank? Van Aarle et al. (1997) assess that monetary unification reinforces the strategic position of the common central bank, which is then alone to face many fiscal authorities (as long as they fail to cooperate). In these conditions, the reaction of fiscal authorities can be stronger in order to reduce their own public indebtedness level, as they anticipate that the monetary reaction to their own fiscal situation is weaker, and fiscal discipline can be improved. Nevertheless, in a monetary union, the common central bank cannot reasonably commit to a given level of inflation rate. So, there is an incentive to increase prices if average public debt levels are high in the monetary union, in order to lighten the weight of this indebtedness. Lenders are aware of this temptation, and so, they can charge a higher nominal interest rate *ex ante*, making the risk of a higher inflation rate self-fulfilling. Therefore, empirically, the monetary authority balances inflation's benefits against its costs. Higher inflation has benefits because it reduces the real value of nominal debt and thus reduces the amount of distortionary taxes that must be raised by each country's government in order to repay the debt. However, a higher inflation rate also has costs, because it distorts allocations and thus reduces output.

Furthermore, Leith and Wren-Lewis (2006) show that the strategic dominant position of the common central bank can be put into question in the framework of a monetary union. Indeed, the monetary authority can abandon its active targeting of inflation to ensure the solvency of at most one fiscal authority, and then, this will result in price level indeterminacy and/or indefinite transfers of wealth between the countries forming the monetary union. Fiscal shocks have limited impact on output and inflation provided the fiscal authorities meet the (weak) requirements of fiscal solvency. However, when monetary policy is forced to abandon its active targeting of inflation, then fiscal shocks have a much greater impact on both output and inflation. Indeed, the 'no-bailout' provision in the Maastricht's Treaty may be at odds with other functions of the ECB, such as the smooth functioning of the payments system. So, if public debts are high and if many countries in the monetary union are in fiscal distress, pressure may be put on the central bank to keep interest rates low, in order to minimize the cost of a financial crisis. Therefore, the risk of monetary accommodation increases with the public debt levels of the member countries of the monetary union.

Nevertheless, Aguiar et al. (2014) demonstrate that a high-debt country may be less vulnerable to self-fulfilling debt crises and have higher welfare when it belongs to a monetary union with an intermediate mix of high- and low-debt members, than one where all other members are low-debt. Indeed, a fraction of high debt countries imply that the common central bank doesn't only consider the goal of price stability, but it also considers a role of lender of last resort and it is liable to intervene in case of indebtedness crisis. This contrasts with the conventional wisdom that all countries should prefer a union with low-debt members, as such a union can credibly deliver low inflation. In the same way, among multiple potential equilibria regarding the link between monetary policy and the inter-temporal budgetary constraint, Jeanne (2012) distinguishes two forms of monetary dominance. According to the first (soft, or preventive) form of monetary dominance, in the United-States or in Japan for example, the government adjusts its fiscal policy so as to avoid having to choose between a default or debt monetization. In the second case (hard form of monetary dominance), favored by the European authorities in the statutes of the ECB, in the extreme situation where this choice has to be made, the monetary authority should let the government default rather than monetizing the debt. In this context, the authors show that hard monetary dominance may reduce the probability of fiscal adjustment, make default more likely, and, if the fiscal consolidation is not perfectly credible, may increase the probability of inflation.

Mitra (2007) derives an interest rate rule for monetary policy in an inflation-targeting policy regime, in which the interest rate response of the central bank towards an increase in expected inflation falls (less response to expected inflation) as public debts increase beyond a certain threshold level. Indeed, with a high and growing government debt, taxes are not supposed to be able to back debt shocks entirely. So, government spending is expected to be reduced in the future in line with real debt service costs. The 'constraint' on monetary policy then operates through an altered policy transmission mechanism: the fiscal authority puts pressure indirectly on the monetary authority to decrease its interest rate, which alters the IS curve. In the same way, Diaz et al. (2008) study the effects of nominal debt on the optimal sequential choice of monetary policy. When the stock of debt is nominal, the incentive to generate unanticipated inflation increases the cost of outstanding debt even if no unanticipated inflation episodes occur in equilibrium. Without full commitment, to deplete the outstanding stock of debt progressively until these extra costs disappear is part of a sequential optimal policy. Nominal debt is therefore a burden on monetary policy, not only because it must be serviced, but also because it creates a time inconsistency problem that distorts interest rates.

Besides, Beetsma and Bovenberg (1999) use a dynamic two periods model of discretionary monetary and fiscal policy-making in a monetary union. They show that if discretionary monetary policy (the common central bank is unable to commit) implies an inflation bias, monetary unification boosts the accumulation of public debt. This additional debt accumulation is welfare reducing if governments are sufficiently myopic (higher valorization of the current period than the society), but not if they represent the social preferences of their citizens. So in the presence of myopic governments, debt ceilings play a useful role in avoiding excessive debt accumulation in a monetary union, and they allow a conservative, independent central bank to focus on price stability. In the same way, Chari and Kehoe (2007) show that if the monetary authority can commit regarding its future monetary policy, fiscal constraints can only impose costs. However, a benevolent monetary authority which cannot commit finds it optimal to set high inflation rates when the inherited debt levels of the member countries are large. There is then a free rider problem in fiscal policy (higher common nominal interest rate which is a cost for other fiscal authorities), as the governments conduct excessively lax budgetary policies and have too high public debt levels, and fiscal constraints may thus be desirable.

The monetary policy should mainly stabilize inflation, and this is in the statutes of all central banks. However, this Taylor principle can be violated in case of irresponsible governments and if the public debt is too high. So, Leith and Wren-Lewis (2000) show that with a low steady state of debt, the burden of the stabilization is shared between the monetary and budgetary authorities. But in an economy with high steady-state debt, the optimal discretionary monetary policy cuts the interest rate in the first period in response to a cost-push shock, in order to reduce the burden of the public debt (Fiscal Theory of the Price Level). In the same way, Kirsanova et al. (2005) study the interactions of fiscal policy and monetary policy when they stabilize a single economy against shocks in a dynamic setting. If both policy-makers are benevolent, the best outcome is achieved when monetary policy does nearly all of the stabilization. In the same way, if a regime of fiscal leadership exists, then the outcome would be very nearly as good as when both policy-makers are benevolent. However, if the monetary authority is benevolent, but the fiscal authority strongly discounts the future (more impatient and shorter planning horizon), or aims for an excessive level of output, then a Nash equilibrium will result in large welfare losses. An inflationary shock would imply an excessively tight monetary policy (high interest rates), excessive fiscal expansion, and a risk of rapid accumulation of public debts.

On the contrary, Van Aarle et al. (1997) show that the strategic position of the common central bank is not weakened by monetary unification. They use a dynamic game between symmetric national governments and a single monetary authority, where the governments first optimize according to economic objectives (activity, etc.), and afterwards optimize in order to satisfy their intertemporal budgetary constraint. Then, they show that debt adjustment is quicker in the framework of a monetary union, while inflation as well as fiscal deficits are lower. Therefore, in absence of commitment and coordination of fiscal authorities, there would be no fiscal indiscipline related to monetary unification, as fiscal authorities are constrained to be more active in the stabilization of asymmetric shocks.

In the same way, Stehn and Vines (2008) analyze optimal monetary and fiscal policy in a New-Keynesian model with public debt and also with inflation persistence (possibility of a hybrid Phillips curve with a strong backward component). Then, they show that with high degrees of inflation persistence, the monetary policy is not less active with high debt levels. Indeed, with a high degree of inflation persistence, it becomes impossible to carry out a monetary policy which violates the Taylor principle but is nevertheless consistent with the control of inflation, and the interest rate increases after a cost-push shock. Therefore, the authors also show that optimal fiscal policy is then more active to complement this more constrained monetary policy, if the degree of inflation persistence and public debt levels are both high: they cut budgetary spending more strongly, and less public debt is accumulated. Furthermore, this optimal budgetary policy is more active in a discretionary framework, where commitment is not allowed.

Leith and Wren-Lewis (2011) also examine the interactions between multiple national fiscal policy-makers and a single monetary policy maker in response to shocks to government debt in some or all of the countries of a monetary union. They assume that national governments respond to excess debt in an optimal manner, but that they do not have access to a commitment technology. This implies that national fiscal policy gradually reduces debt: the lack of a commitment technology precludes a random walk in steady state debt, but the need to maintain national competitiveness avoids excessively rapid debt reduction (surprise inflation is not an option). If the central bank can commit, it adjusts its policy only slightly in response to higher debt, allowing national fiscal policy to undertake most of the adjustment. However if it cannot commit, then optimal (time-consistent) monetary policy involves using low interest rates to rapidly reduce debt, with significant welfare costs. Therefore, the authors show that in these circumstances, the central bank would do better to ignore national fiscal policies (union wide debt and the national fiscal responses to it) in formulating its policy.

Finally, Corsetti and Dedola (2016) consider a model where welfare maximizing monetary and fiscal authorities optimally choose their policies under discretion. Default from the governments can occur via haircuts (losses for bond holders), and default from the central bank can occur through inflation reducing the real value of debt. However, unconventional monetary (balance sheet) policies may be helpful for a backstop of belief-driven public debt crisis, as long as the credibility of the central bank to honor its own low interest rates liabilities is not put into question. The authors study such policies, which rely on reducing borrowing costs *ex-ante*, at the time of debt issuance, and which can reduce the expectations of monetary accommodation and of high inflation rates. According to the authors, for the efficiency of such a backstop, governments should have access to the benefit of a backstop only provided the fiscal authorities are sufficiently adverse to inflation, and/or if they agree to strict conditionality, ensuring stability of public finances.

In the framework of this large economic literature, the current chapter aims at providing a simple theoretical and analytical analysis of the width of public debt externalities in the context of a monetary union, according to the characteristics of the monetary policy of the common central bank, and to its sensibility to budgetary pressures.

3. A Modelling of Public Debt Externalities

We use a simple analytical modelling of public debt externalities in the framework of a monetary union, in particular passing through the impact of public indebtedness levels of the various member countries on the common monetary policy. The monetary union consists of n participating countries. We mainly study the situation of a small country (i) member of this monetary union, among a continuum of (infinitesimal small) economies, which cannot influence global economic variables for the whole monetary union denoted by an asterisk[1]. We will only relax this assumption in the

[1] In the economic literature, a monetary union is often considered as atomistic with respect to the rest of the world. In this chapter, we also consider that it is the case for a member country (i) with respect to all the monetary union, except in section 5.3.

context of an influential country in section 5.3; each individual fiscal policy will then be important, beyond the aggregate union wide fiscal policy.

Whereas the common central bank sets monetary policy for the entire union (the instrument is then the interest rate), fiscal policies are defined at a decentralized, national level by each government (the instruments are the budgetary expenditures). All economies are structurally homogeneous, symmetric with home bias in consumption, and each economy produces a single perfectly substitutable good. We consider that the 'law of one price' is verified regarding consumption goods; without barriers to commodity trade, the inflation rate is uniform across the union. Labor is immobile internationally. For simplicity, the possibility of nominal wages rigidity is ignored. Finally, in order to simplify the modelling, we also avoid the external interaction of monetary union countries with outside countries.

3.1. Households

We suppose a representative household in the country (i), which provides labor, and which consumes goods. In a given period (t), this representative household/consumer in the country (i) maximizes an inter-temporal utility function:

$$max \sum_{k=t}^{\infty} \beta^{k-t} E_t[U_{i,k}] \quad (1)$$

Where: $E_t()$ is the rational expectation operator conditional on information available at date (t), and (β) is the time discount factor of the private sector. Prices of goods, interest rates, taxation rates and wages are then taken as given by the representative household.

This maximization is subject to the life time and inter-temporal nominal budgetary constraint, for whatever date (t) considered for the actualization. If we suppose complete financial markets, a household flow budgetary constraint for each period (t) takes the form[2]:

$$P_{i,t}C_{i,t} + B_{i,t} + \frac{1}{(1+r_t)}E_t(A_{i,t+1}) = (1-t_i^l)W_{i,t}L_{i,t} + A_{i,t} + (1+r_{i,t-1}^b)B_{i,t-1} \quad (2)$$

With, in the country (i) in period (t): ($C_{i,t}$): real consumption; ($P_{i,t}$): level of consumer prices; ($W_{i,t}$): nominal hourly wage rate; (t_i^l): labor income tax rate; ($L_{i,t}$): hours worked by the household; (r_t): riskless common nominal interest rate; ($r_{i,t}^b$): interest rate on bonds from the government; ($B_{i,t}$): nominal value of bonds (portfolio of all claims on the governments); ($A_{i,t}$): nominal wealth of the household invested on the financial markets (including shares in firms).

Each period, consumption expenditure, financial wealth invested on the financial markets and purchases of government bonds are equal to labor revenues, previous financial wealth and gains from government bonds holding from the previous period. For simplicity, we suppose that these bonds are only riskless one-period nominal government bonds. Besides, for households, a perfect arbitrage and a same return between detention of public debt and of financial wealth implies: ($r_{i,t}^b = r_t$). Summing to have an inter-temporal budgetary constraint, assuming a non-Ponzi game for the government [$\lim_{n\to\infty}\frac{1}{(1+r_t)^n}E_t(B_{i,t+n}) = 0$] and that the net present value of financial wealth is bounded [$\lim_{n\to\infty}\frac{1}{(1+r_t)^n}E_t(A_{i,t+n}) = 0$], we obtain:

$$P_{i,t}C_{i,t} + E_t[\sum_{k=t}^{\infty}\frac{P_{i,k+1}C_{i,k+1}}{(1+r_k)\ldots(1+r_t)}]$$

---

[2] Indeed, [$\frac{1}{(1+r_t)}$] is the 'price' of carrying the wealth (A_{t+1}) in period (t+1), as the actualization of the sum: $\frac{1}{(1+r_t)}E_t(A_{i,t+1})$ will give ($A_{i,t+1}$) in period (t).

$$= (1 - t_i^l)W_{i,t}L_{i,t} + (1 - t_i^l)E_t[\sum_{k=t}^{\infty} \frac{W_{i,k+1}L_{i,k+1}}{(1 + r_k) \dots (1 + r_t)}] + A_{i,t}$$

$$+(1 + r_{t-1})B_{i,t-1} < \infty \quad (3)$$

Current consumption and anticipated consumption levels after the current period (t) mustn't exceed current financial wealth and revenues of previous detention of public bonds, current real activity revenues and anticipated revenues for all future periods. Therefore, in this model, we allow for the possibility to borrow from one period to another, but we limit anticipated future revenues in order to avoid the possibility of Ponzi schemes.

We also suppose that the utility function of a representative household has the form:

$$U_{i,t} = \frac{\alpha_c \theta}{(\theta-1)} C_{i,t}^{\frac{(\theta-1)}{\theta}} + \frac{\alpha_g \theta}{(\theta-1)} (G_{i,t})^{\frac{(\theta-1)}{\theta}} - \frac{\alpha_l}{(1+\varphi)} L_{i,t}^{(1+\varphi)} \quad (4)$$

With $(G_{i,t})$: real public expenditure of the government of the country (i) in period (t).

The indices $(0<\alpha_c<1)$, $(0<\alpha_g<1)$ and $(0<\alpha_l<1)$ are the respective weights given to consumption of private goods, public goods and leisure in the utility function.

Utility is an increasing and concave function of $(C_{i,t})$, an index of the household's consumption of all domestic or foreign goods supplied; $(\theta>1)$ is the elasticity of intertemporal substitution. Utility is also an increasing and concave function of public goods and services provided in the home country $(G_{i,t})$. Finally, utility is a decreasing and convex function of the hours worked $(L_{i,t})$, where $(\varphi \geq 0)$ is the inverse of the Frisch elasticity of labor supply.

In this context, the result of the maximization of equation (1) under the constraint (3) implies the following first order Euler condition, regarding timing of consumption expenditure decisions and inter-temporal allocation of consumption between periods, for whatever periods (t) and (t+k):

$$\frac{1}{P_{i,t}}\frac{\partial U_{i,t}}{\partial C_{i,t}}=\frac{\beta(1+r_t)}{E_t(P_{i,t+1})}\frac{\partial E_t(U_{i,t+1})}{\partial C_{i,t+1}}$$
$$=\frac{\beta^k(1+r_{t+k-1})...(1+r_t)}{E_t(P_{i,t+k})}\frac{\partial E_t(U_{i,t+k})}{\partial C_{i,t+k}} \quad (5)$$

Furthermore, combining equations (4) and (5), (∀t), we have:

$$C_{i,t}=\left[\frac{E_t(P_{i,t+1})}{\beta(1+r_t)P_{i,t}}\right]^{\theta}E_T(C_{i,t+1}) \quad (6)$$

So, in logarithms and in variations from their long run equilibrium values (lower case letters are in log deviations from steady state), with ln(1+x)~x provided (x=interest or inflation rate) is sufficiently small; we obtain the following private consumption:

$$c_{i,t}=E_t(c_{i,t+1})-\theta[\hat{r}_t-E_t(\pi_{i,t+1})] \quad (7)$$

For each variable X, its deviation in period (t) from the steady state (X_i) is (in lower case letters): $x_{i,t}=lnX_{i,t}-lnX_i=\frac{X_{i,t}-X_i}{X_i}$. The inflation rate for consumption prices is: $\pi_{i,t}=\frac{P_{i,t}-P_{i,t-1}}{P_{i,t-1}}$. We suppose that the steady state inflation rate is null. Besides, we note: ($\hat{r}_t=r_t-r$) the deviation of the current from the steady state interest rate.

We can also mention that equation (6) implies: $[\beta^{\theta}(1+r)^{\theta}=1]$. So, the equilibrium long term nominal interest rate verifies: $\left[r=\frac{1-\beta}{\beta}\right]$.

In the same way, for the whole monetary union, we have:

$$c_t^*=E_t(c_{t+1}^*)-\theta[\hat{r}_t-E_t(\pi_{t+1}^*)] \quad (8)$$

where asterisks denote variables for the whole monetary union.

Besides, for the representative household in the country (i), the maximization of equation (1) under the constraint (3) implies the following optimal substitution between private consumption, public consumption and working time, $(\forall k)$[3]:

$$\frac{\partial U_{i,t+k}}{\partial C_{i,t+k}} = -\frac{P_{i,t+k}}{(1-t_i^l)W_{i,t+k}} \frac{\partial U_{i,t+k}}{\partial L_{i,t+k}} = \frac{\partial U_{i,t+k}}{\partial G_{i,t+k}} \tag{9}$$

So, according to equations (4) and (9), in logarithms and in variations from their long run equilibrium values, labor supply is as follows[4]:

$$l_{i,t} = \frac{1}{\varphi}\left(w_{i,t} - p_{i,t}\right) - \frac{1}{\varphi\theta} c_{i,t} \tag{10}$$

It increases with the real wage, but it decreases with the disutility of working time (φ).

Furthermore, regarding variations of private and public consumption, with equations (4) and (9), in variations from their long term equilibrium values, we obtain[5]:

$$c_{i,t} = g_{i,t} \tag{11}$$

Therefore, given private consumption implicitly defined by the Euler equation and chosen by the representative household, the government should chose a level of public consumption increasing exactly at the same pace. Therefore, public expenditure is endogenously defined by households' behavior, in the framework of our model.

Besides, we suppose that the 'law of one price' prevails: 'pricing to market' and discrimination between domestic or foreign producers is not possible. Prices of goods consumed are the same in a given country, whatever the place where they have been produced; there is perfect

---

[3] We use equations (3) and (32), which imply: $\frac{\partial U_{i,t}}{\partial (P_{i,t}C_{i,t})} = \frac{\partial U_{i,t}}{\partial (t_i^l W_{i,t} L_{i,t})} = \frac{\partial U_{i,t}}{\partial (P_{i,t}G_{i,t})}$.

[4] $\frac{\partial U_{i,t}}{\partial L_{i,t}} = -\alpha_l L_{i,t}^{\varphi} = -\frac{(1-t_i^l)W_{i,t}}{P_{i,t}} \frac{\partial U_{i,t}}{\partial C_{i,t}} = -\frac{(1-t_i^l)W_{i,t}}{P_{i,t}} \alpha_c (C_{i,t})^{-\frac{1}{\theta}}$.

[5] $\frac{\partial U_{i,t}}{\partial G_{i,t}} = \alpha_g (G_{i,t})^{-\frac{1}{\theta}} = \frac{\partial U_{i,t}}{\partial C_{i,t}} = \alpha_c (C_{i,t})^{-\frac{1}{\theta}}$. $G_{i,t} = \left(\frac{\alpha_g}{\alpha_c}\right)^{\theta} C_{i,t}$

substitutability between domestic and foreign goods. Therefore, as suggested by Gali and Monacelli (2008), or as in Leith and Wren-Lewis (2011), we decompose the consumption of households in the country (i) ($C_{i,t}$) between the share (1-η) of goods produced in the home country ($C_{i,t}^{i}$), (1-η) being a measure of home bias in consumption decisions, and the share (η) of imported goods produced in all the monetary union ($C_{i,t}^{*}$), (η) being an indicator of openness of the national country. So, we have:

$$C_{i,t} = \frac{\left(C_{i,t}^{i}\right)^{(1-\eta)} \left(C_{i,t}^{*}\right)^{\eta}}{(1-\eta)^{(1-\eta)}\,\eta^{\eta}} \tag{12a}$$

$$c_{i,t} = (1-\eta)c_{i,t}^{i} + \eta\, c_{i,t}^{*} \tag{12b}$$

In the same way, the consumer price index ($P_{i,t}$) can be divided between prices of domestically produced goods ($P_{i,t}^{i}$) and prices of goods produced in the monetary union (P_{t}^{*}).

$$P_{i,t} = \left(P_{i,t}^{i}\right)^{(1-\eta)} \left(P_{t}^{*}\right)^{\eta} \tag{13a}$$

$$p_{i,t} = p_{i,t}^{i} + \eta\left(p_{t}^{*} - p_{i,t}^{i}\right) \tag{13b}$$

So, we have the following relation between national inflation measured in terms of consumer price index ($\pi_{i,t}$) or in terms of producer price index ($\pi_{i,t}^{i}$):

$$\pi_{i,t} = p_{i,t} - p_{i,t-1} = \pi_{i,t}^{i} + \eta\left(\pi_{t}^{*} - \pi_{i,t}^{i}\right) \tag{14}$$

Therefore, consumer prices increase more than producer prices if the competitiveness and the terms of trade improve, if the country (i) is very open (η is high) with a faster increase in prices of imported goods in comparison with domestically produced goods.

Furthermore, for the representative household in the country (i), the optimal allocation of expenditure between the national country (i) and the rest of the monetary union implies:

$$P_{i,t}^{i} C_{i,t}^{i} = (1-\eta) P_{i,t} C_{i,t} \tag{15a}$$

$$P_t^{*} C_{i,t}^{*} = \eta P_{i,t} C_{i,t} \tag{15b}$$

In the same way, regarding consumption by households in the monetary union of goods produced in the home country ($C_{*,t}^{i}$) and in the whole monetary union ($C_{*,t}^{*}$), we have:

$$P_{i,t}^{i} C_{*,t}^{i} = \eta P_t^{*} C_t^{*} \tag{16a}$$

$$P_t^{*} C_{*,t}^{*} = (1-\eta) P_t^{*} C_t^{*} \tag{16b}$$

Finally, by combining equations (7) and (8), and using (13b) and (14), we obtain[6]:

$$c_{i,t} = c_t^{*} + \theta\left(p_t^{*} - p_{i,t}\right) = c_t^{*} + \theta(1-\eta)\left(p_t^{*} - p_{i,t}^{i}\right) \tag{17}$$

Therefore, consumption in the national country increases more than in the rest of the monetary union if inflation is higher in the foreign countries, all the more as the intertemporal substitutability of private consumption (θ) is high and countries are less open (η small).

Equation (17) also implies:

$$C_{i,T} \sim C_T^{*} \left(\frac{P_T^{*}}{P_{i,T}}\right)^{\theta} \tag{18}$$

---

[6] $c_{i,t} - E_t(c_{i,t+1}) = c_t^{*} - E_t(c_{t+1}^{*}) + \theta[p_t^{*} - E_t(p_{t+1}^{*})] - \theta[p_{i,t} - E_t(p_{i,t+1})]$.

3.2. Firms

We suppose a continuum of firms in the country (i) producing a differentiated good in a monopolist competition setting. However, equation (19) below only models the production of one representative firm in the country (i). This firm defines prices in order to maximize its profit, taking other variables as given. Capital is supposed to be fixed in the short run, whereas labor supply is defined according to the maximization program of households in equation (10). It is the only factor of production which is variable in the short run, and we abstract from capital accumulation in this chapter. Besides, public expenditure is also a factor raising public input; production increases with public goods and services supplied by the government ($0 < z < 1$). So, the production function has the following form, for the representative firm in the country (i):

$$Y_{i,t} = A_{i,t} L_{i,t}^{1-\nu} G_{i,t}^{z} \quad 0 < n < 1 \tag{19}$$

and in terms of variation from its long run equilibrium value:

$$y_{i,t} = a_{i,t} + (1-\nu) l_{i,t} + z g_{i,t} \tag{20}$$

with, in the country (i) in period (t): ($A_{i,t}$): productivity shock, evolving exogenously over time; ($Y_{i,t}$): real production level; (v): decreasing returns in the production function.

This firm maximizes its nominal profit: $\Pi_{i,t} = P_{i,t}Y_{i,t} - W_{i,t}L_{i,t}$. Labor is paid at its marginal product. So, the maximization of the profit and equation (19) imply:

$$P_{i,t}\frac{\partial Y_{i,t}}{\partial L_{i,t}} = (1-\nu) A_{i,t} P_{i,t} \left(L_{i,t}\right)^{-\nu} G_{i,t}^{z} = W_{i,t} > 0 \tag{21a}$$

$$\frac{W_{i,t}L_{i,t}}{P_{i,t}Y_{i,t}} = (1-\nu) \tag{21b}$$

Therefore, by combining equations (20) and (21b), we obtain:

$$\left(w_{i,t} - p_{i,t}\right) = a_{i,t} - \nu l_{i,t} + z g_{i,t} \tag{22}$$

Furthermore, we consider a Calvo-type framework of staggered prices, where a fraction (0<α<1) of goods prices remain unchanged each period, whereas prices are adjusted for the remaining fraction (1-α) of goods. Monopolistically competitive firms choose their nominal prices to maximize profits subject to constraints on the frequency of future price adjustments, and taking into account that prices may be fixed for many periods. So, if we suppose that firms are initially at their equilibrium level (minimizing absolute levels would then not be different), they minimize the following loss function in terms of variation:

$$Min_{p_{i,t}^{i,r}} \sum_{k=0}^{\infty} (\alpha\ \beta)^k E_t (p_{i,t}^{i,r} - \widetilde{p_{i,t+k}^{i,r}})^2 \tag{23}$$

Where ($\widetilde{p_{i,t}^{i,r}}$) is the logarithm (percentage deviation from steady state) of the optimal price that a firm (i) will set in period (t) if there were no price rigidity. It is the price that will allow a maximal profit for the firm, according to the prices of production factors and of its budgetary constraint, which thus doesn't need to be mentioned in the optimization problem.

The firm minimizes expected losses in profit for all future periods (t+k) due to the fact that it will not be able to set a frictionless optimal price in this period (t+k).These losses are subject to the actualization rate (β), as closer profits are given a higher weight than more distant ones. Besides, the probability that the price ($p_{i,t}^{i}$) will be fixed for (k) periods, until the period (t+k), is (α^k). Thus, by deriving according to the reset price ($p_{i,t}^{i,r}$), we have:

$$p_{i,t}^{i,r} = (1 - \alpha\ \beta) \sum_{k=0}^{\infty} (\alpha\ \beta)^k E_t (\widetilde{p_{i,t+k}^{i,r}}) \tag{24}$$

The optimal strategy of the firm (i) is to fix prices at marginal costs: $\widetilde{p_{i,t}^{i,r}} = mc_{i,t}$, where ($mc_{i,t}$) is the variation of the nominal marginal production cost of the firm (i). Furthermore, prices in period (t) are an average of past prices and reset prices:

$$p_{i,t}^{i} = \alpha p_{i,t-1}^{i} + (1-\alpha) p_{i,t}^{i,r} \tag{25}$$

So, by combining equations (24) and (25), we obtain:

$$\begin{aligned} p_{i,t}^{i,r} &= \frac{1}{(1-\alpha)} p_{i,t}^{i} - \frac{\alpha}{(1-\alpha)} p_{i,t-1}^{i} \\ &= \frac{\alpha\,\beta}{(1-\alpha)} E_t\left(p_{i,t+1}^{i}\right) - \frac{\alpha^2\beta}{(1-\alpha)} p_{i,t}^{i} + (1-\alpha\,\beta) mc_{i,t} \end{aligned} \tag{26}$$

Therefore, we have the following equation regarding inflation for producer prices:

$$\pi_{i,t}^{i} = \left(p_{i,t}^{i} - p_{i,t-1}^{i}\right) = \beta\, E_t\left(\pi_{i,t+1}^{i}\right) + \frac{(1-\alpha)(1-\alpha\,\beta)}{\alpha}\left(mc_{i,t} - p_{i,t}^{i}\right) \tag{27}$$

Inflation then depends on expected future inflation, and on the gap between the frictionless optimal price level and the current price level, i.e.: on the real marginal cost. Indeed, inflationary pressures can be due to the fact that prices reset by firms are increased.

We still have to clarify the expression of the real marginal production cost for the representative firm of the country (i) [see for example: Woodford (2003) or Gali (2008)]. According to equation (19), the variable production cost of the quantity ($Y_{i,t}$) is: $W_{i,t}L_{i,t} = W_{i,t}\left(\frac{Y_{i,t}}{A_{i,t}G_{i,t}^{z}}\right)^{\frac{1}{1-\nu}}$. So, differentiating this expression, the nominal marginal production cost of the quantity ($Y_{i,t}$) is:

$$\frac{\partial(W_{i,t}L_{i,t})}{\partial Y_{i,t}} = \frac{W_{i,t}}{A_{i,t}^{\frac{1}{1-\nu}} G_{i,t}^{\frac{z}{1-\nu}} (1-n)} (Y_{i,t})^{\frac{\nu}{1-\nu}} \tag{28}$$

So, in logarithms and in variations from their long run equilibrium values, if we suppose that the variation of the productivity shock ($A_{i,t}$) is a white noise which cannot be anticipated by the firm to fix production costs, we obtain the following real marginal production cost:

$$(mc_{i,t} - p_{i,t}^{i}) = (w_{i,t} - p_{i,t}^{i}) - \frac{z}{(1-\nu)} g_{i,t} + \frac{\nu}{(1-\nu)} y_{i,t} \quad (29)$$

Equations (10), (11), (13b), (20), (22) and (29) imply [see equations (C6) and (C7)]:

$$\left(mc_{i,t} - p_{i,t}^{i}\right) = \left(p_{i,t} - p_{i,t}^{i}\right) + \frac{1}{(1-\nu)} a_{i,t} = \eta \left(p_t^{*} - p_{i,t}^{i}\right) + \frac{1}{(1-\nu)} a_{i,t} \quad (30)$$

Finally, by combining equations (27) and (30), for the country (i), we have:

$$\pi_{i,t}^{i} = \beta E_t\left(\pi_{i,t+1}^{i}\right) + k_1 \eta \left(p_t^{*} - p_{i,t}^{i}\right) + \varepsilon_{i,t}^{s} \; with{:}\; k_1 = \frac{(1-\alpha)(1-\alpha\beta)}{\alpha} \quad (31)$$

with: ($\varepsilon_{i,t}^{s} = \frac{k_1}{(1-\nu)} a_{i,t}$): supply shock, which is a white noise, related to the unanticipated productivity or technological shock ($A_{i,t}$) in the production function (19).

Therefore, real marginal production costs and inflation increase with the higher excess of prices above their long run equilibrium values in the other countries of the monetary union than in the national country (catching up).

3.3. Budgetary Policy of the Government

In our model, the specificity of a monetary union relies on the fact that there is only one common monetary policy and nominal interest rate, but

(n) idiosyncratic and strategic fiscal policies (which would only influence the global budgetary situation in section 5.3). Taxations rates are fixed at the national level by the budgetary authorities, while budgetary expenditure is the one satisfying equation (9). Distortionary taxation (contrary to lump-sum taxation) allows a departure from Ricardian equivalence between increasing current taxation rates or the public debt. The budgetary constraint of the government then becomes an effective policy constraint, and the public debt is an endogenous variable of the system. In this chapter, to simplify, we only consider the labor income taxation rate paid by households. We also suppose that all government debt is held domestically, and is risk free nominal debt (not state contingent), in conformity with most empirical observations. We also abstract from monetary creation and from seigniorage revenues, which are quite small today.

For the government of the country (i), the budgetary constraint is then the following:

$$B_{i,t} = (1 + r_{t-1})B_{i,t-1} + P_{i,t}G_{i,t} - t_i^l W_{i,t}L_{i,t} \qquad (32)$$

($B_{i,t}$): nominal public debt of country (i)'s government at the end of period (t).

Besides, in nominal terms and in proportion of GDP, using equation (21b), we obtain:

$$\frac{B_{i,t}}{P_{i,t}Y_{i,t}} = \frac{(1+r_{t-1})(1+y_{i,t-1})}{(1+\pi_{i,t})(1+y_{i,t})}\frac{B_{i,t-1}}{P_{i,t-1}Y_{i,t-1}} + \frac{G_{i,t}}{Y_{i,t}} - (1-\nu)t_i^l \qquad (33)$$

Solving this equation (33) forwards, with: $[\lim_{n\to\infty} \frac{1}{(1+r_t)^n} E_t(B_{i,t+n}) = 0]$, we can obtain the following variation of the nominal debt to GDP ratio $(BB_{i,t} = \frac{B_{i,t}}{P_{i,t}Y_{i,t}})$[7]:

$$BB_{i,t} = E_t\left\{\sum_{n=0}^{\infty} \frac{(1+\pi_{i,t+n+1})\dots(1+\pi_{i,t+1})}{(1+r_{t+n})\dots(1+r_t)} \frac{(1+y_{i,t+n+1})}{(1+y_{i,t})}\left[(1-\nu)t_i^l - \frac{G_{i,t+n+1}}{Y_{i,t+n+1}}\right]\right\}$$

$$= E_t\left\{\beta \sum_{n=0}^{\infty} \frac{\beta^n (C_{i,t})^{\frac{1}{\theta}}}{(C_{i,t+n+1})^{\frac{1}{\theta}}}\left[(1-\nu)t_i^l - \frac{G_{i,t+n+1}}{Y_{i,t+n+1}}\right]\right\} \quad (34)$$

Therefore, the steady state long run value of the debt to GDP ratio (BB_i) is as follows:

$$BB_i = \beta \sum_{n=0}^{\infty} \beta^n [(1-\nu)t_i^l - \frac{G_i}{Y_i}] = \frac{\beta}{1-\beta}[(1-\nu)t_i^l - \frac{G_i}{Y_i}] \quad (35)$$

Besides, log-linearizing equation (33), as $(\pi_{i,t})$, $(y_{i,t})$ and (r_t) are small, using equation (35), in variations from their long term equilibrium values, we obtain:

$$bb_{i,t} = (1+r)\left(bb_{i,t-1} + y_{i,t-1} - y_{i,t} - \pi_{i,t} + \widehat{r_{t-1}}\right) + \frac{G_i}{BB_i Y_i}\left(g_{i,t} - y_{i,t}\right) + e_{i,t}^b$$

$$= (1+r)\left(bb_{i,t-1} + y_{i,t-1} - y_{i,t} - \pi_{i,t} + \widehat{r_{t-1}}\right) + \frac{(1-\beta)}{\beta[\frac{Y_i}{G_i}(1-\nu)t_i^l - 1]}\left(g_{i,t} - y_{i,t}\right) + e_{i,t}^b \quad (36)$$

---

[7] Equations (4) and (5) imply: $\frac{(1+\pi_{i,t+n+1})\dots(1+\pi_{i,t+1})}{(1+r_{t+n})\dots(1+r_t)} = \frac{\beta^{n+1}(C_{i,t})^{\frac{1}{\theta}}}{(C_{i,t+n+1})^{\frac{1}{\theta}}}$ and we suppose that: $E_t(y_{i,t+n+1}) \sim y_{i,t}$.

With $(e^b_{i,t})$: shock on the public debt to GDP ratio which is a white noise, for example due to an exogenous variation in public expenditure.

3.4. Definition of the Global Equilibrium

We are now going to derive the equilibrium on the goods market regarding global demand. In this chapter, we omit investment and capital accumulation, and exports are assimilated to demand of consumption goods by foreign consumers. So, using equations (13a), (15a), (16a) and footnote 5, clearing on the goods market in the country (i) requires:

$$
\begin{aligned}
Y_{i,t} &= C^i_{i,t} + C^i_{*,t} + G_{i,t} \\
&= \left[(1-\eta)\frac{(P^*_t)^{\eta}}{\left(P^i_{i,t}\right)^{\eta}} + \eta\frac{(P^*_t)^{1-\theta(1-\eta)}}{\left(P^i_{i,t}\right)^{1-\theta(1-\eta)}} + \left(\frac{\alpha_g}{\alpha_c}\right)^{\theta}\right] C_{i,t} \\
&= \left(\frac{P^*_t}{P^i_{i,t}}\right)^{\eta}\left[(1-\eta) + \eta\left(\frac{P^*_t}{P^i_{i,t}}\right)^{(1-\eta)(1-\theta)} + \left(\frac{P^i_{i,t}}{P^*_t}\right)^{\eta}\left(\frac{\alpha_g}{\alpha_c}\right)^{\theta}\right] C_{i,t} \qquad (37)
\end{aligned}
$$

Therefore, in logarithms and in variations, using equation (17), we obtain:

$$
\begin{aligned}
y_{i,t} &= c_{i,t} + \eta[1-(1-\eta)(\theta-1)]\left(p^*_t - p^i_{i,t}\right) + \varepsilon^d_{i,t} \\
&= y^*_t + [\theta - \eta(2-\eta)(\theta-1)]\left(p^*_t - p^i_{i,t}\right) + \varepsilon^d_{i,t} \qquad (38)
\end{aligned}
$$

$$
where:\ \varepsilon^d_{i,t} = \ln\left[(1-\eta)\left(\frac{P^*_t}{P^i_{i,t}}\right)^{[(1-\eta)(\theta-1)-1]} + \eta\left(\frac{P^i_{i,t}}{P^*_t}\right) + \left(\frac{P^i_{i,t}}{P^*_t}\right)^{(2-\theta+\eta\theta)}\left(\frac{\alpha_g}{\alpha_c}\right)^{\theta}\right]
$$

is a white noise positive demand shock, related to variations in relative prices and in competitiveness of the national country inside the monetary union, and to variations of the preferences between public and private goods of the representative consumer.

And at the level of the whole monetary union, we obtain:

$$y_t^* = c_t^* + \varepsilon_t^{*d} \ with\text{: } \varepsilon_t^{*d} = \ln\left[1 + \left(\frac{\alpha_g}{\alpha_c}\right)^{\theta}\right] \quad (39)$$

Let's define $(x_{i,t})$ as the differential between economic growth in the country (i) and in the rest of the monetary union: $(x_{i,t} = y_{i,t} - y_t^*)$. So, using equations (31) and (38), the supply function is as follows, in differential with long run equilibrium values:

$$\pi_{i,t}^i = \beta\, E_t\left(\pi_{i,t+1}^i\right) + k_1 k_2 x_{i,t} + \varepsilon_{i,t}^s \ with\text{: } k_2 = \frac{\eta}{[\theta - \eta(2-\eta)(\theta - 1)]} \quad (40)$$

In the same way, for the whole monetary union, we obtain:

$$\pi_t^* = \beta\, E_t(\pi_{t+1}^*) + \varepsilon_t^{*s} \quad (41)$$

Equation (40) is the simplest form of the New-Keynesian Phillips curve in open economy. In this equation, $(k_1 k_2)$ is an indicator of price flexibility, and is the elasticity of prices to the level of real economic activity. This parameter decreases with the indicator of price-stickiness (α), the longer the average time interval between price changes. It increases with the impatience of households to consume (it decreases with β), and with the degree of openness of the national country (η). Indeed, openness implies that national output is more sensitive to the terms of trade, and then that in case of economic growth, the weaker price-competitiveness of the national country can efficiently contribute to reduce tensions on national economic activity, marginal costs and inflation. On the contrary, price flexibility decreases with the intertemporal elasticity of substitution of households' expenditure (θ).

Regarding the demand equation, whereas $(x_t^* = 0)$ for the whole monetary union, the differential of economic growth is as follows for the national country (i) (see Appendix A for a precise determination of this equation):

$$x_{i,t} = E_t\left(x_{i,t+1}\right) - [\theta - \eta(2-\eta)(\theta-1)]\left[E_t(\pi^*_{t+1}) - E_t\left(\pi^i_{i,t+1}\right)\right] + \varepsilon^d_{i,t} \tag{42}$$

In this equation, $[\theta - \eta(\theta-1)(2-\eta)]$ is the real interest rate elasticity of the output-gap, the inter-temporal elasticity of substitution of private spending in open economy.

So, according to equation (42), higher future expected output increases current output and consumption, because households prefer to smooth consumption, and then higher future revenues raise their current consumption and current output. Current output is also a decreasing function of the excess of the real interest rate above its natural level, because of the inter-temporal substitution of consumption. So, if future expected inflation is higher in the national country than in the foreign partner countries in the monetary union, the real interest rate decreases more in the national country, which favors a higher level of private consumption and economic activity in the national country.

Finally, using equations (11), (14), (36), (A2) in Appendix A, (C1) and (C2) in Appendix C, with: $[E_t\left(\varepsilon^{*d}_{t+k}\right) = E_t\left(\varepsilon^d_{i,t+k}\right) = 0$ for k≥1], $[\beta(1+r) = 1]$, we obtain[8]:

$$\begin{aligned} bb_{i,t} &= \beta E_t\left(bb_{i,t+1}\right) + (\theta-1)[\hat{r}_t - E_t(\pi^*_{t+1})] - \varepsilon^{*d}_t + \varepsilon^b_{i,t} \\ &+(1-\eta)E_t\left(\pi^i_{i,t+1} - \pi^*_{t+1}\right) + E_t\left(x_{i,t+1} - x_{i,t}\right) \\ &+ \frac{(1-\beta)}{\left[\frac{Y_i}{G_i}(1-\nu)t^l_i - 1\right]} \frac{\eta[1-(\theta-1)(1-\eta)]}{[\theta-\eta(\theta-1)(2-\eta)]} E_t(x_{i,t+1}) \end{aligned} \tag{43}$$

Where: $(\varepsilon^b_{i,t} = -\beta e^b_{i,t+1})$ is a white noise shock on the public debt to GDP ratio.

Therefore, the public debt to GDP ratio increases if the current output gap in the national country is temporary weaker than its future expected level. It increases if the real interest rate is higher in the monetary union

[8] We have: $E_t\left(c_{i,t+1} - y_{i,t+1}\right) = -\frac{\eta[1-(\theta-1)(1-\eta)]}{[\theta-\eta(\theta-1)(2-\eta)]} E_t\left(x_{i,t+1}\right)$.

that its equilibrium level, increasing the cost of the reimbursement of this public debt. On the contrary, a symmetric positive demand shock can reduce the public debt in all member countries of the monetary union.

4. Externalities of the Public Debt in a Monetary Union

The previous model can now provide the framework to analyze public debt externalities in the context of a monetary union. Appendix B defines the equilibrium excess of economic growth, inflation rate and public debt to GDP ratio in the national country (i). Appendix C defines other equilibrium variables in the national country (i) and in the whole monetary union.

Currently, in the European Economic and Monetary Union (EMU), national governments and fiscal authorities cannot play the role of Stackelberg leader vis-à-vis the European Central Bank (ECB). Indeed, they have distinct interests, and the current European institutional framework doesn't allow an effective coordination between these authorities. So, Hughes Hallett (2005) assesses that the evidence suggests, in the EMU, 'weak monetary leadership—or more likely, a straightforward non-cooperative game'. Therefore, we suppose the following strategic interaction and non-cooperative game between the monetary and fiscal authorities. In order to suit to the European framework, we consider that the budgetary policies of the national governments are defined by the budgetary constraints in equations (11) and (36). Taking into account these inter-temporal constraints, and the equilibrium budgetary policies of the governments (which remain at the Nash solution), we will suppose that the central bank is a Stackelberg leader, and can chose accordingly its equilibrium monetary policy.

4.1. Monetary Policy of the Common Central Bank

We suppose that the main goal (α_π^M) of the central bank (as for the ECB in Europe) is to stabilize the inflation rate in the whole monetary union (for example: in the Euro Area) around an inflation target (zero). Regarding the tradition of Taylor rules, the central bank can also give a non-negligible weight to stabilizing economic activity (α_y^M), whereas interest rate smoothing (α_i^M) corresponds to the empirical limitation of fluctuations of the nominal interest rate. Besides, Kirsanova et al. (2005) are reluctant to introduce a public debt goal in the loss function of the central bank, as in their backward-looking modeling, it could imply economic cycles with a higher volatility of economic activity and inflation. However, as in Beetsma and Vermeylen (2007) for example, in our forward-looking model, we consider that the central bank can have a secondary goal: minimizing variations in the public debt levels of the member countries (α_b^M), as these public debts could affect price levels in the monetary union (Fiscal Theory of the Price Level). Indeed, inflation can mechanically decrease the real cost of the public debt service for highly indebted governments, which have therefore interest to exert some pressure on the central bank in order to allow a higher inflation rate. So, we suppose that the loss function of the central bank is as follows:

$$L_t^M = E_t \sum_{k=t}^{\infty} \beta^{k-t} \{\alpha_\pi^M \pi_k^{*2} + \alpha_y^M (y_k^* - y^*)^2 + \alpha_i^M \widehat{\iota_k}^2 + \alpha_b^M bb_k^{*2}\} \tag{44}$$

Here, (α_b^M) is the relative weight given by the central bank to the goal of stabilizing the average public debt to GDP ratio in the monetary union, in comparison with the price stability goal, even if it is not in the mandate of the ECB and other central banks. This parameter is therefore an indicator of the lack of independence of the central bank from the governments: the central bank is fully independent if ($\alpha_b^M = 0$), whereas it becomes more dependent as this parameter increases. Indeed, for the governments, the concern about the public debt level can be due to the fact that a high public debt can increase inequalities regarding inter and intra-generations income redistribution, increase tax distortions, or imply crowding-out effects on capital accumulation. Furthermore, according to the parameter (α_b^M), countries with higher public debt levels exert more influence on the conduct of the common monetary policy. We also suppose that the long term public debt to GDP ratio is stable: $(bb_i = bb^* = 0)$.

Given the loss function in equation (44) of the common central bank, what is the equilibrium monetary policy, and the fiscal externalities due to this common monetary policy?

Using equations (B7) and (C1) in Appendixes B and C, $\left[\frac{\partial \pi^*_{t+k}}{\partial \widehat{\iota_t}} = \frac{\partial \pi^i_{i,+k}}{\partial \widehat{\iota_t}} = 0\right]$. Current average supply shocks influence the current average inflation rate in the monetary union, but not the long term inflation rate which is supposed to be null. So, in the framework of our model, a variation of the nominal interest rate of the common central bank cannot influence the average inflation rate in the monetary union. The monetary authority can only impact and stabilize symmetric demand shocks, but it cannot stabilize supply shocks. Besides, $\left[\frac{\partial \widehat{\iota_{t+k}}}{\partial \widehat{\iota_t}} = 0 \; for \; k > 0\right]$, as the variation of the current nominal interest rate is supposed to be independent from its past variations if monetary policy is discretionary.

Using equations (C2) and (C4) in Appendix C, $\left[\frac{\partial y^*_t}{\partial \widehat{\iota_{t+k}}} = \frac{\partial y_{i,t}}{\partial \widehat{\iota_{t+k}}} = -\theta \; for \; k \geq 0\right]$; an increase of the current nominal interest rate decreases current economic activity in all member countries of the monetary union. Indeed, it increases the real interest rate, and therefore, because of the intertemporal substitution of private consumption in the behavior of households, it increases sparing to the detriment of private consumption.

Using equation (B8) in Appendix B, $\left[\frac{\partial bb^*_t}{\partial \widehat{\iota_{t+k}}} = \frac{\partial bb_{i,t}}{\partial \widehat{\iota_{t+k}}} = (\theta - 1)\beta^k > 0 \; for \; k \geq 0\right]$; an increase of the current nominal interest rate increases the current public debt to GDP ratio in all member countries of the monetary union. Indeed, it increases the cost of the reimbursement of this public debt for the following period, and so, there is an incentive to increase immediately the public indebtedness (when the cost is weaker) instead of delaying it.

So, if the central bank minimizes its loss function in equation (44), it chooses the following variation of the nominal interest rate:

$$\widehat{\iota_t} = \frac{\alpha_y^M \theta}{\alpha_i^M}(y_t^* - y^*) - \frac{\alpha_b^M(\theta-1)}{\alpha_i^M} bb_t^* \tag{45}$$

Therefore, the monetary policy implies that the nominal interest rate tries to stick to the equilibrium long term interest rate (i). Nevertheless, in comparison with this long term level, the nominal interest rate increases if average economic activity in the monetary union increases quicker than its long term tendency; the more contractionary monetary policy then has a contra-cyclical role in avoiding expansionary and inflationary tensions. Besides, the nominal interest rate decreases if the average public debt to GDP ratio increases in the monetary union, in order to reduce the weight of this public debt for the following period.

We can also mention that interest rates responses to economic activity or public debt deviations increase with the intertemporal elasticity of substitution of private spending (θ). To the contrary, the weight given to the goal of limiting interest rates fluctuations (α_i^M) reduces obviously the responses of monetary policy to activity or public debt deviations.

Therefore, using equations (45), (B8) and (C2) in Appendixes B and C, if we suppose that expected variations of the interest rate for the future periods are null $[E_t(\widehat{\iota_{t+k}}) = 0\ for\ k \geq 1]$, the variation of the nominal interest rate in comparison with its long term level chosen by the common central bank is as follows:

$$\widehat{\iota_t} = \frac{[\alpha_y^M \theta + \alpha_b^M(\theta-1)]}{[\alpha_i^M + \alpha_y^M \theta^2 + \alpha_b^M(\theta-1)^2]} \varepsilon_t^{*d} - \frac{\alpha_b^M(\theta-1)}{[\alpha_i^M + \alpha_y^M \theta^2 + \alpha_b^M(\theta-1)^2]} \varepsilon_t^{*b} \tag{46}$$

So, the nominal interest rate increases after an average symmetric positive demand shock in the monetary union (ε_t^{*d}), as the central bank then conducts a more contractionary contra-cyclical monetary policy. To the contrary, the nominal interest rate decreases after a positive shock on the average public debt to GDP ratio in the monetary union, in order to lighten the future weight of the reimbursement of this public debt. These interest rates variations are obviously reduced by the goal of interest rate smoothing (α_i^M), and are less than proportional to demand or public debt shocks. The interest rate is also less reduced, after a positive shock on the average public debt to GDP ratio in the monetary union, if stabilizing economic activity is a more important goal for the governments $\left[\partial\left(\frac{\partial \hat{\iota}_t}{\partial \varepsilon_t^{*b}}\right)/\partial \alpha_y^M > 0\right]$. However, interest rates fluctuations are accentuated, and monetary policy is more active, if public indebtedness in the monetary union (α_b^M) is a non-negligible goal for the central bank, and if the latter is therefore less independent from budgetary pressures $\left[\partial\left(\frac{\partial \hat{\iota}_t}{\partial \varepsilon_t^{*d}}\right)/\partial \alpha_b^M > 0 \; and \; \partial\left(\frac{\partial \hat{\iota}_t}{\partial \varepsilon_t^{*b}}\right)/\partial \alpha_b^M < 0\right]$[9].

4.2. Consequences for Economic Activity and the Labor Market

This monetary reaction function influences economic activity. Indeed, according to equations (46), and (C4) and (C5) in Appendix C, we obtain:

$$y_{i,t} = y^* + \left(\varepsilon_{i,t}^d - \varepsilon_t^{*d}\right) + \frac{\left[\alpha_i^M - \alpha_b^M(\theta - 1)\right]}{\left[\alpha_i^M + \alpha_y^M\theta^2 + \alpha_b^M(\theta - 1)^2\right]}\varepsilon_t^{*d} + \frac{\alpha_b^M\theta(\theta-1)}{\left[\alpha_i^M+\alpha_y^M\theta^2+\alpha_b^M(\theta-1)^2\right]}\varepsilon_t^{*b} \tag{47}$$

$$c_{i,t} = g_{i,t} = y^* - \frac{\theta\left[\alpha_y^M\theta + \alpha_b^M(\theta - 1)\right]}{\left[\alpha_i^M + \alpha_y^M\theta^2 + \alpha_b^M(\theta - 1)^2\right]}\varepsilon_t^{*d}$$

---

[9] The derivatives of equation (46) show that the effect of the height of the intertemporal elasticity of substitution of private consumption (θ) on the monetary reaction function is ambiguous.

$$+\frac{\alpha_b^M \theta(\theta-1)}{[\alpha_i^M+\alpha_y^M \theta^2+\alpha_b^M (\theta-1)^2]}\varepsilon_t^{*b} \tag{48}$$

Indeed, in the framework of our model, private and public consumption expenditure vary at the same pace in all member countries of the monetary union. However, an asymmetric positive demand shock in a given country (i) ($\varepsilon_{i,t}^d - \varepsilon_t^{*d}$) can increase the relative economic activity in this country [see equation (47)], as well as its labor demand and supply and its real wage. Indeed, equations (C10) and (C11) in Appendix C imply:

$$l_{i,t} = \frac{\left(\alpha_i^M + \alpha_y^M \theta\right)}{(1+\varphi)\left[\alpha_i^M + \alpha_y^M \theta^2 + \alpha_b^M (\theta-1)^2\right]}\varepsilon_t^{*d} + \frac{1}{(1+\varphi)}\left(\varepsilon_{i,t}^d - \varepsilon_t^{*d}\right)$$
$$+\frac{(\theta-1)}{\theta(1+\varphi)}y^* + \frac{\alpha_b^M(\theta-1)^2}{(1+\varphi)\left[\alpha_i^M+\alpha_y^M \theta^2+\alpha_b^M (\theta-1)^2\right]}\varepsilon_t^{*b} \tag{49}$$

$$\left(w_{i,t} - p_{i,t}\right) = \frac{\left[\varphi\alpha_i^M - \alpha_y^M \theta - (1+\varphi)\alpha_b^M(\theta-1)\right]}{(1+\varphi)\left[\alpha_i^M + \alpha_y^M \theta^2 + \alpha_b^M (\theta-1)^2\right]}\varepsilon_t^{*d}$$
$$+\frac{\varphi}{(1+\varphi)}\left(\varepsilon_{i,t}^d - \varepsilon_t^{*d}\right)$$
$$+\frac{(1+\varphi\theta)}{\theta(1+\varphi)}y^* + \frac{(1+\varphi\theta)\alpha_b^M(\theta-1)}{(1+\varphi)\left[\alpha_i^M+\alpha_y^M \theta^2+\alpha_b^M (\theta-1)^2\right]}\varepsilon_t^{*b} \tag{50}$$

Besides, an average or symmetric positive demand shock (ε_t^{*d}) in the monetary union implies a contractionary monetary policy (increase of the interest rate). In these conditions, private and public consumption are reduced in the same proportions in all member countries of the monetary union, because of this contractionary monetary policy and of the increase of the real interest rate. Furthermore, the contra-cyclical monetary policy stabilizes variations of economic activity, which are less than proportional to the demand shock. Economic activity can be higher if the increase of the interest rate is limited by interest rate smoothing $\left[\partial\left(\frac{\partial y_{i,t}}{\partial \varepsilon_t^{*d}}\right)/\partial\alpha_i^M = \partial\left(\frac{\partial c_{i,t}}{\partial \varepsilon_t^{*d}}\right)/\partial\alpha_i^M = \partial\left(\frac{\partial g_{i,t}}{\partial \varepsilon_t^{*d}}\right)/\partial\alpha_i^M > 0\right]$, whereas it is better stabilized, and it can even decrease, like private and public consumption, if the variation of the interest rate is strongly accentuated by budgetary pressures and by the lack of independence of the central bank $\left[\partial\left(\frac{\partial y_{i,t}}{\partial \varepsilon_t^{*d}}\right)/\partial \alpha_b^M = \partial\left(\frac{\partial c_{i,t}}{\partial \varepsilon_t^{*d}}\right)/\partial \alpha_b^M = \partial\left(\frac{\partial g_{i,t}}{\partial \varepsilon_t^{*d}}\right)/\partial \alpha_b^M < 0\right]$.

A symmetric positive demand shock (for example, on private investment or net exports towards the rest of the world) always increases labor supply and demand in the monetary union, whereas the effect on the real wage is more ambiguous [see equations (49) and (50)]. Obviously, like for economic activity, they are both higher if interest rate smoothing constrains the contractionary monetary policy and the increase of the nominal interest rate, whereas they are reduced by budgetary pressures $\left[\partial\left(\frac{\partial l_{i,t}}{\partial \varepsilon_t^{*d}}\right)/\partial \alpha_b^M < 0 \; and \; \partial\left(\frac{\partial w_{i,t}-p_{i,t}}{\partial \varepsilon_t^{*d}}\right)/\partial \alpha_b^M < 0\right]$. Therefore, it seems that a less independent central bank, caring about public debt levels in the member countries of the monetary union, is more active and better mitigates the expansionary (deflationary) effect of a positive (negative) demand shock on economic activity and on the labor market, and therefore, that it is a source of macro-economic stability and of attenuation of economic cycles regarding demand shocks.

A shock increasing the average public debt-to-GDP ratio in the monetary union (ε_t^{*b}) implies an expansionary monetary policy (weaker interest rate) in order to lighten the weight of this public debt. So, this monetary policy increases economic activity in all member countries of the monetary union $\left[\partial\left(\frac{\partial y_{i,t}}{\partial \varepsilon_t^{*b}}\right)/\partial \alpha_b^M = \partial\left(\frac{\partial c_{i,t}}{\partial \varepsilon_t^{*b}}\right)/\partial \alpha_b^M = \partial\left(\frac{\partial g_{i,t}}{\partial \varepsilon_t^{*b}}\right)/\partial \alpha_b^M > 0\right]$, provided the central bank is not fully independent and cares about public indebtedness of the member countries ($\alpha_b^M > 0$). So, this monetary policy also increases labor demand and supply and the real wage on the labor market. However, the traditional goals of the central bank, interest rate smoothing and stabilizing output, mitigate and reduce these expansionary effects of monetary policy. Therefore, the fact that the common central bank cares about public debt levels ($\alpha_b^M > 0$) implies macroeconomic cycles which would not exist without such concern $\left(\frac{\partial y_{i,t}}{\partial \varepsilon_t^{*b}} = \frac{\partial l_{i,t}}{\partial \varepsilon_t^{*b}} = 0 \; if \; \alpha_b^M = 0\right)$ and without any variation of the nominal interest rate.

Finally, what are the consequences of the monetary policy defined in section 4.1 on the variation of the public debt to GDP ratio in each member country of the monetary union? Using equations (46) and (B8) in Appendix B, we obtain:

$$bb_{i,t} = -\left(\varepsilon_{i,t}^{d} - \varepsilon_t^{*d}\right) - \frac{\left(\alpha_i^M + \alpha_y^M \theta\right)}{\left[\alpha_i^M + \alpha_y^M \theta^2 + \alpha_b^M (\theta - 1)^2\right]} \varepsilon_t^{*d}$$

$$+\left(\varepsilon_{i,t}^{b} - \varepsilon_t^{*b}\right) + \frac{\left(\alpha_i^M + \alpha_y^M \theta^2\right)}{\left[\alpha_i^M + \alpha_y^M \theta^2 + \alpha_b^M (\theta - 1)^2\right]} \varepsilon_t^{*b} \qquad (51)$$

So, a positive demand shock reduces the current public debt to GDP ratio, if it is a global and average symmetric shock (ε_t^{*d}), but also if this shock is asymmetric and higher in the national country (i) than in the other member countries of the monetary union ($\varepsilon_{i,t}^{d} > \varepsilon_t^{*d}$). However, after a positive average demand shock (ε_t^{*d}), the effect is less than proportional. The public debt to GDP ratio decreases more strongly in all member countries of the monetary union as interest rate smoothing is a more important goal for the central bank $\left[\partial \left(\frac{\partial bb_{i,t}}{\partial \varepsilon_t^{*d}}\right) / \partial \alpha_i^M < 0\right]$. Indeed, monetary policy is then less active and contractionary, and the weaker increase of the nominal interest rate avoids an excessive increase of the cost of the reimbursement of the public debt. On the contrary, variations of public debt to GDP ratios are, obviously, more limited if the central bank gives a non-negligible weight to stabilizing these ratios $\left[\partial \left(\frac{\partial bb_{i,t}}{\partial \varepsilon_t^{*d}}\right) / \partial \alpha_b^M > 0\right]$ and is more sensible to budgetary pressures (if α_b^M is high), or if the intertemporal elasticity of substitution of private consumption is high $\left[\partial \left(\frac{\partial bb_{i,t}}{\partial \varepsilon_t^{*d}}\right) / \partial \theta > 0\right]$.

Obviously, a positive shock on the public debt increases the current public debt to GDP ratio, if it is a global and average symmetric shock

(ε_t^{*b}), but also if this shock is asymmetric and higher in the national country (i) than in the other member countries of the monetary union ($\varepsilon_{i,t}^b > \varepsilon_t^{*b}$). However, after a positive shock on the average public debt (ε_t^{*b}), the effect is less than proportional. The public debt to GDP ratio increases more strongly in all member countries of the monetary union if interest rate smoothing $\left[\partial\left(\frac{\partial bb_{i,t}}{\partial \varepsilon_t^{*b}}\right)/\partial \alpha_i^M > 0\right]$ or if stabilizing economic activity $\left[\partial\left(\frac{\partial bb_{i,t}}{\partial \varepsilon_t^{*b}}\right)/\partial \alpha_y^M > 0\right]$ has a higher weight for the central bank. Indeed, monetary policy is then less active and expansionary, and the limited decrease of the nominal interest rate reduces the relief for the cost of the reimbursement of the public debt. On the contrary, variations of public debt to GDP ratios are, obviously, more limited if the central bank gives a non-negligible weight to stabilizing these ratios $\left[\partial\left(\frac{\partial bb_{i,t}}{\partial \varepsilon_t^{*b}}\right)/\partial \alpha_b^M < 0\right]$ and if it is more sensible to budgetary pressures (if α_b^M is high), and/or if the intertemporal elasticity of substitution of private consumption is high $\left[\partial\left(\frac{\partial bb_{i,t}}{\partial \varepsilon_t^{*b}}\right)/\partial \theta < 0\right]$.

Therefore, it is quite obvious that in case of symmetric demand or public debt shocks, variations of public debt to GDP ratios in the member countries of the monetary union can be reduced if the central bank is influenced by political pressures, cares about public indebtedness, and conducts therefore a more active monetary policy.

5. Various Parameters Influencing Fiscal Externalities

Some institutional factors strongly influence the previous results mentioned in section 4 regarding public debt externalities, and therefore, we are now going to review them successively: the institutional independence of the central bank (we will take the example of the ECB), the case of commitment of the central bank, and the possibility that the central bank be concerned with the situation of each specific member country in the monetary union.

5.1. The Institutional Independence of the ECB

Our modeling has shown that an independent central bank (α_b^M is near zero) conducts a less active monetary policy. In particular, it is then immune from shocks on average public indebtedness in the monetary union; then, such shocks cannot influence economic activity, private or public consumption, or the situation of the labor market. That is why in order to reduce fiscal externalities between the member countries of the EMU, the European authorities have institutionally ensured the independence of the European Central Bank. Indeed, Article 130 of the Treaty on the Functioning of the European Union states that:

> "When exercising the powers and carrying out the tasks and duties conferred upon them by the Treaties and the Statute of the ESCB and of the ECB, neither the European Central Bank, nor a national central bank, nor any member of their decision-making bodies shall seek or take instructions from Union institutions, bodies, offices or agencies, from any government of a Member State or from any other body. The Union institutions, bodies, offices or agencies and the governments of the Member States undertake to respect this principle and not to seek to influence the members of the decision-making bodies of the European Central Bank or of the national central banks in the performance of their tasks".

So, the institutional framework for the single monetary policy aims at protecting the ECB from all types of political influence; this independence of the ECB consists of five main pillars. Beyond the institutional independence mentioned in the previous article, the statutes of the European System of Central Banks (ESBC) protect the personal independence of the ECB's Executive Board members: they are appointed for a non-renewable term of eight years and can only be removed from office in case of serious misconduct. Third, the ECB and the national central banks have a financial and organizational independence: they have their own financial resources, and they are free to organize their internal structure. Fourth, the ECB has its own legal personality. Fifth, the ECB benefits from a functional and operational independence. It is assigned all necessary competencies to achieve its primary objective of price stability, and the Euro-system enjoys exclusive competence for monetary policy in the Euro Area. Furthermore, the ECB is prohibited from lending directly to the public sector, in order to be protected from pressure of public authorities. Indeed, Article 125 of the previous Treaty states:

> "The Union shall not be liable for or assume the commitments of central governments, regional, local or other public authorities, other bodies governed by public law, or public undertakings of any Member State, without prejudice to mutual financial guarantees for the joint execution of a specific project".

Extensive empirical evidence and theoretical analyses have shown that independent central banks are better capable of maintaining low inflation rates. So, the Treaty on the Functioning of the EU gives the ECB the very clear and limited mandate to maintain price stability in the euro area, and its institutional independence is intended to preserve it from short-term political influence when fulfilling this mandate. However, there is a flaw with the previous 'no bailout' clause (Article 125). Because commercial banks are an essential source of funding for the governments, the ECB is intended to refuse liquidity to banks domiciled in insolvent members States. Thus, the ECB is founded on rules that prevent it from serving as lender of last resort; but no insolvency procedures are then provided for Euro Area members States. Nevertheless, in such an undefined framework, the ECB accepted as collateral debt liabilities guaranteed by the Greek State, for example, a sequence of loans that Greece was unable to repay, whereas a truly independent central bank should have refused such collaterals. Besides, following the public debt crisis in Greece in 2010, the use of funds to reimburse national central banks in France or Germany deepened the problem of insolvency of the Greek government. The decision to issue new loan tranches, without cutting off liquidities, was political, and during this crisis, the decisions of the ECB were mostly governed by the governments of Europe's creditor countries.

On 26 July 2012, in the context of the debt crisis, Mario Draghi, President of the ECB, assesses the following famous sentence: "*Within our mandate, the ECB is ready to do whatever it takes to preserve the euro. And believe me, it will be enough*". This sentence was enough to allow a decrease of interest rate spreads on governments bonds of peripheral countries, and to open again the credit channel. Besides, in the post financial crisis era, like other central banks, the ECB has been entrusted with powers and responsibilities going beyond its traditional monetary policy mandate. For example, the ECB started acting in the areas of macro- and micro-prudential supervision and crisis management, and it has adopted unconventional monetary policy measures (Quantitative Easing, Outright Monetary Transactions). In the context of this new role of Supervisor, critical voices then claim that the ECB has over-stretched its mandate, blurring or even crossing the line into fiscal and economic policy, putting into question its effective empirical independence.

The primacy of national competence in the field of macro-prudential policy is clarified in Article 127(5) of the Treaty, which states that "*the ESCB shall contribute to the smooth conduct of policies pursued by the competent authorities relating to the stability of the financial system*". This implies that, in general, the Euro-system has only a contributory role to the formulation of macro-prudential policies, a competence which remains essentially national. The implication of the ESCB in the management of a crisis is more a contributory task rather than an own competence, and the ECB is not policy-maker in this field. However, last years have shown that the institutional independence of the ECB is more difficult to comply with empirically, in times of crisis management. Indeed, Buiter and Rahbari (2012) show that since 2010, the ECB has been acting as sovereign Lender of Last Resort through its Securities Market Program purchases of periphery sovereign debt (Greek, Portuguese, Irish, Spanish and Italian government debt securities) in the secondary markets (article 125 prevents purchases on the primary market). Through the heavily subsidized (cheap and attractive credit conditions regarding interest rates) bank funding it provided through Longer Term Refinancing Operations, the ECB has also indirectly fostered the purchase by domestic banks in the primary issue markets of the sovereign debt of their own country. The authors also mention a 'financial repression' from the ECB, requiring banks (for example: in Italy or in Spain) to purchase more of their own government's debt than they would voluntarily and at below-market yields.

In the framework of our modelling, the monetary policy of a less independent central bank ($\alpha_b^M > 0$) is more active, which obviously reduces fluctuations in public debt to GDP ratios. However, we have also shown that this can be source of instability for economic activity and for the labor market, in case of shocks on average public indebtedness, which characterizes a situation of public debt crisis.

5.2. The Case of Commitment of the Central Bank

We are now going to study the consequences of a potential commitment of the central bank on the previous macro-economic equilibrium defined in section 4. If the central bank can commit, according to equation (44), the monetary policy to implement in period (t+n), which verifies $\left[\frac{\partial L_t^M}{\partial \widehat{\iota_{t+n}}} = 0\right]$, is the following, using equations (C2) and (B8):

$$\left[\alpha_i^M \beta^n + \alpha_y^M \theta^2 \sum_{k=0}^{n} \beta^k + \alpha_b^M (\theta - 1)^2 \sum_{k=0}^{n} \beta^k \left(\frac{1}{1+i}\right)^{2(n-k)}\right] \widehat{\iota_{t+n}}$$
$$= -\alpha_y^M \theta^2 \sum_{j=0}^{n-1} \beta^j \sum_{k=j}^{n-1} \widehat{\iota_{t+k}}$$
$$- \alpha_b^M (\theta - 1)^2 \sum_{j=0}^{n-1} \beta^j \sum_{k=j}^{n-1} \left(\frac{1}{1+i}\right)^{n+k-2j} \widehat{\iota_{t+k}}$$

$$+\sum_{k=0}^{n}\left[\alpha_y^M\theta\beta^k+\alpha_b^M(\theta-1)\beta^k\left(\frac{1}{1+i}\right)^{n-k}\right]\varepsilon_{t+k}^{*d}$$
$$-\alpha_b^M(\theta-1)\sum_{k=0}^{n}\beta^k\left(\frac{1}{1+i}\right)^{n-k}\varepsilon_{t+k}^{*b} \quad (52)$$

Therefore, monetary policy in case of commitment is time-inconsistent, as the policy that should be implemented in period (t+n) given data of period (t) is effectively different from the policy that will be effectively implemented in period (t+n) if discretionary re-optimization were allowed. In case of commitment, monetary policy should react less to demand or public debt shocks, it should be less active. Indeed, a discretionary re-optimization implies a more reactive monetary policy, which is more contractionary is case of positive demand shocks, and more expansionary in case of positive shocks on the public debt-to-GDP ratio. Indeed, comparing equations (46) and (52), we obtain:

$$\left|\frac{\partial\widehat{\iota_{t+n}}}{\partial\varepsilon_{t+n}^{*d}}\right| = \frac{\beta^n\left[\alpha_y^M\theta+\alpha_b^M(\theta-1)\right]}{\left[\alpha_i^M\beta^n+\alpha_y^M\theta^2\sum_{k=0}^{n}\beta^k+\alpha_b^M(\theta-1)^2\sum_{k=0}^{n}\beta^k\left(\frac{1}{1+i}\right)^{2(n-k)}\right]} < \left|\frac{\partial\widehat{\iota_t}}{\partial\varepsilon_t^{*d}}\right| \quad (53)$$

$$\left|\frac{\partial\widehat{\iota_{t+n}}}{\partial\varepsilon_{t+n}^{*b}}\right| = \frac{\alpha_b^M(\theta-1)\beta^n}{\left[\alpha_i^M\beta^n+\alpha_y^M\theta^2\sum_{k=0}^{n}\beta^k+\alpha_b^M(\theta-1)^2\sum_{k=0}^{n}\beta^k\left(\frac{1}{1+i}\right)^{2(n-k)}\right]} < \left|\frac{\partial\widehat{\iota_t}}{\partial\varepsilon_t^{*b}}\right| \quad (54)$$

$$As{:}\ \alpha_y^M\theta^2\sum_{k=0}^{n-1}\beta^k+\alpha_b^M(\theta-1)^2\sum_{k=0}^{n-1}\beta^k\left(\frac{1}{1+i}\right)^{2(n-k)}>0$$

In case of commitment, all interest rates are fixed for the future periods, and the sequence of interest rates chosen for all periods between (t) and (t+n) depends on all other interest rates and shocks during the whole period. So, the interest rate for a given period (t+n) depends on all demand and public debt shocks between the periods (t) and (t+n). In this context, using equations (C4) and (52), regarding the effect of an average demand shock in the period (t+n) on economic activity during the same period (t+n), we obtain:

$$\frac{\partial y_{i,t+n}}{\partial \varepsilon_{t+n}^{*d}} = 1 - \theta \frac{\partial \widehat{\iota_{t+n}}}{\partial \varepsilon_{t+n}^{*d}}$$

$$= \frac{\left[\alpha_i^M \beta^n + \alpha_y^M \theta^2 \sum_{k=0}^{n-1} \beta^k + \alpha_b^M (\theta-1)^2 \sum_{k=0}^{n-1} \beta^k \left(\frac{1}{1+i}\right)^{2(n-k)} - \alpha_b^M (\theta-1)\beta^n\right]}{\left[\alpha_i^M \beta^n + \alpha_y^M \theta^2 \sum_{k=0}^{n} \beta^k + \alpha_b^M (\theta-1)^2 \sum_{k=0}^{n} \beta^k \left(\frac{1}{1+i}\right)^{2(n-k)}\right]}$$

$$> \frac{\partial y_{i,t}}{\partial \varepsilon_t^{*d}} \qquad (55)$$

So, in case of commitment, monetary policy is less active (contractionary) after an average and symmetric positive demand shock in the monetary union, and then, economic activity is higher in a given country (i) for all future periods. On the contrary, monetary policy is less active (expansionary) after an average and symmetric public debt shock in the monetary union, if the monetary authority is concerned about public indebtedness in the member countries of the monetary union (α_b^M>0). Economic activity is then weaker in a given country (i) for all future periods. Indeed, regarding the effect of an average public debt shock in the period (t+n) on economic activity during the same period (t+n), we obtain:

$$\frac{\partial y_{i,t+n}}{\partial \varepsilon_{t+n}^{*b}}$$

$$= \frac{\alpha_b^M \theta(\theta-1)\beta^n}{\left[\alpha_i^M \beta^n + \alpha_y^M \theta^2 \sum_{k=0}^{n} \beta^k + \alpha_b^M (\theta-1)^2 \sum_{k=0}^{n} \beta^k \left(\frac{1}{1+i}\right)^{2(n-k)}\right]}$$

$$< \frac{\partial y_{i,t}}{\partial \varepsilon_t^{*b}} \tag{56}$$

Therefore, commitment would imply the risk to increase economic fluctuations and to reduce the future well-being, if monetary policy is less active, in case of symmetric demand shocks. On the contrary, commitment would reduce potential economic fluctuations in case of average public debt shocks. So, a potential commitment from the central bank would only be beneficial in case of average public debt shocks in all member countries of the monetary union and if the central bank cares about these shocks, because macro-economic fluctuations and fiscal externalities would then be reduced.

Besides, using equations (52) and (B8), we also obtain the following expected variation of the public debt to GDP ratio in a given country (i) in a future period (t+n), after an expected demand or public debt shock in this future period:

$$\frac{\partial bb_{i,t+n}}{\partial \varepsilon_{t+n}^{*d}} = (\theta - 1)\frac{\partial \widehat{\imath_{t+n}}}{\partial \varepsilon_{t+n}^{*d}} - 1$$
$$= -\frac{\left[\left(\alpha_i^M + \alpha_y^M \theta\right)\beta^n + \alpha_y^M \theta^2 \sum_{k=0}^{n-1} \beta^k + \alpha_b^M (\theta - 1)^2 \sum_{k=0}^{n-1} \beta^k \left(\frac{1}{1+i}\right)^{2(n-k)}\right]}{\left[\alpha_i^M \beta^n + \alpha_y^M \theta^2 \sum_{k=0}^{n} \beta^k + \alpha_b^M (\theta - 1)^2 \sum_{k=0}^{n} \beta^k \left(\frac{1}{1+i}\right)^{2(n-k)}\right]}$$
$$< \frac{\partial bb_{i,t}}{\partial \varepsilon_t^{*d}} \tag{57}$$

$$\frac{\partial bb_{i,t+n}}{\partial \varepsilon_{t+n}^{*b}}$$
$$= \frac{\left[\alpha_i^M \beta^n + \alpha_y^M \theta^2 \sum_{k=0}^{n} \beta^k + \alpha_b^M (\theta - 1)^2 \sum_{k=0}^{n-1} \beta^k \left(\frac{1}{1+i}\right)^{2(n-k)}\right]}{\left[\alpha_i^M \beta^n + \alpha_y^M \theta^2 \sum_{k=0}^{n} \beta^k + \alpha_b^M (\theta - 1)^2 \sum_{k=0}^{n} \beta^k \left(\frac{1}{1+i}\right)^{2(n-k)}\right]}$$
$$> \frac{\partial bb_{i,t}}{\partial \varepsilon_t^{*b}} \tag{58}$$

So, fluctuations of public debt to GDP ratios in all future periods would be accentuated if the common central bank can commit, in case of symmetric demand or public debt shocks, because monetary policy is then less active.

Independence is a statute which goal is to shield the decision-making process of the ECB from short-term political pressures in order to enable it effectively to pursue the aim of price stability. This independence is therefore a necessary condition for allowing commitment in the definition of monetary policy. So, the literature on rules versus discretion points out that decision-makers who are subject to political election cycles tend to act in a more short-sighted manner when exercising their mandate. This short-termism creates an inflation bias, making it difficult to credibly promise actions which will validate low inflation expectations over time. To overcome this time-inconsistency problem, monetary policy needs to be delegated to an institution which is sufficiently detached from these cycles.

However, commitment is more a theoretical concept than an empirically useful framework. Indeed, as other central banks, the ECB cannot credibly tie its hands regarding the monetary policy that it will conduct for distant periods. Besides, in the framework of our model, commitment to a given monetary policy implies the risk to increase fluctuations of public debt to GDP ratios, as well as to accentuate macro-economic cycles in case of demand shocks (public debt shocks are without effect as long as the central bank is independent and $\alpha_b^M = 0$). Therefore, commitment regarding the common monetary policy of the central bank doesn't seem to be the solution to better insulate a country from fiscal externalities coming from its partners in a monetary union.

5.3. A Central Bank Concerned with the Relative Situations of the Countries

A last situation that we want to study is the one where the central bank is not concerned with the deviation of the average public debt to GDP ratio (or inflation, or economic activity) in the whole monetary union, but with the average deviation of each individual public debt to GDP ratio (or inflation rate, or economic activity) in the member countries of the monetary union. Therefore, in this framework, each individual country can have an impact on the monetary policy of the common central bank, which increases with its relative size. So, if there are (n) member countries in the monetary union, the central bank minimizes the following loss function:

$$L_t^M = E_t \sum_{k=t}^{\propto} \beta^{k-t} \left\{ \alpha_\pi^M \sum_{j=1}^{n} \pi_{j,k}^2 + \alpha_y^M \sum_{j=1}^{n} \left(y_{j,k} - y^*\right)^2 + n\alpha_i^M \widehat{\iota_k}^2 + \alpha_b^M \sum_{j=1}^{n} bb_{j,k}^2 \right\} \tag{59}$$

So, using equations (B8) and (C4) in Appendixes B and C, the common central bank then chooses the following variation of the nominal interest rate, where a shock in an individual member country (j) affects the common monetary policy, according to its relative share (1/n) in the monetary union:

$$\widehat{\iota_t} = \frac{\left[\alpha_y^M \theta + \alpha_b^M (\theta - 1)\right]}{n\left[\alpha_i^M + \alpha_y^M \theta^2 + \alpha_b^M (\theta - 1)^2\right]} \sum_{j=1}^{n} \varepsilon_{j,t}^d - \frac{\alpha_b^M (\theta-1)}{n\left[\alpha_i^M + \alpha_y^M \theta^2 + \alpha_b^M (\theta-1)^2\right]} \sum_{j=1}^{n} \varepsilon_{j,t}^b \tag{60}$$

In this context, using equations (C4) and (C5), variations of economic activity, private and public consumption are as follows:

$$y_{i,t} = y^* - \frac{\theta\left[\alpha_y^M \theta + \alpha_b^M (\theta - 1)\right]}{n\left[\alpha_i^M + \alpha_y^M \theta^2 + \alpha_b^M (\theta - 1)^2\right]} \left[\varepsilon_{i,t}^d - \frac{1}{(n-1)} \sum_{j \neq i} \varepsilon_{j,t}^d\right] + \left[\varepsilon_{i,t}^d - \frac{1}{(n-1)} \sum_{j \neq i} \varepsilon_{j,t}^d\right] + \frac{\left[\alpha_i^M - \alpha_b^M (\theta - 1)\right]}{(n-1)\left[\alpha_i^M + \alpha_y^M \theta^2 + \alpha_b^M (\theta - 1)^2\right]} \sum_{j \neq i} \varepsilon_{j,t}^d$$

$$+\frac{\alpha_b^M\theta(\theta-1)}{[\alpha_i^M+\alpha_y^M\theta^2+\alpha_b^M(\theta-1)^2]}\left[\frac{1}{n}\left(\varepsilon_{i,t}^b-\frac{1}{(n-1)}\sum_{j\neq i}\varepsilon_{j,t}^b\right)+\frac{1}{(n-1)}\sum_{j\neq i}\varepsilon_{j,t}^b\right] \quad (61)$$

$$c_{i,t}=g_{i,t}=y^*$$
$$-\frac{\theta\left[\alpha_y^M\theta+\alpha_b^M(\theta-1)\right]}{\left[\alpha_i^M+\alpha_y^M\theta^2+\alpha_b^M(\theta-1)^2\right]}\left[\frac{1}{n}\left(\varepsilon_{i,t}^d-\frac{1}{(n-1)}\sum_{j\neq i}\varepsilon_{j,t}^d\right)+\frac{1}{(n-1)}\sum_{j\neq i}\varepsilon_{j,t}^b\right]$$
$$+\frac{\alpha_b^M\theta(\theta-1)}{[\alpha_i^M+\alpha_y^M\theta^2+\alpha_b^M(\theta-1)^2]}\left[\frac{1}{n}\left(\varepsilon_{i,t}^b-\frac{1}{(n-1)}\sum_{j\neq i}\varepsilon_{j,t}^b\right)+\frac{1}{(n-1)}\sum_{j\neq i}\varepsilon_{j,t}^b\right] \quad (62)$$

So, a positive demand shock in the foreign countries ($\varepsilon_{j,t}^d$) reduces private and public consumption, whereas a positive shock on the public debt to GDP ratio in the foreign countries ($\varepsilon_{j,t}^b$) increases economic activity and consumption, but all the more as (n) is weak, in comparison with a central bank only concerned with average variables in the monetary union [we compare equations (61) and (62) with equations (47) and (48)]. The effect of foreign shocks is reduced by the size of the monetary union, as each country has then a weaker impact on the common monetary policy, and a big country is more immune from the influence of foreign demand and public debt shocks. It is the same for the variation of the public debt to GDP ratio: a positive shock on the foreign public debt to GDP ratio increases whereas a positive foreign demand shock reduces the national public indebtedness, all the more as the size of monetary union is small (n is weak).

Regarding asymmetric shocks, an asymmetric shock on the national public debt to GDP ratio influences economic activity, private and public consumption exactly in the same way as a foreign shock, whereas it has no impact in equations (47) and (48) if the central bank cares only about average variables. Then, a positive national and asymmetric shock on the public debt to GDP ratio increases labor demand and supply and the real wage in the national country, exactly like a foreign shock. In the same way, if the central bank cares about national variables, an asymmetric national demand shock influences private and public consumption like a foreign demand shock, whereas it had no influence in the previous section 4.

The main difference in comparison with section 4 is that, when the central bank cares about national variables, the impact of an asymmetric positive national demand shock to sustain national economic activity is reduced. The increase of economic activity is now less than proportional to the asymmetric demand shock. Indeed, equation (61) implies:

$$0 < \frac{\partial y_{i,t}}{\partial\left[\varepsilon_{i,t}^{d} - \frac{1}{(n-1)}\sum_{j\neq i}\varepsilon_{j,t}^{d}\right]} = 1 - \frac{\theta\left[\alpha_{y}^{M}\theta + \alpha_{b}^{M}(\theta-1)\right]}{n\left[\alpha_{i}^{M} + \alpha_{y}^{M}\theta^{2} + \alpha_{b}^{M}(\theta-1)^{2}\right]} < 1 \qquad (63)$$

So, a national asymmetric positive demand shock is more efficient in order to increase national economic activity, and to limit the decrease of private and public consumption, if the common nominal interest rate only weakly increases, that is to say: if (n) or (α_{i}^{M}) are high. The common central bank then reacts less to the shock in the national country, as the relative size of this country is limited in the monetary union, as its impact is weaker, or because of the importance of the goal of interest rate smoothing. On the contrary, economic activity, private and public consumption are reduced if the central bank cares about public indebtedness in the member countries of the monetary union (if α_{b}^{M} is high).

In this context, after a positive asymmetric national demand shock, the increase of labor supply and demand and of the real wage is weaker if the central bank cares about national variables. Besides, this increase is still more limited if monetary policy is more active and contractionary, i.e., if (α_{b}^{M}) is high whereas (α_{i}^{M}) and (n) are weak. Indeed, using equations (60), (C10) and (C11), we obtain:

$$0 < \frac{\partial l_{i,t}}{\partial\left[\varepsilon_{i,t}^{d} - \frac{1}{(n-1)}\sum_{j\neq i}\varepsilon_{j,t}^{d}\right]}$$

$$= \frac{1}{(1+\varphi)} - \frac{(\theta-1)[\alpha_y^M\theta+\alpha_b^M(\theta-1)]}{n(1+\varphi)[\alpha_i^M+\alpha_y^M\theta^2+\alpha_b^M(\theta-1)^2]} \quad (64)$$

$$\frac{\partial(w_{i,t}-p_{i,t})}{\partial\left[\varepsilon_{i,t}^d-\frac{1}{(n-1)}\sum_{j\neq i}\varepsilon_{j,t}^d\right]}$$
$$= \frac{\varphi}{(1+\varphi)} - \frac{(1+\varphi\theta)[\alpha_y^M\theta+\alpha_b^M(\theta-1)]}{n(1+\varphi)[\alpha_i^M+\alpha_y^M\theta^2+\alpha_b^M(\theta-1)^2]} \quad (65)$$

Furthermore, using equations (60) and (B8), we have:

$$-1 < \frac{\partial bb_{i,t}}{\partial\left(\varepsilon_{i,t}^d-\frac{1}{(n-1)}\sum_{j\neq i}\varepsilon_{j,t}^d\right)}$$
$$= -1 + \frac{(\theta-1)[\alpha_y^M\theta+\alpha_b^M(\theta-1)]}{n[\alpha_i^M+\alpha_y^M\theta^2+\alpha_b^M(\theta-1)^2]} < 0 \quad (66)$$

$$0 < \frac{\partial bb_{i,t}}{\partial\left(\varepsilon_{i,t}^b-\frac{1}{(n-1)}\sum_{j\neq i}\varepsilon_{j,t}^b\right)} = 1 - \frac{\alpha_b^M(\theta-1)^2}{n[\alpha_i^M+\alpha_y^M\theta^2+\alpha_b^M(\theta-1)^2]} < 1\,) \quad (67)$$

So, if the common central bank takes into account national variables, fluctuations of public debt to GDP ratios are reduced in case of asymmetric public debt or demand shocks. The public debt to GDP ratio decreases less than proportionally in case of asymmetric positive national demand shocks, whereas it increases less than proportionally in case of asymmetric positive national public debt shocks. Furthermore, these fluctuations of public debt to GDP ratios are reduced by the goal of interest rate smoothing (α_i^M) and by the size of the monetary union (n). On the contrary, they are increased by the weight given to the goal of limiting fluctuations of public debt to GDP ratios (α_b^M) and by the height of the inter-temporal elasticity of substitution of private consumption (θ).

Therefore, our model shows that a central bank concerned with the situation of each individual member country, and not only with average economic variables in the monetary union, allows a better stabilization of economic variables after an asymmetric demand shock in one of the member countries. However, such a concern for national variables also implies new macro-economic fluctuations for the national country in case of an asymmetric shock on its own public debt to GDP ratio, provided the central bank cares about public indebtedness ($\alpha_b^M > 0$), which were absent if the central bank only cares about average variables in the monetary union.

CONCLUSION

The common central bank conducts a contractionary monetary policy (increase of the nominal interest rate) in case of an average symmetric demand shock, whereas it conducts an expansionary monetary policy (decrease of the nominal interest rate) in case of an average positive shock on the public debt to GDP ratio in the member countries of the monetary union. So, one channel of transmission of public debt externalities in a monetary union is due to the fact that, if the global public indebtedness increases, the common central bank could be constrained to reduce its nominal interest rate, in order to reduce the weight of the future reimbursement of this public debt (monetary accommodation). Furthermore, in case of demand or public debt shocks, fluctuations of interest rates would be all the more accentuated as the central bank is not immune from budgetary pressures, and as stabilizing public debt levels in the member countries of the monetary union is a secondary and implicit goal for this central bank. In the current context of the strong economic crisis implied by the COVID-19 health crisis, and of the necessary increase of public debt levels in all European countries, our model can therefore contribute to justify the necessity, for the ECB, to sustain economic growth by a decrease of its interest rates.

It is quite obvious that in case of symmetric demand or public debt shocks, variations of public debt to GDP ratios in the member countries of the monetary union can be reduced if the central bank is influenced by political pressures, cares about public indebtedness, and conducts therefore a more active monetary policy. Besides, such a less independent central bank is more active, and it better mitigates the expansionary (deflationary) effect of a positive (negative) demand shock on economic activity and on the labor market, and therefore, it is a source of macro-economic stability and of attenuation of economic cycles regarding demand shocks. However, the fact that the common central bank cares about public debt levels implies that monetary policy becomes active and reacts to public debt shocks, and therefore, for such shocks, it introduces macroeconomic cycles which would not exist without such concern.

Furthermore, beyond these first results, we show that the institutional independence of the central bank is a first way to limit the effect of potential budgetary pressures, and to reduce macro-economic fluctuations and fiscal externalities. However, the European public debt crisis has shown (and the current COVID-19 crisis will certainly show) that this independence is difficult to sustain empirically in the framework of the management of a serious crisis. In the framework of our modelling, budgetary pressures imply that the monetary policy of the central bank is more active, which obviously reduces fluctuations of public debt to GDP ratios. However, we have also shown that it can be a source of instability for economic activity and for the labor market, in case of shocks on average public indebtedness, particularly in a context of public debt crisis. On the contrary, a potential and theoretical monetary commitment would imply that monetary policy is less active, which accentuates fluctuations of public debt to GDP ratios in case of demand or public debt shocks. Besides, if the central bank could commit, it would also increase macro-economic fluctuations in case of demand shocks (public debt shocks are then reduced, but they are without effect as long as the central bank is independent). Therefore, commitment regarding the common monetary policy of the central bank doesn't seem to be the solution to better insulate a member country of a monetary union from fiscal externalities.

Finally, if the common central bank doesn't care about average variables but about the situation of each member country of the monetary union, a national and asymmetric shock in a member country has an impact on the common monetary policy proportional to its relative weight in the monetary union. Fluctuations of public debt to GDP ratios are then reduced in case of asymmetric demand or public debt shocks. Besides, an asymmetric demand shock implies a weaker impact on national economic activity, on labor supply and demand and on the real wage. Therefore, our model shows that a central bank concerned with the situation of each individual country, and not only with average economic variables in the monetary union, allows a better stabilization of economic variables after an asymmetric demand shock in one of the member countries. However, such a concern for national variables also implies new macro-economic fluctuations for the national country after a shock on its own public debt to GDP ratio, provided the central bank cares about public indebtedness, which were absent if the central bank only cares about average variables in the monetary union.

To conclude, our results thus contribute to put light on the strength of fiscal spill-overs, in particular going through public indebtedness levels, between the member countries of a monetary union, and on the incapacity to really insulate a member country from these fiscal externalities. These externalities justify, in the economic literature, the benefits of a potential coordination of budgetary policies in a monetary union… but we leave this interrogation and this subject for another paper.

APPENDIX A: DETERMINATION OF THE DEMAND EQUATION

Equations (7) and (14) imply:

$$c_{i,t} = E_t\left(c_{i,t+1}\right) - \theta\hat{r}_t + \theta E_t\left(\pi^i_{i,t+1}\right) + \theta\,\eta\, E_t\left(\pi^*_{t+1} - \pi^i_{i,t+1}\right) \quad \text{(A1)}$$

Equations (17) and (39) imply: $(p^*_t - p^i_{i,t}) = \frac{1}{\theta(1-\eta)} c_{i,t} - \frac{1}{\theta(1-\eta)} y^*_t + \frac{1}{\theta(1-\eta)} \varepsilon^{*d}_t$, and then, with equation (38), we have:

$$c_{i,t} = \frac{\theta(1-\eta)}{[\theta-\eta(\theta-1)(2-\eta)]}\left(y_{i,t}-\varepsilon_{i,t}^{d}\right)$$
$$+\frac{\eta[1-(1-\eta)(\theta-1)]}{[\theta-\eta(\theta-1)(2-\eta)]}\left(y_t^*-\varepsilon_t^{*d}\right) \quad \text{(A2)}$$

So, by combining equations (A1) and (A2), as $[E_t(\varepsilon_{i,t}^{d}) = 0\ for\ t \geq 1]$, we obtain:

$$y_{i,t} = E_t(y_{i,t+1}) + \frac{\eta[1-(1-\eta)(\theta-1)]}{\theta(1-\eta)}\left[E_t(y_{t+1}^*) - y_t^* + \varepsilon_t^{*d}\right] + \varepsilon_{i,t}^{d}$$
$$-\frac{[\theta-\eta(\theta-1)(2-\eta)]}{(1-\eta)}\left[\widehat{r}_t - E_t(\pi_{i,t+1}^{i}) - \eta\, E_t(\pi_{t+1}^*) + \eta\, E_t(\pi_{i,t+1}^{i})\right] \quad \text{(A3)}$$

Therefore, with $(y_{i,t} = x_{i,t} + y_t^*)$, using (A3), we can obtain the differential of economic growth in the country (i) in comparison with the rest of the monetary union:

$$x_{i,t} = E_t(x_{i,t+1}) - \frac{\eta}{(1-\eta)k_2}\left[\widehat{r}_t - (1-\eta)E_t(\pi_{i,t+1}^{i}) - \eta\, E_t(\pi_{t+1}^*)\right]$$
$$+\frac{\eta}{\theta(1-\eta)k_2}\left[E_t(y_{t+1}^*) - y_t^* + \varepsilon_t^{*d}\right] + \left(\varepsilon_{i,t}^{d} - \varepsilon_t^{*d}\right) \quad \text{(A4)}$$

For the whole monetary union, we have: $x_t^* = 0$ (A5)

And thus, using (A4) and (A5), the differential of economic growth for the whole monetary union is:

$$x_t^* = E_t(x_{t+1}^*) + \frac{\eta}{\theta(1-\eta)k_2}\left[E_t(y_{t+1}^*) - y_t^* + \varepsilon_t^{*d}\right]$$
$$-\frac{\eta}{(1-\eta)k_2}\left[\widehat{r}_t - E_t(\pi_{t+1}^*)\right] = 0 \quad \text{(A6)}$$

So, equations (A3) or (A6) imply the following demand equation for the monetary union:

$$y_t^* = E(y_{t+1}^*) - \theta\widehat{r}_t + \theta E_t(\pi_{t+1}^*) + \varepsilon_t^{*d} \quad \text{(A7)}$$

Therefore, using equations (A4) and (A7), the differential of economic growth for the national country (i) is as follows:

$$x_{i,t} = E_t\left(x_{i,t+1}\right) - [\theta - \eta(2-\eta)(\theta-1)]\left[E_t(\pi^*_{t+1}) - E_t\left(\pi^i_{i,t+1}\right)\right] + \left(\varepsilon^d_{i,t} - \varepsilon^{*d}_t\right) \quad \text{(A8)}$$

APPENDIX B: EXCESS OF ECONOMIC ACTIVITY, INFLATION RATE AND PUBLIC DEBT

Equation (A8) implies:

$$x_{i,t} = E_t\left(x_{i,t+1}\right) + k_3 E_t\left(\pi^i_{i,t+1}\right) - k_3 E_t(\pi^*_{t+1}) + \varepsilon^d_{i,t} - \varepsilon^{*d}_t \quad \text{(B1)}$$
$$with\ k_3 = [\theta - \eta(2-\eta)(\theta-1)]$$

Equations (40) and (B1) imply:

$$\pi^i_{i,t} = k_1 k_2 E_t\left(x_{i,t+1}\right) + (\beta + k_1 k_2 k_3) E_t\left(\pi^i_{i,t+1}\right) - k_1 k_2 k_3 E_t(\pi^*_{t+1}) + k_1 k_2\left(\varepsilon^d_{i,t} - \varepsilon^{*d}_t\right) + \varepsilon^s_{i,t} \quad \text{(B2)}$$

Equations (43) and (B1) imply:

$$bb_{i,t} = \beta E_t\left(bb_{i,t+1}\right) + (\theta-1)[\hat{r}_t - E_t(\pi^*_{t+1})] + k_4 E_t\left(x_{i,t+1}\right) + (k_3 - 1 + \eta) E_t\left(\pi^*_{t+1} - \pi^i_{i,t+1}\right) + \varepsilon^b_{i,t} - \varepsilon^d_{i,t} \quad \text{(B3)}$$
$$with\ k_4 = \frac{(1-\beta)}{\left[\frac{Y_i}{G_i}(1-\nu)t^l_i - 1\right]} \frac{\eta[1-(\theta-1)(1-\eta)]}{[\theta - \eta(\theta-1)(2-\eta)]}$$

So, we have to solve the following system:

$$\begin{pmatrix} x_{i,t} \\ \pi_{i,t}^{i} \\ bb_{i,t} \end{pmatrix} = A \begin{pmatrix} E_t(x_{i,t+1}) \\ E_t(\pi_{i,t+1}^{i}) \\ E_t(bb_{i,t+1}) \end{pmatrix} + \begin{pmatrix} -k_3 & 0 \\ -k_1k_2k_3 & 0 \\ -(\theta - k_3 - \eta) & (\theta - 1) \end{pmatrix} \begin{pmatrix} E_t(\pi_{t+1}^{*}) \\ \widehat{r_t} \end{pmatrix} + \begin{pmatrix} 1 & -1 & 0 & 0 \\ k_1k_2 & -k_1k_2 & 1 & 0 \\ -1 & 0 & 0 & 1 \end{pmatrix} \begin{pmatrix} \varepsilon_{i,t}^{d} \\ \varepsilon_t^{*d} \\ \varepsilon_{i,t}^{s} \\ \varepsilon_{i,t}^{b} \end{pmatrix} \quad \text{(B4)}$$

$$A = \begin{pmatrix} 1 & k_3 & 0 \\ k_1k_2 & (\beta + k_1k_2k_3) & 0 \\ k_4 & -(k_3 - 1 + \eta) & \beta \end{pmatrix} \quad A^n = \begin{pmatrix} a_{1,n} & a_{2,n} & a_{3,n} \\ a_{4,n} & a_{5,n} & a_{6,n} \\ a_{7,n} & a_{8,n} & a_{9,n} \end{pmatrix}$$

With: $\lim_{n\to\infty} x_{i,n} = \lim_{n\to\infty} \pi_{i,n}^{i} = \lim_{n\to\infty} bb_{i,n} = 0$, and $E_t(\varepsilon_{i,t}^{d}) = E_t(\varepsilon_{i,t}^{s}) = E_t(\varepsilon_{i,t}^{b}) = 0$ for (t≥1), this implies:

$$\begin{pmatrix} x_{i,t} \\ \pi_{i,t}^{i} \\ bb_{i,t} \end{pmatrix} = \sum_{n=t}^{\infty} A^{n-t} \begin{pmatrix} -k_3 & 0 \\ -k_1k_2k_3 & 0 \\ (k_3 - \theta + \eta) & (\theta - 1) \end{pmatrix} \begin{pmatrix} E_t(\pi_{n+1}^{*}) \\ \widehat{r_n} \end{pmatrix} + \begin{pmatrix} 1 & -1 & 0 & 0 \\ k_1k_2 & -k_1k_2 & 1 & 0 \\ -1 & 0 & 0 & 1 \end{pmatrix} \begin{pmatrix} \varepsilon_{i,t}^{d} \\ \varepsilon_t^{*d} \\ \varepsilon_{i,t}^{s} \\ \varepsilon_{i,t}^{b} \end{pmatrix} \quad \text{(B5)}$$

So, with $(a_{3,n} = a_{6,n} = 0)\ and\ (a_{9,n} = \beta^n)$ $(\forall n)$, we have the following equilibrium economic variables:

$$x_{i,t} = -\sum_{n=t}^{\infty}\left[k_3 a_{1,n-t} + k_1k_2k_3 a_{2,n-t}\right] E_t(\pi_{n+1}^{*}) + (\varepsilon_{i,t}^{d} - \varepsilon_t^{*d}) \quad \text{(B6)}$$

$$\pi_{i,t}^{i} = -\sum_{n=t}^{\infty}\left[k_3 a_{4,n-t} + k_1k_2k_3 a_{5,n-t}\right] E_t(\pi_{n+1}^{*}) + k_1k_2\varepsilon_{i,t}^{d} - k_1k_2\varepsilon_t^{*d} + \varepsilon_{i,t}^{s} \quad \text{(B7)}$$

$$bb_{i,t} = -\sum_{n=t}^{\infty}\left[k_3 a_{7,n-t} + k_1 k_2 k_3 a_{8,n-t} - (k_3 - \theta + \eta)\beta^{n-t}\right]E_t(\pi^*_{n+1})$$
$$+(\theta - 1)\sum_{n=t}^{\infty}\beta^{n-t}E_t(\widehat{r_n}) - \varepsilon^d_{i,t} + \varepsilon^b_{i,t} \quad \text{(B8)}$$

APPENDIX C: EQUILIBRIUM ECONOMIC VARIABLES

Equation (41) implies:

$$\pi^*_t = \sum_{k=0}^{\infty} \beta^k E_t(\varepsilon^{*s}_{t+k}) = \varepsilon^{*s}_t \quad \text{(C1)}$$

Equations (11), (39) and (A7) imply:

$$y^*_t = y^* - \theta\sum_{k=0}^{\infty} E_t(\widehat{r_{t+k}} - \pi^*_{t+k+1}) + \varepsilon^{*d}_t = y^* - \theta\sum_{k=0}^{\infty} E_t(\widehat{r_{t+k}}) + \varepsilon^{*d}_t \quad \text{(C2)}$$

$$c^*_t = g^*_t = y^*_t - \varepsilon^{*d}_t = y^* - \theta\sum_{k=0}^{\infty} E_t(\widehat{r_{t+k}}) \quad \text{(C3)}$$

Equations (B6), (C1) and (C2) imply:

$$y_{i,t} = x_{i,t} + y^* - \theta\sum_{k=0}^{\infty} E_t(\widehat{r_{t+k}}) + \varepsilon^{*d}_t = y^* - \theta\sum_{k=0}^{\infty} E_t(\widehat{r_{t+k}}) + \varepsilon^d_{i,t} \quad \text{(C4)}$$

Equations (11), (A2), (B6), (C2) and (C4) imply:

$$c_{i,t} = g_{i,t} = y^* - \theta\sum_{k=0}^{\infty} E_t(\widehat{r_{t+k}}) + \frac{\theta(1-\eta)}{[\theta-\eta(\theta-1)(2-\eta)]}(x_{i,t} + \varepsilon^{*d}_t - \varepsilon^d_{i,t}) = c^*_t \quad \text{(C5)}$$

Equations (10), (11), (20) and (22) imply:

$$\theta(\varphi+\nu)y_{i,t}=\theta(1+\varphi)a_{i,t}-(1-z\theta-\nu-z\theta\varphi)c_{i,t} \quad \text{(C6)}$$

$$\theta(\varphi+\nu)\left(w_{i,t}-p_{i,t}\right)=\theta\varphi a_{i,t}+(\nu+z\theta\varphi)c_{i,t} \quad \text{(C7)}$$

$$\theta(\varphi+\nu)l_{i,t}=\theta a_{i,t}-(1-z\theta)c_{i,t} \quad \text{(C8)}$$

So, equations (C4), (C5) and (C6) imply:

$$a_{i,t}=\frac{(1-z\theta-\nu-z\theta\varphi+\theta\varphi+\theta\nu)}{\theta(1+\varphi)}\left[y^{*}-\theta\sum_{k=0}^{\infty}E_t(\widehat{r_{t+k}})\right]+\frac{(\varphi+\nu)}{(1+\varphi)}\varepsilon_{i,t}^{d} \quad \text{(C9)}$$

Equations (C5), (C8) and (C9) imply:

$$l_{i,t}=\frac{(\theta-1)}{\theta(1+\varphi)}\left[y^{*}-\theta\sum_{k=0}^{\infty}E_t(\widehat{r_{t+k}})\right]+\frac{1}{(1+\varphi)}\varepsilon_{i,t}^{d} \quad \text{(C10)}$$

Equations (C5), (C7) and (C9) imply:

$$\left(w_{i,t}-p_{i,t}\right)=\frac{(1+\varphi\theta)}{\theta(1+\varphi)}\left[y^{*}-\theta\sum_{k=0}^{\infty}E_t(\widehat{r_{t+k}})\right]+\frac{\varphi}{(1+\varphi)}\varepsilon_{i,t}^{d} \quad \text{(C11)}$$

References

Aguiar M., Amador M., Fahri E., Gopinath G. (2014), "Coordination and Crisis in Monetary Unions", *NBER Working Papers*, n°20277, July.

Beetsma, R., & Bovenberg, A. L. (1999). Does monetary unification lead to excessive debt accumulation? *Journal of Public Economics*, vol.74, n°3: 299–325.

Beetsma, R. M. W. J., and K. Vermeylen (2007), "The effect of monetary unification on public debt and its real return", *Public Choice*, vol.133: 393-415.

Bernoth, K., Von Hagen, J., & Schuknecht, L. (2004). "Sovereign risk premia in the European Government Bond Market", *European Central Bank Working Paper*, n°369, June.

Broner, F., A. Erce, A. Martin and J. Ventura (2014), "Sovereign debt markets in turbulent times: Creditor discrimination and crowding out effects", *Journal of Monetary Economics,* 61(C), pp. 114-142.

Buiter, W. and E. Rahbari (2012), "The European Central Bank as Lender of Last Resort for Sovereigns in the Eurozone", *Journal of Common Market Studies*, vol.50, n°s2, September: 6-35.

Chang, R. (1990). International coordination of fiscal deficits. *Journal of Monetary Economics*, vol.25, n°3, June: 347–366.

Chari, V., & Kehoe, P. J. (2007). On the need for fiscal constraints in a monetary union. *Journal of Monetary Economics*, vol.54, n°8, November: 2399-2408.

Chari, V. V. and Kehoe, P. J. (2008). Time Inconsistency and Free-Riding in a Monetary Union. *Journal of Money, Credit and Banking*, vol.40, n°7:1329-1356.

Constancio V., "Contagion and the European Debt Crisis", *Financial Stability Review*, Banque de France. April. 109-122.

Cooper, R., Kempf, H., and Peled, D. (2010,a). Regional debt in monetary unions: Is it inflationary? *European Economic Review*, vol.54, n°3: 345-358.

Cooper, R., Kempf, H., and Peled, D. (2010,b). *Insulation Impossible: Fiscal Spillovers in a Monetary Union.* Centre d'Economie de la Sorbonne, Working Papers, 2010-45.

Corsetti G. and L. Dedola (2016), "The Mystery of the Printing Press: Monetary Policy and Self-fulfilling debt crisis", *Journal of the European Economic Association*, vol.14, n°6, December: 1329-1371.

Diaz J., G. Giovannetti, R. Marimon and P. Teles (2008). Nominal Debt as a Burden on Monetary Policy., *Review of Economic Dynamics*, 11(3): 493-514.

Galí, J. 2008. *Monetary Policy, Inflation, and the Business Cycle: An Introduction to the New Keynesian Framework.* Princeton: Princeton University Press.

Gali, J. & Monacelli, T. (2008). Optimal Monetary and Fiscal Policy in a Currency Union. *Journal of International Economics*, vol.76, n°1: 116–132.

Gande, A., & Parsley, D. (2005). "News spillovers in the sovereign debt market". *Journal of Financial Economics*, *75*(3), 691–734.

Giuliodori, M., & Beetsma, R. (2004). *What are the spill-overs from fiscal shocks in Europe? An empirical analysis*, European Central Bank, Working Paper, n°325, March.

Hughes Hallett, A. (2005), 'In Praise of Fiscal Restraint and Debt Rules: What the Euro Zone might Do Now', *CEPR Discussion Paper*, n°5043.

Jeanne, Olivier. (2012). "Fiscal Challenges to Monetary Dominance in the Euro Area: A Theoretical Perspective". *Financial Stability Review*, Banque de France. April. 143-150.

Kirsanova, T., Stehn, S. J. & Vines, D. (2005), 'The interactions between fiscal policy and monetary policy', *Oxford Review of Economic Policy,* vol.21, n°4, Winter: 532-564.

Landon, S., Smith, C. A. (2007), "Government Debt Spillovers in a Monetary Union", *North American Journal of Economics and Finance*, n°18: 135-154.

Leith, C., & Wren-Lewis, S. (2000). Interactions between monetary and fiscal policy rules. *The Economic Journal*, vol.110, n°462, March: C93–108.

Leith, Campbell & Wren-Lewis, Simon, 2006. "Compatibility between monetary and fiscal policy under EMU", *European Economic Review*, vol.50, n°6, August: 1529-1556.

Leith, Campbell & Wren-Lewis, Simon, 2011. "Discretionary policy in a monetary union with sovereign debt," *European Economic Review,* vol. 55, n°1, January: 93-117.

Mitra, S. (2007): Is the Quantity of Government Debt a Constraint for Monetary Policy?, *IMF Working Paper*, WP/07/62, March.

Stehn, Sven Jari & Vines, David, 2008. "Debt Stabilisation Bias and the Taylor Principle: Optimal Policy in a New Keynesian Model with Government Debt and Inflation Persistence," *CEPR Discussion Papers*, n°6696.

Van Aarle, B., Bovenberg, A. L., & Raith, M. (1997). Is there a tragedy of a Common Central Bank? A dynamic analysis. *Journal of Economic Dynamics and Control*, vol.21, n°2-3: 417–447.

Woodford, M. (2003). *Interest and Prices: Foundations of a Theory of Monetary Policy,* Princeton: Princeton University Press.

In: Public Debt
Editor: Antoine Bélanger

ISBN: 978-1-53619-326-8

Chapter 2

IS THERE A LEVEL OF PUBLIC DEBT THAT IMPAIRS ECONOMIC GROWTH? IN SEARCH OF A THEORY

Roberto Tamborini and Matteo Tomaselli
Department of Economics, University of Trento, Trento, Italy

ABSTRACT

Beyond inconclusive empirical research, this chapter examines the theoretical literature concerning public debt and economic growth finding no univocal and straightforward answer. No meaningful assessment of debt and its effect on growth at any point in time is possible without reference to the whole debt trajectory and the specific state of the economy along the trajectory. An orderly and consistent analysis may be developed along two coordinates of debt assessment: sustainability/ unsustainability, and efficiency/inefficiency. In our view, research should concentrate on the study of specific conditions and cases, and abandon the pursuit of a general law.

Keywords: public debt, debt burden, debt sustainability, economic growth, endogenous growth models

1. Introduction

Policymakers and economists have long been engaged in the debate about the evaluation of public debt, and its impact on economic activity and growth. The large fiscal imbalances created worldwide by the Great Recession of 2008-09 revived general interest in the issue and moved the attention from the poor and developing countries to the developed ones. The epicenter became Europe, and the Euro Zone in particular, where the Great Recession was followed by acute sovereign debt crises between 2010 and 2012. As a result, many countries implemented, or were forced to implement, also in compliance with the Euro Zone fiscal rules, restrictive fiscal policies aiming at reducing their budget deficit and, eventually, their public debt.

If not dictated by immediate threats, fiscal consolidation, the so-called "austerity", was also prescribed as a requisite for reinstating sound growth conditions before prolonged fiscal stimuli to the economy became self-defeating as public debt was growing too high.

"There should be little question that European economies share the need to reduce public deficits and debts from levels that, as confirmed by a growing strand of empirical literature (Reinhardt and Rogoff 2009, Kumar and Woo 2012) are likely to be harmful for growth in the medium term [...]." (Buti and Pench 2012, 45)

Reinhart and Rogoff 2010, in a large panel of countries, identified a critical threshold of 90% of the debt-to-GDP ratio beyond which debt is harmful to growth. Several countries in the world, notably in the Euro Zone, were fast approaching that threshold or already were well beyond. The Reinhart-Rogoff finding has spurred a buoyant empirical research in search of the debt threshold above which growth is jeopardized by public debt. Hitherto results of these researches are inconclusive or controversial.

In the first place, the Reinhart-Rogoff work was criticized with regard to the implied causality (Irons and Bivens 2010),[1] and then for some methodological and statistical problems (Herndon, Ash and Pollin 2013).[2] Further works support the existence of critical debt-to-GDP ratios under various time and space observational fields (but there is no agreement on their level: see, among others, Pattillo, Poirson, Ricci 2011; Baum, Checherita-Westphal and Rother 2012; Checherita-Westpahl and Rother 2012). Some authors point out the existence of a positive relationship between debt and growth above a certain threshold (Minea and Parent 2012). A third group of studies do not completely deny the existence of a negative relationship between the two variables, but rather claim that a general threshold is unlikely to exist, and it provides no guidance towards the adoption of widespread policies of debt reduction (e.g., Bowdler and Esteves 2013; Pescatori, Sandri and Simon 2014). Country-specific characteristics, contingencies and events play a prominent role, thus prompting a branch of literature that attempts to comprehensively understand the debt-growth relationship and its determinants (Panizza and Presbitero 2014; Eberhardt and Presbitero 2015).

In retrospect, one may say that the empirical pursuit of the debt-to-GDP threshold harmful to growth lacks deeper foundational work. Why should we expect a negative public debt-growth relationship in the first place? If such a relationship exists, why should it take the specific form of a threshold of the debt-GDP ratio, and why should we expect this threshold to be equally valid across time and space?

To address these questions, we refocus attention on the possible theoretical underpinnings of the (negative) debt-growth relationship. In this chapter we explore the rather extended range and vintages of theoretical explanations that can be found in the literature, which presents itself as a scattered, heterogeneous and rather coarse constellation of theories, models and case studies. With the aim to provide the reader with an effective guide

[1] Their application of the Granger causality test has showed that debt does not cause growth and growth does not cause debt.

[2] The analysis was spoiled by coding errors, selective exclusion of available data, and unconventional weighting of summary statistics.

in the search for explanation of the debt- growth relationship, the material is organized according to *distinct though possibly connected channels* through which debt can impinge on growth negatively: the effects of debt being kept on a solvency path and those due to debt being on an unsustainable path.

The first block, presented in section 2, concerns the evolution of the notion of "debt burden" in public finance where the relevant debt-growth channel goes through the consequences of *policies aimed at consolidating debt and secure its solvency*. Debt management essentially consists of choosing a sustainable future path of expenditures and taxation; hence the problem is how various forms of expenditure and taxation affect economic activity and growth (e.g., Zagler and Dürnecker 2003).

The second block, in section 3, gathers another specialized literature concerned with the *consequences of expected or effective debt default*. Of course, there are overlaps across this classification, which inevitably involves some degree of arbitrariness. Yet the debt-growth channels involved are quite different from the previous ones. In many cases, default is a policy choice of the government as a result of trading off the costs/benefits of default with those of solvency (see, among others, Buiter and Rahbari 2013, and Reihnart and Rogoff 2009 for a historical overview). Default may be unexpected, anticipated or even self-generated by creditors; each case has its own specific impact on the economy quite different in nature than those mentioned above.

One main problem emerging from these strands of literature is that a consistent theoretical framework for the debt-growth nexus is missing. Therefore, in section 4 we introduce a third block where the evolution of debt and its effect on growth are cast in an intertemporal horizon such that the whole debt trajectory and the specific state of the economy along the trajectory can be examined. We provide a guideline to this approach by means of a fiscal model of endogenous growth freely inspired to Barro (1990) and Diamond (1965). In Barro (1990) endogenous growth is sustained by productive public expenditure fully covered by taxation. To introduce debt, we adopt a sequential economy with two-period generations *à la* Diamond (1965) where public expenditure is financed by debt in the first period and the debt burden in covered by taxation in the second period. An advantage of this framework is that the debt-growth relationship can be analyzed in four scenarios centered on the notions of *efficiency/inefficiency*, *sustainability/unsustainability* of debt, including the case of "voluntary" default.

Our conclusion, to be found in section 5, is that the literature that we have been able to examine and organize, on the one hand offers a rich variety of explanations and insights to researchers of the debt-growth relationship, but on the other it does not provide any one-way conclusion: the relationship may be negative, positive, or even no relationship may exist. Even less is theoretically founded the existence of a general debt-to-GDP threshold above which growth is consistently stifled. Each country's specific characteristics, circumstances, and events have an overwhelming importance that cannot be encapsulated in a single general law. Research should concentrate on the former and abandon the pursuit of the latter.

2. Public Finance and the Debt Burden View

2.1. Debt Burden and Debt Service

The idea that public debt may represent a burden for the economic system has distant origins in public finance. Its focus is on who and how should pay for debt, and with what consequences on the economy. Note that the concept of debt burden is broader than, and should not be confused with, the concept of debt sustainability (to be introduced later in section 3.1) though the two may be related. The impact of debt repayment on the economy, according to different repayment strategies, is of course central to this analysis.

The debt burden is usually identified and described by some indicators, and the most common involve the debt service: the interest-to-debt ratio, the interest-to- GDP ratio, the interest-to-taxation ratio, or the interest-to-export ratio. The amount of external debt with respect to the total outstanding debt is considered as a measure of the external burden, a relevant indicator when the focus is on the foreign creditors.

In the mid-1950s, Sun (1954) distinguished between three interrelated concepts of debt burden: psychological (subjective, and related to people's confidence in the government debt policies and in the stability of the economy), financial (referred to the amount of taxes required to repay the principal and the interest charges), and real economic burden (related to a decrease in national income, a decline in production, etc.). Sun concluded that the effective burden of the public debt depends on the economic conditions, and that some principles must be respected in order to minimize it. The analysis turned to incentives in Meade (1958), who argued that a reduction in public domestic debt can improve economic incentives, but there could be a cost if the economic conditions worsen in the short-run.

Particularly relevant is the approach put forward by Bohn (1995, 1998). It is based on the fiscal policy reaction function that relates the primary balance, as the control variable, to outstanding debt in such a way that the latter is kept on a path converging to some finite level (e.g., Greiner, Koeller and Semmler 2007; Ghosh et al. 2013; Passamani, Tamborini and Tomaselli 2015 for applications to the Euro Zone countries). One main merit of this approach is that it allows for a relatively simple and measurable "fiscal effort" that should consistently be borne by the government (i.e., the relevant economic subjects) over time.

This can easily be seen by means of the standard dynamic equation of the debt/GDP ratio. If D_t is the amount of debt at time t, the corresponding debt-to- GDP ratio is $d_t \equiv D_t/Y_t$, and its change over the previous year is given by (approximately)

$$\Delta d_t = (i_t - g_{nt})d_{t-1} - b_t - \mu_t + v_t \quad (1)$$

where i_t is the average interest payment (interest rate for short) on debt, g_{nt} is the nominal growth rate of GDP, and b_t, μ_t, v_t are, respectively, the GDP-ratios of the fiscal primary balance, the monetization of debt, and exogenous changes in the amount of debt. A primary surplus $b_t > 0$ generates a negative impulse to the debt/GDP ratio, and vice versa a primary deficit $b_t < 0$. The government's commitment to debt control implies that b_t is targeted to achieving a specified path of d_t, i.e., Δd^*_t. Therefore,

$$b^*_t = (i_t - g_{nt})d_{t-1} - \Delta d^*_t - \mu_t + v_t \tag{2}$$

is the necessary fiscal effort in terms of primary surplus.

As long as $v_t = 0$, the above expression shows that the extent of the fiscal effort is determined by some key factors. The first is the debt-path target. For instance, the minimal requirement of debt stability, $\Delta d^*_t = 0$, implies that b^*_t is entirely dependent on the remaining factors. The reformulation of fiscal rules in the Euro Zone introduced with the so-called Six Pack and Fiscal Compact, state that Δd^*_t should be set on a decreasing path equal to 1/20th of the difference between the outstanding debt $d_{t\text{-}1}$ and 60%. To the extent that $\Delta d^*_t < 0$, the fiscal effort should be greater.

The second factor that may determine a greater fiscal effort is the outstanding debt $d_{t\text{-}1}$ (note therefore that in the Euro Zone it weighs twice). The third critical factor is the interest-growth gap $(i_t - g_{nt})$ — also known as "snowball effect". If high debt is accompanied by high interest payments and low growth, the resulting interest-growth gap magnifies the required fiscal effort. Finally, a fourth factor is the extent to which the government has access to debt monetization μ_t. As is well known, for the EZ governments $\mu_t = 0$.

The extent of the fiscal effort may underpin the notion that the debt burden (i.e., $d_{t\text{-}1}$ in equation (2)) may depress growth provided that it is explained how the creation of a primary surplus depresses growth. We shall return to the point later in this section.

Before the financial and the debt crises in which many advanced countries have been entangled, the debt-growth relationship was of particular interest to the Heavily Indebted Poor Countries (HIPC): many works have analyzed how the debt burden, or the "debt overhang", affects economic development, and whether the debt relief programs would have been useful and, in case, which was the best way to implement them. The debate around the HIPCs and debt relief programs goes beyond the scope of our chapter, however a few cases are worth mentioning.

Starting with the Costa Rica's and the Mexico's defaults at the beginning of the 80s, the growth of the debt burden for high indebted countries has been recognized as an issue. Kamin, Khan and Levine (1989) gauged whether Argentina, Chile, Brazil, and Mexico had been better off in terms of GDP path for having borrowed considerable amounts before experiencing the debt crises, concluding that these countries were in fact worse off. Cunningham (1993) proposed one of the first empirical analysis investigating the effect of debt burden on economic growth, in which the debt burden was measured as the rate of change in the long-run debt service to public and publicly guaranteed ratio. Its main empirical finding indicates that the debt burden negatively affects economic growth.

This conclusion is in line with the concept of debt overhang, initially proposed by Krugman (1988), according to whom the relationship between the sovereign debt and the national product is described by an inverted U relationship. Thus, above a certain level of the public debt, both the debtor and the creditor countries could find it convenient to forgive a part of the debt. In addition, the incentive to invest in the country may be reduced when public debt becomes "large".

Some authors have focused mainly on the external debt component, which is often deemed to be the most relevant component as it implies a real transfer from the debtor to the creditor country. According to Karagol (2002, 40), "foreign debt acts like a tax when the debt situation is such that an improvement in the economic performance of the indebted country has the side product of higher debt repayments", and he found that, for the specific case of Turkey, external debt service has a negative short-run impact on economic growth. External debt, generated by large and persistent current account deficits, has also been indicated as the driver of the Euro Zone sovereign debt crises (Alcidi and Gros 2011; Gros 2013).

In summary, the debt burden view points out several channels whereby (high) public debt may directly or indirectly hamper economic growth and country's development. In fact, this has been the situation in which the high indebted poor countries have been entangled, and for which initiatives of debt reduction or even debt forgiveness were widely proposed and studied in the last decades. However, this literature is essentially empirical and applied to historical cases, with no commitment to any particular theory of the debt-growth relationship. If anything, these studies are important because they add further strength to the warning that specific conditions play a crucial role that can hardly be absorbed into a general law.

2.2. Consolidation Policies

A corollary of the burden view is that, sooner or later, the government will be forced to implement some consolidation policy, i.e., a fiscal restriction aimed at reducing debt and bringing it onto a sustainable path. The connection between this argument and the conclusion that, therefore, high debt impairs growth is less straightforward than one may think at first sight. The fiscal-effort equation (2) may provide simple and useful guidance.

To begin with, an analytical shift occurs from a stock to a flow approach, for the reason that a fiscal restriction is a change in the government budget (more surplus or less deficit) aimed at reducing the outstanding debt (or, more commonly, the debt-GDP ratio). Hence, the initial stock conditions should matter, which are, however, seldom specified.

In this perspective, the front line has long been represented by the traditional Keynesian vs. neoclassical models of fiscal expansions or restrictions, revolving around the extent of "crowding out" (in case of expansions) or "crowding in" (in case of restrictions) of private expenditure. Note that, generally, these models yield mirror effects in the two cases.

As is well known, Keynesian models (e.g., in the IS-LM class) predict that fiscal restrictions have a net negative effect on economic activity. Typically, the net negative effect results from the direct impact of the fiscal restriction on GDP via aggregate demand, amplified by the Keynesian multiplier, and the indirect, though incomplete, "crowding in" of private expenditure by way of a lower interest rate. This standard result, however, has a tenuous relation with the debt-growth issue as is embodied in equation (2).

First, the role of the debt stock is, at best, indirect and implicit in that a "large" debt will require a "large" restriction. In the basic IS-LM setup at least, the interest-rate effect is not related to the stock of debt, but to the stock money: with a fixed stock of money, the contraction of economic activity reduces the transaction demand for money which is satisfied by a lower interest rate. Second, the endogenous variable is current GDP, not its long-run growth rate, and it is not specified whether the fiscal restriction is permanent or transitory. This connection, however, may be provided by the notion of "hysteresis" such that a temporary demand-led downturn may be translated into a long-run loss of output capacity on the supply side (DeLong and Summers 2012; Fatàs and Summers 2018).

The traditional neoclassical approach is well-known for predicting a small or null effect of fiscal expansions owing to their "crowding-out" effect on private expenditure (see for instance Bernheim 1989 for a reassessment). It is less noticed that, since the mechanisms involved operate symmetrically, fiscal contractions are expected to have small or null effect on economic activity, with the consequence that the debt burden may not be *per se* conducive for lower growth.

In fact, this class of earlier neoclassical models is characterized by perfectly rational consumers with a finite lifespan, with access to a perfect capital market, where the consumption level is determined by a utility maximization process. Analysis focuses on the amount of loanable funds in the capital market. In this context, a fiscal surplus decreases lifetime consumption. However, provided that the economic resources remain fully employed, less consumption implies higher saving. The interest rate falls to keep investments equal to savings, crowding-in private expenditure.

Note two important caveats, however. The first is that the extent of crowding- out or crowding-in is largely seen as an empirical matter, and in some circumstances fiscal imbalances may retain some limited Keynesian effects on economic activity (Bernheim 1989). The second is that, as in the Keynesian counterparty, there is no explicit treatment of the debt stock and its effects on growth over time.

The modern neoclassical approach, that we can date back to the path-breaking works on "Ricardian Equivalence" by Barro (1974, 1989a, 1989b), lend further theoretical strength to the notion that budgetary adjustments along the government's intertemporal budget constraint are neutralized by compensatory adjustments on the private side.[3] Barro (1979) proposed a specific model incorporating the Ricardian Equivalence and an empirical analysis supporting it, while in Barro (1989b, 1) he concluded that the Ricardian Equivalence is a "good first-order approximation to reality", supported also by the empirical evidence.

There are noteworthy differences with earlier neoclassical models. One is that households are characterized by a sort of "inter-generational altruism", as if they were living infinitely. If current public expenditure is financed by resorting to public debt, the current generation will leave the necessary amount of money to the following generation in order to compensate the future increment in taxes. Thus, Ricardian Equivalence has also the strong implication that public deficits have no effects on the interest rate, provided that households firmly believe that the government's intertemporal budget will be honored. Hence, the hallmark of traditional neoclassical theory (and quite a popular argument about the negative effects of high indebtedness) is muted. Moreover, if creating a deficit is neutral on economic activity, creating the surplus when the debt service falls due will also be neutral (taxpayers have already hoarded the equivalent of taxation). Hence Ricardian Equivalence does not seem an appropriate support to the view that high debt reduces growth as a consequence of consolidation policies. However, various aspects of this

[3] They may not be neutral on the supply side of the economy as long as intertemporal shifts between consumption and leisure are also considered.

approach have raised doubts and debates also in the neoclassical camp fostering research of caveats and limitations to this theory.[4]

A variant in the same vein was introduced in the 1990s under the name of "expansionary fiscal consolidations", or "Non-Keynesian effects of fiscal policy", and it explicitly maintains that consolidation policies *are not necessarily harmful for growth* but, on the contrary, may have a positive effect. Giavazzi and Pagano (1990, 1995), and Alesina and Perotti (1995) were among the first who put forward and test this hypothesis empirically, followed more recently by Alesina and Ardagna (2010, 2013), and others. Their main conclusion, the fact that "even drastic fiscal adjustments are not associated with major recessions" (Alesina and Perotti, 1995, 24), has recently been recovered in support of the Euro Zone austerity policies.[5]

Though framed within the modern intertemporal approach, the reasons why from Ricardian neutrality fiscal restrictions become expansionary remain unclear. A possibility may be that the public sector *is not (no longer) on its intertemporal budget constraint*. A simple device is an unexpected shock that raises outstanding debt. In that moment, the private agents discover that fiscal consolidation (the present value of future public surpluses) should be *larger* than previously expected. On the other hand, "Non-Keynesian" consolidation stories may in fact be due to several favorable Keynesian side conditions, regarding in particular the concomitant stance of monetary and exchange-rate policies (e.g., Favero et al. 2011; Perotti 2012; Blyth 2013, chap. 3). That a fiscal contraction accompanied by expansionary monetary policy and exchange-rate depreciation may end up with a neutral, or net positive, effect on GDP has been well known ever since the basic Mundell-Fleming model (Foresti and Marani 2014).

---

[4] As reported by Bernheim (1989), the Ricardian paradigm needs unrealistic assumptions to hold that make it implausible. Ricardian equivalence has also been tested in experimental laboratories by resorting, in general, to an overlapping generations design. Cadsby and Frank (1991) supported the validity of the Ricardian equivalence, but further developments found evidence of departures if more articulated experimental designs are employed (see Slate et al. 1995; Ricciuti and Di Laurea 2003).

[5] See Blyth (2013, 205 ff.) for a recollection of the evolution of this idea.

As a matter of fact, this strand of literature was born, and has remained, essentially empirical being based on analyses of success stories of fiscal consolidations followed by fast recovery. Indeed, these analyses boil down to the choice of a growth-friendly consolidation design: large, front-loaded, with expenditure cuts rather than tax hikes (Alesina and Ardagna 2010, 2013; Carnot 2013). With reference to the fiscal-effort equation (2), the effect of b^*_t on the growth rate g_{nt} depends not so much on its absolute dimension but on its composition. Public expenditure cuts do not impinge on the level of economic activity because households consume more in anticipation of less future taxes. The recommendation of a large and front-loaded consolidation relies on the argument that incomplete or delayed consolidation raises the present value of future fiscal surpluses; this is matched with less current spending and more hoarding by the private sector with a depressive effect on economic activity.

If the government fails to adopt the right consolidation design, then the conclusion may be that debt repayment has a negative effect on growth. Yet this conclusion also means that it is not the level of debt *per se* that can be pointed to as the determinant of future growth. Moreover, like the other approaches discussed so far, the focus is on short-run effects on economic activity, not on long-run determinants of growth.

Search for empirical support remains highly controversial as it intersects with the ever-lasting endeavor to estimate fiscal multipliers (Hebous 2011; Gechert, Hughes Hallet and Rannenberg 2015). In parallel with a progressive revaluation of the Keynesian view, based on sizeable fiscal multipliers especially during downturns, some recent studies have cast doubts on the reliability of expansionary consolidations, and, more importantly, on their general value (IMF 2010). Perotti (2012) studies four individual episodes in different countries. He shows that all these episodes were in fact associated with an increase in growth but the explanation of why this occurred was to be found in the specific conditions of those countries. In line with this finding, Guajardo, Leigh and Pescatori (2016) argue that once changes in fiscal policy are motivated by a "desire to reduce the budget deficit and not by responding to prospective economic conditions", there is little evidence of any expansionary effects. Jordà and

Tylor (2016) also conclude that a fiscal consolidation is always associated with a fall in real GDP over a period of five years. The Euro Zone is a natural observational field of large fiscal consolidations, and the prevalent assessments yield negative effects on subsequent growth at least in the short to medium run (Berti, de Castro and de Salto 2013; in't Veld 2013; Beetsma et al. 2015).[6]

If the fiscal consolidation has Keynesian effects, the debt/GDP ratio may rise instead of falling, as in fact happened throughout the Euro Zone. This effect therefore envisages a possible reverse causality between higher debt ratio and lower growth that should be taken account in empirical estimations. As shown by Nuti (2013) and Tamborini (2013), this reverse causality occurs when the fiscal multiplier is greater than the reciprocal of the initial debt/GDP ratio.

Consider again the dynamic equation of the debt/GDP ratio (1), and assume that $\mu_t = v_t = 0$. Let the interest rate be on its trend value i, and □ = $\Delta g_{nt}/\Delta b_t < 0$ be the Keynesian fiscal multiplier; this gives the deviation of nominal growth from trend Δg_{nt}, given a change in the primary balance ratio Δb_t. Hence $g_{nt} = g_n + \phi\Delta b_t$. This fact entails that the change in the debt ratio becomes

$$\begin{aligned}\Delta d_t &= (i - g_n - \phi\Delta b_t)d_{t\text{-}1} - (b_{t-1} + \Delta b_t)\\ &= [(i - g_n)d_{t\text{-}1} - b_{t-1}] - (1 + \phi d_{t\text{-}1})\Delta b_t \qquad (3)\end{aligned}$$

The term in square brackets yields the debt path with unchanged fiscal effort. The point is that an *increase* in fiscal effort ($\Delta b_t > 0$) generates a negative impulse to the debt/GDP ratio only if $(1 + \phi d_{t\text{-}1}) > 0$, or $|\phi| < 1/d_{t\text{-}1}$. Hence, a combination of high outstanding debt and strong fiscal multiplier can eventually produce both *less growth* and higher debt/GDP

---

6 As to the wide debate on austerity see e.g., Corsetti (ed.) 2012, Buti and Carnot (2013), Tamborini 2015b.

ratio due to a *reverse causality* effect. Note that when the debt/GDP ratio is large, even a relatively small multiplier may produce this effect.

2.3. Fiscal Space

Another particular, indirect debt-growth channel that can be found in this context relates to the so-called "fiscal space". This is a measure of the extent of fiscal expansion a government enjoys given its outstanding debt and some target or constraint on it (different indicators have been proposed by Aizenman and Hutchison (2012), Ghosh et al. (2013) and Buti and Carnot (2016), among others). This notion, indirectly, subscribes to the Keynesian view that fiscal expansions do have anti-cyclical properties.

The different indicators converge to the point that the higher the debt, the lower the fiscal space. Consequently, high debt inhibits the stabilisation capacity of the government. Persistent under-stabilisation may impinge on growth in the long run if other phenomena are considered such as hysteresis (DeLong and Summers 2012; Fatàs and Summers 2018).

Overall, one may argue that high debt may have a negative effect on economic activity in the short-to-medium run, and possibly on long-run growth, to the extent that an *unanticipated* fiscal restriction becomes necessary, or limits to anti-cyclical fiscal space are to be met. However, this conclusion is not univocal, and, somewhat paradoxically, it finds some support more from the Keynesian view, based on "large" fiscal multipliers, than from the neoclassical camp. Indeed, if Ricardian Equivalence holds, the result is fiscal super-neutrality: both fiscal expansions and subsequent consolidations are neutral on aggregate economic activity at any point along the time path. If we observe a consolidation action, and this is not neutral, some condition(s) of Ricardian Equivalence should not hold.

3. Unsustainable Debt, (Self-Fulfilling) Expectations, and Default

As previously explained, a critical point that is often blurred in the search for the debt-growth relationship is whether it goes through the fiscal policies that are adopted to service the debt or through the consequences of the debt being unsustainable and bound to default. This latter channel is examined here. A further distinction to be considered is between the negative effects on growth in the run-up of the debt crisis, and those due to the actual default.

3.1. Sustainability

A formal definition of sustainability, based on financial first principles, states that the outstanding value of debt should not exceed the discounted value of the current and futures expected primary surpluses. This definition is fraught with several implementation problems (e.g., the choice of the appropriate discount rate, time horizon, and budget items) leading to controversial if not inconclusive judgements. Therefore, less demanding, empirically based, criteria have been put forward.

Liviatan (1984) proposed a "macro-absorption" approach for the sustainability of the debt burden, and classified the debt burden indicators into three categories: naive, simple, and composite. Naive indicators concern the total amount of debt and the related measures, such as the interest rate and the maturity; simple indicators involve the debt service and the related ratios, while composite indicators are weighted averages of naive and simple indicators, and aim at better identifying the debt burden and the approaching of a default. Further developments include, among others, Collignon and Mundschenk (1999), Arnone and Presbitero (2007), Fincke and Greiner (2012).

Major international agencies and institutions, notably the International Monetary Fund and the European Commission, have developed sophisticated methods of sustainability analysis (IMF 2012; European Commission 2014). They build on projections of macroeconomic, fiscal and financial variables that are sensitive to the kind of hypotheses used in the models. Every kind of assumption involves a certain degree of scrutiny so, to deal with uncertainty, assessments are typically, in the form of different scenarios upon various policy assumption. The saga of the Greek debt crisis witnesses how controversial the assessment of sustainability may be.

In the approach put forward by Bohn (1995, 1998), introduced above in section 2.1, the focus falls on the fiscal effort borne by the government, i.e., the primary- balance ratio over GDP necessary to achieve a target debt path (see equation (2)). In this regard, the composition of the effort (e.g., more taxes *vs.* less expenditure) may matter as suggested by the studies on the expansionary fiscal consolidations. The critical point is that the evaluation of sustainability of debt is not simply a technical matter, but it also depends on the (political) assessment of the costs and benefits of the consolidation policies (or the costs and benefits of some degree of default), which leads to the political economy literature on the solvency/default choice of governments that we shall consider below.

3.2. Sovereign Risk and the Confidence Channel

Macro-models with sovereign risk belonging to the so-called "New Keynesian Macroeconomics", or "New Neoclassical Synthesis", developed since the early '90s, may be regarded as adding a new, "micro-founded" channel to the debt burden view; examples are Corsetti et al. (2010, 2013) and, with reference to the Euro Zone, Buti and Pench (2012). They also offer a clearer identification of the departure point from fiscal expansions/consolidations neutrality in the standard Neo-Ricardian framework. That is to say, at some point in time, agents *do not have full confidence* that the government will honor its intertemporal budget.

The key feature of these models is the connection between the level of the debt- GDP ratio, its sustainability assessment on the part of investors in sovereign bonds, and how this is translated into a risk premium. In turn, the risk premium is transmitted to the long-term interest rate impinging upon private expenditure (for consumption and/or capital goods). As is the hallmark of this school, we find a composition of Keynesian and neoclassical features. It should be noted that the involvement of the interest rate is not due to the excess absorption of loanable funds (a *flow* concept that was involved in the Keynesian-neoclassical dispute about the "crowding-out" effect of fiscal imbalances), but to the increasing sovereign risk of debt (a *stock* concept).

According to Buti and Pench (2012), the key factors can be encapsulated in a formula of the "*stock* fiscal multiplier" like the following

[1 − confidence] / [1 + (monetary policy) + (competitiveness) − (financial constraints)] (4)

Confidence relates to the forward-looking-ness of investors, i.e., their probability assessment of future default, and hence the demand for risk premium. Higher debt triggers lower confidence, higher risk premium and interest rate, and hence a dragging anchor on economic activity. Other factors that affect this "debt multiplier" relate to the Keynesian side of these models: the monetary policy stance (an accommodative stance helps reduce the interest rate and sustain aggregate demand) and competitiveness gains via real exchange rate depreciation (which also sustain the foreign component of aggregate demand). Finally, financial constraints, another typical New Keynesian feature, inhibit Ricardian neutrality and amplify the impact of the interest rate on aggregate demand.

Reasoning in reverse, one may obtain further conditions for expansionary fiscal consolidations. Assume that the economy is in a state of high "debt multiplier" as represented by expression (4). Accordingly, output is depressed. If the government enacts an *unanticipated fiscal restriction* that lowers the probability of future default, investors demand a lower risk premium. The domestic private sector enjoys a lower interest rate and anticipates the lower path of future taxes: both spur expenditure. The higher the confidence, the smaller the multiplier of the consolidation, or it may even turn into a positive net effect. Unsurprisingly, such a rich set of factors yield nuanced results, and, once again, results are conditional on the state of economy and other side elements (Corsetti et al. 2010, 2013).[7]

A test of this channel of the debt-growth relationship is provided by Fragetta and Tamborini (2019) who estimate the impact of austerity (increases in the structural primary balance) on growth in a panel of European countries from 2010 to 2015, controlling for other possible explanatory factors that have been indicated in the literature together with, or instead of, austerity. The authors find that the negative effect of austerity on growth is always statistically significant together with changes in the debt/GDP ratio. However, they warn that since austerity was associated with increasing debt/GDP ratios, as explained above the reverse causality hypothesis cannot be excluded.

3.3. Default as a Government's Choice

With regard to debt sustainability and default risk, it is necessary to remind that, as is clear from equation (1), a sovereign government can always achieve any desired debt-path target provided that it has full control over expenditure, taxation and possibly monetization. The problem lies in the costs associated with these instruments. Therefore, default is better understood *as a policy choice* of the government trading off the costs of default with those of solvency (Gros 2012; Buiter and Rahbari 2013; Tomz and Wright 2013; Tamborini 2015).

A partial or total default on public debt, either explicit (a refusal to pay back the capital and a subsequent reduction in the outstanding amount of debt) or implicit (through high inflation rates — or even hyperinflation —

---

[7] "In relatively extreme cases where fiscal strains are severe and monetary policy is constrained for an extended period, fiscal tightening may even exert an expansionary effect. That being said, fiscal retrenchment is no miracle cure. Indeed, all our simulations feature a deep recession even if tighter fiscal policy, under the aforementioned conditions, may stimulate economic activity *relative to an even bleaker baseline*" (Corsetti et al. 2010, 41, italics added). The confidence channel has also been tested, and partially supported, through laboratory experiments: see Geiger et al. (2016), Mittone and Tomaselli (2017).

that conspicuously diminish the real sovereign debt), is an extreme occurrence influenced also by the general financial and political situation as well as by agents' behavior and expectations. Default may be unexpected, anticipated or even self-generated by creditors; each case has its own specific impact on the economy.

The economic consequences of default may be severe but concentrated in time, whereas the benefits of freeing the economy from the burden of debt may unfold over time. Behavioral aspects can play a role in terms of agents' belief about past debt efficiency, agents' expectations about current sustainability, and agents' confidence level about future debt repayments, though they are not deemed to be always founded. Notably, these aspects have the potential to be self-fulfilling, thus leading to the actual default that could otherwise have been avoided.

The historical literature about sovereign defaults is vast and it goes beyond the purpose of this chapter (see Reinhart and Rogoff 2009; a mainly quantitative and a mainly qualitative literature reviews are respectively provided by Stähler 2013 and Tomz and Wright 2013), but it may be useful to briefly recall the most recent case of the sovereign debt crisis in the Euro Zone between 2010 and 2012.

Throughout the euro's first decade, countries like Belgium, Italy, and Greece were characterized by high public debt-to-GDP ratios. Meanwhile, "emerging" and fast-growing countries like Spain and Ireland started from very low levels of public debt but rapidly rising levels of private debts. Initially, investors regarded sovereign debts in the Eurozone as substantially equivalent prompting a remarkable convergence of interest rates towards the German safe rate. They became increasingly worried about debt sustainability after the Papandreu government's disclosure of the huge deterioration of Greek public finances, and after the sharp rise in the debt/GDP ratios due to the financial crisis and bank bailouts in other countries (notably Spain and Ireland), leading to a dramatic increase in the interest rates of the bonds of the so-called "periphery countries" (Greece, Ireland, Italy, Portugal, Spain). The New Keynesian models mentioned above have been designed to capture these events. Their negative debt-growth relationship is the result of the combined effects on consumption and/or investment of higher interest rates and the anticipation of fiscal consolidation or default (as already discussed, the conclusions about the growth effects of consolidation are instead ambivalent).

The concomitant flourishing of empirical studies has also raised a number of challenges. In the first place, the relationship between the level (or growth rate) of public debt, the rise of risk premia, and speculative attacks turns out to be of dubious nature. Others have instead pointed out that speculative attacks have been driven by analogy with the "original sin" of many developing countries which issue debt in a foreign currency (De Grauwe and Ji 2012, 2013). This argument brings an institutional factor to the forefront: sovereign debt in euros is "foreign denominated" for Euro Zone countries because the issuers do not have a central bank in control of the currency. A third problematic area concerns the transmission channels of risk premia across countries. In this regard, there is evidence that post-2009 spreads not only reflected country-specific fundamentals, but were also highly sensitive to "systemic risk" and other exogenous factors (Manganelli and Wolswijk 2009; Attinasi, Checherita-Westphal and Nickel 2009; Caceres, Guzzo and Segoviano 2010). In particular, research has focused on "contagion", that is, the transmission of high spreads across countries via non-fundamental channels (Constancio 2012; Arghyrou and Kostunica 2012).

3.4. Self-Fulfilling Expectations

Finally, the issue of self-fulfilling default expectations should be considered in its connection with the determination of the level of debt, or of the debt burden, that may trigger the sequence of events that may force a government into heavy fiscal consolidation or default. It may be recalled that the ECB President Mario Draghi opened his famous "whatever-it-takes" speech by saying that

> "[...] we are in a situation now where you have large parts of the euro area in what we call a "bad equilibrium", namely an equilibrium in

> which you may have self-fulfilling expectations that feed upon themselves and generate very adverse scenarios. So, there is a case for intervening, in a sense, to "break" these expectations" (Draghi 2012, 4)

The introduction of self-fulfilling expectations in macroeconomic models dates back to the 1980s (Farmer 1993). In general, they also entail multiple equilibria, the selection of which depends of the state of expectations. In our context, the typical mechanism is one where, as default expectations arise, the cost of debt solvency also rises (e.g., because of higher risk premium) thus making the government default decision more likely.

The seminal study in our context is represented by the influential paper by Calvo (1988), who recognized that expectations about debt default may determine the equilibrium that is reached by the economy. Many other applications followed up to nowadays, and it is not possible to cite all of them. The Euro Zone crisis has also prompted new contributions.

De Grauwe (2012) presents a model of exogenous expectations determining an area of threat of self-fulfilling speculative attacks. Gros (2012) introduces a political-economy model of investors' subjective expectations of default affecting the market interest rate and the likelihood to observe multiple equilibria. Moreover, creditors may find it profitable to forgive part of a country's debt to avoid the default, in line with the debt overhang theory. By following the same methodology, Tamborini (2015) shows that multiple equilibria can arise as a consequence of investors' heterogeneous beliefs about primary balance sustainability, where the risk premium is higher the larger is the share of "pessimistic" investors about the level of fiscal effort beyond which the government prefers default. This model clarifies how the level of debt, its burden and sustainability are largely conditioned by the distribution of investors' beliefs. When pessimistic investors prevail, fostering more ambitious consolidation plans is likely to be counterproductive as greater, instead of smaller, risk premium is the result, which triggers the reverse causality between higher debt/GDP ratio and lower GDP.

Empirical evidence of self-fulfilling speculative attacks is uneasy to collect. De Grauwe and Ji (2013), and Passamani, Tamborini and Tomaselli (2015) can be mentioned among the studies that detect the phenomena presented above. Overall, research on the EZ crisis delivers a problematic picture of the "confidence channel" of the debt-growth relationship as far as its the connection between the debt level and the "fundamentals" of its sustainability are concerned. On the other hand, whatever the motivations behind rising risk premia, there is also evidence that 1) high debt levels may be more easily involved in confidence crises, 2) market pressure is a major vehicle for large fiscal consolidations, 3) these are likely to have strong and prolonged negative effects on economic activity (e.g., Born et al. 2018, Tomaselli and Tamborini 2019).

4. Four Scenarios for the Debt-Growth Relationship

On the basis of the previous literature review, it is not possible to reach a univocal conclusion regarding the debt-growth relationship. Even less is theoretically founded the existence of a general debt-to-GDP threshold above which growth is consistently stifled. We now move to a further strand of literature, which sets the debt-growth relationship in a fully developed intertemporal framework in which the debt life and the output growth are examined jointly.

4.1. Debt in Intertemporal Perspective

An important contribution coming from public finance is that public debt should be evaluated along its whole-time path rather than at a specific point in time. Debt is created for a reason or purpose, then it unfolds its effects over time, and these effects may, or may not, contribute to debt repayment. All these aspects are to be considered when assessing the relationship between debt and growth, whereas the sheer measurement of the debt level at some point may be uninformative or misleading.

To be more specific, when tracking the debt/GDP ratio it should be first recognized that this is given by to the joint trajectories (D_{t-k}, ..., D_{t-1}), (Y_{t-k}, ..., Y_{t-1}), determined by the underlying sequence of budgetary policies and their consequences on the economy. The observed values D_t/Y_t may be the outcome of an *efficient* or *inefficient* trajectory, while subsequently they may turn out to be either *sustainable* or *unsustainable*.

In this literature, the debt trajectory can be considered efficient if the use of debt is consistent with its purpose in terms of general criteria of economic efficiency, and if it has no distortionary effects on social equity and social welfare. Efficiency implies sustainability *ex ante*, the long-term solvency constraint represented by the condition that the present value of the future government deficits and surpluses converge to zero as t tends towards infinity. However, debt on an efficient trajectory may turn out to be unsustainable *ex post* owing to unforeseen events. Two other scenarios are possible: debt may be inefficient but sustainable, debt may both inefficient and unsustainable. These four scenarios have quite different implications in terms of growth and, what is more important, the level of debt and the corresponding level of the debt-to-GDP ratio along the trajectory are irrelevant on their own.

An early example of this kind of analysis is the cyclical stabilisation role of fiscal policy theorized by Musagrave (1959). If debt is created during a slump and repaid during the recovery in order to equalize national income over the business cycle, both efficiency and sustainability (and intergenerational equity) are achieved. The time profile of debt may be quite different in different specific conditions.

Modigliani (1961) instead pointed out that an increase in the national debt (both internal and external) can be advantageous for the current generation, but it places a burden on future generations entailing a reduction in the available stock of private capital, thus causing a decrease in the future flows of goods and services. Analogous conclusions were reached by Bowen, Davis and Kopf (1960), according to whom, even if the repayment of the debt principal is continuously delayed, each current generation bears a burden represented by the taxes used to pay debt interests.

Another classic topic in this line of literature is the so-called "golden rule" of public finance (Musgrave 1964). This rule is the object of a long-standing branch of public finance which we need not examine here, whereas it is important to note how it fits in our four scenarios. As is well known, the rule states that the balance between current expenditure and revenues should be nil, while public debt is only allowed as a means to finance productive investment. Here the efficiency- sustainability criteria are even more transparent. Productive investment is realized as growth-enhancing debt-based expenditure, and efficiency requires the equality between marginal product and social cost. Sustainability should be guaranteed by equality between the marginal increase in revenues due to additional growth and the debt service. Equity lies in the fact that the generation paying for debt also enjoys a higher level of income.

In this context, Diamond (1965) was the first who studies the effects of debt on economic growth properly. Diamond divided debt into external debt (borrowed from foreign lenders) and internal debt (borrowed from domestic lenders). External debt has negative effects on growth in the long run because of the taxes needed to finance interest payments. Taxes are levied on domestic lenders whereas interests are paid to the foreign ones. Initially, taxes reduce consumers' total lifetime income, and hence consumption. As a further consequence, taxes reduce savings and the capital stock. Internal debt, on the other hand, entails both effects as well as a reduction in the capital stock due to the fact that individuals substitute government debt for physical capital in their portfolios. Therefore, public debt crowds out private capital.

The 1990s have seen the emergence of discordant views. Some authors proposed models leading to opposite conclusions with respect to those of Diamond. For instance, Dotsey and Mao (1994) introduced distortionary taxation,[8] and in fact, debt turned out to crowd-in investments. Ludvingson (1996) analyzed deficit- financed fiscal policies in a forward-looking general equilibrium model and showed that the economy's response to an increase in government expenditure depends on how it is financed. In particular, distortionary taxes may lead to a decline in output, consumption and investments, while deficits may increase output and consumption. Moreover, deficit-financed cuts in income taxation may increase investments although agents expect future taxes to be higher (due to the substitution between leisure and labor), a conclusion supported also by Lin (2000). Therefore, according to this branch of works, there are no crowding-out effects and the impact of government debt on growth can be positive.

In this perspective, endogenous growth theory deserves a specific treatment. This approach spread during the 1990s attempting to explain how long-term growth can be generated without relying solely on exogenous or "residual" technological changes as in the Solow foundational model. This strand of literature is relevant to our topic because, following the model proposed by Barro (1990), it examines how fiscal variables interact with the variables that generate endogenous growth. Interaction can be indirect (this is typically the case of taxation) or direct to the extent that public expenditure can sustain endogenous growth. This latter case is particularly important because it marks a shift of approach with respect to the neoclassical views examined above which typically see public expenditure as sheer consumption of resources.

The Barro model obtains a typical inverted U function of the relationship between public expenditure and growth, with an optimal level of expenditure (taxation) that maximizes growth. Public expenditure is fully covered by taxation and taxation depresses growth. Below the optimal level of public expenditure, the government does not exploit its

---

[8] According to Kneller (1999), distortionary taxes in this context are those which affect the investment decisions of agents (with respect to physical and/or human capital), creating tax wedges and hence distorting the steady-state rate of growth. Non-distortionary taxation, on the other hand, does not affect savings and investment decisions and therefore has no effects on the growth rate.

growth-enhancing effect, beyond that point the growth-depressing effect of taxation prevails. On the other hand, the bulk of this literature is concerned with the effects of fiscal variables on growth along a balanced budget path, showing a rich variety of results and policy implications (see Zagler and Dürnecker 2003 for an accurate survey), which however are not immediately suitable for analysis of the debt-growth problem.

More to the point, Teles and Cesar-Mussolini (2014) proposed an endogenous growth model in which the effect of fiscal policy on economic growth is negatively affected by the level of the debt-to-GDP ratio. This effect works via the debt interest: a portion of young people's savings is extracted and paid to elderly people, who do not save, thus implying an allocation exchange between generations. The negative effects of government debt on growth have been shown also by Saint-Paul (1992) and, by studying the impact of fiscal constraints (limited tax and debt capacity) on growth, Aizenman, Kletzer and Pinto (2007) reached similar conclusions: lower maximal tax rate and higher outstanding debt can lower the growth rate, supporting the fact that differences in growth rates can stem from differences in fiscal policy constraints.

In the subsequent sections we shall characterize and discuss the debt-growth relationship in the four scenarios centered on the efficiency-sustainability criteria recalled above within the intertemporal setup of the fiscal models of endogenous growth, on which we graft public debt as a means to finance productive public expenditure. As will be seen, the model also embeds some specific debt-growth relationships previously presented.

4.2. Endogenous Growth with Efficient and Sustainable Public Debt

We propose a fiscal model of endogenous growth freely inspired to Barro (1990) and Diamond (1965). Barro (1990), as said above, represents a new standard model of growth sustained by productive public expenditure fully covered by taxation.[9] To introduce debt in this setup, we adopt a sequential economy with two-period generations *à la* Diamond (1965)[10] where public expenditure is financed by debt in the first period and the debt burden in covered by taxation in the second period. The key assumption in the Barro model is that the economy consists of competitive firms producing an aggregate output Y according to a neoclassical (Cobb-Douglas) production function augmented by productive public expenditure, where productive means a kind of expenditure in public goods that can raise private factors' productivity (typical examples are infrastructures, education, research, health care, etc.). We reformulate the Barro production function in terms of *private* capital K, and *public* capital K_G (i.e., the stock of public goods mentioned above):

$$Y_t = A_t K_t^{\alpha} K_{Gt}^{\beta} L_t^{\beta},\ \alpha + \beta = 1 \tag{5}$$

In order to introduce public debt, we first treat the economy as a sequence of two-period generations. The generation starting in period t is endowed with labor L_t and private capital K_t. Labour is supplied inelastically in each period and normalized to 1. Likewise, for the time being, we set the scale factor at constant value $A_t = 1$ in each period. The depreciation rate of private and public capital is 100% and gestation time is one period.

If the private sector realizes net investment in addition to depreciation by the amount I_t, the private capital stock $K_{t+1} = K_t + I_t$ will be operative in t+1. The government, too, can invest in public capital the amount G_t financed by debt, $D_t = G_t$ so that Public capital $K_{Gt+1} = G_t > 1$ will also be operative in t+1. Therefore, feasible production in t+1 will be:

[9] We draw on the version by Barro and Sala-i-Martin (1998, ch. 4).

[10] The difference here is that the generations do not overlap, but we assume that they comply with the intergenerational pact that each generation leaves the same endowment of capital to the next.

$$Y_{t+1} = K_{t+1}^{\alpha} K_{Gt+1}^{\beta} \tag{6}$$

The government fulfils its intertemporal budget constraint by taxing all incomes in period $t+1$ with the flat rate τ. Incomes include the public debt service (principal and interests). Therefore, the following government budget equality holds:

$$\tau Y_{t+1} = (1 - \tau) D_t R^d{}_{t+1} \tag{7}$$

where $R^d{}_{t+1}$ is the unit debt service.

Under the efficient capital market hypothesis, the interest rate is equalized across the private and public sectors, so that, $R^d{}_{t+1} = R_{t+1} \equiv 1+r_{t+1}$ is the gross return to capital, determined as marginal product of private capital, i.e.:

$$R_{t+1} = \alpha \left(\frac{K_{Gt+1}}{K_{t+1}} \right)^{\beta} \tag{8}$$

Given $D_t = K_{Gt+1}$, and $R^d{}_{t+1} = R_{t+1}$, the public budget constraint (7) sets the feasible stock of public capital. Since Y_{t+1} is determined by (6), the result is

$$K_{Gt+1} = K_{t+1} \left(\frac{\tau}{(1-\tau) R_{t+1}} \right)^{1/\alpha} \tag{9}$$

This expression can also be interpreted as the optimal public/private capital ratio $k^*{}_{t+1} \equiv K_{Gt+1}/K_{t+1}$. The complementarity between public and private capital is the first key feature of this economy.

Substituting $k^*{}_{t+1}$ into the interest rate equation (8), the latter results to be

$$R_{t+1} = \alpha'\left(\frac{\tau}{1-\tau}\right)^{\beta}, \alpha' = \alpha^{\alpha} \tag{10}$$

The second notable result is that the marginal product of private capital, and hence the interest rate, are invariant to the capital stock — a result propaedeutic to endogenous growth. The interest rate is however a concave function of the tax rate, which leads to the peculiar relationship between debt and growth in this economy.

To this end, we have first to consider the optimal consumption path of the representative household of the *t*-th generation, which maximizes a time separable logarithmic utility function subject to its two-period budget constraints:

$$\begin{aligned} &(\max_{C_t, C_{t+1}} U(C_t, C_{t+1}) = \log(C_t) + (1+\rho)^{-1}\log(C_{t+1}) \\ &\text{s.t. } C_t = Y_t - I_t - D_t \\ &C_{t+1} = (1-\tau)[Y_{Lt+1} + (K_t + I_t + D_t)R_{t+1}] - W_{t+1} \end{aligned} \tag{11}$$

where Y_{Lt+1} is labor income, $\rho > 0$ is the rate of time preference, and $W_{t+1} \geq 0$ is the final stock of wealth (for simplicity we assume $W_{t+1} = K_t$, i.e., each generation leaves to the next one the same capital endowment received from the previous one).

By combining the first order conditions with respect to C_t, C_{t+1}, we obtain the Euler equation and the optimal consumption path

$$\gamma \equiv \frac{C_{t+1}}{C_t} = \frac{(1-\tau)R_{t+1}}{(1+\rho)} \tag{12}$$

As usual, an increase in the (after tax) interest rate raises γ, while an increase in the rate of time preference decreases it. Substitution of the interest rate equation (10) into (12) yields the growth equation for this economy, namely

$$\gamma = \frac{\alpha'(1-\tau)^{\alpha}\tau^{\beta}}{1+\rho} \tag{13}$$

We thus see the crucial result, namely that growth is a concave function of the tax rate necessary to finance public capital. Concavity reflects the double-edge role of taxation: τ^{β} is the growth-enhancing effect of financing public capital, $(1-\tau)^{\alpha}$ is the growth-depressing effect of taxing capital income. As a consequence, there exists a unique tax rate τ^* that maximizes γ, namely

$$\tau^* = 1 - \alpha \tag{14}$$

which is the same result as in the original Barro model.

The public finance implication is that, given τ^*, each generation has its own optimal public debt which is both sustainable and efficient. In particular, there is neither "crowding out" when debt is created in t (indeed there is crowding-in)[11] nor is there excess fiscal burden in t+1. As to the debt/GDP ratio, it can first be noted that the relevant ratio (in terms of debt burden) for the t-th generation is given by the GDP equation (6), i.e.,

$$d_{t+1} \equiv \frac{K_{Gt+1}}{Y_{t+1}} = \left(\frac{K_{Gt+1}}{K_{t+1}}\right)^{\alpha} \tag{15}$$

Hence, the key variable is the public/private capital ratio. Equation (9) sets the feasible ratio. Substituting R_{t+1} and τ with the respective optimal values (10) and (15) the result is

[11] According to equation (8), as long as $\tau < \tau^*$, raising public capital increases the marginal product of private capital, which allows for a larger private capital stock, and shifts consumption to the future, which generates more saving for capital accumulation.

$$d^*_{t+1} = \left(\frac{\beta}{\alpha^2}\right)^{\alpha} \tag{16}$$

That is to say, the optimal debt/GDP ratio may be whatever is appropriate for each economy and each generation. Different endowments, preferences or technologies, would yield different results, so that no generalization or comparison is meaningful across time or different economies. In other words, *"high" and "low" debt/GDP ratios may equally be efficient and sustainable.*

4.3. Sustainable but Inefficient Debt

The previous model provides an immediate instance of cases in which public debt is sustainable but inefficient in terms of growth. Since the relationship between taxation and growth is concave, the cases in consideration occur whenever public debt, i.e., public capital, is either too low or too high with respect to (16). In the former case, the government fails to exploit the full range of growth-enhancing public investment; in the latter excess investment requires excess taxation that depresses growth.

Therefore, note in the first place that growth may be sub-optimal not only because debt is "too high". In the second place, even when debt is in fact too high, it remains perfectly sustainable. Indeed, lower growth is due to the fact that the government complies with sustainability by levying excess taxation. This, moreover, need not come as an unexpected event but may be fully anticipated. In other words, inefficiency defines a set of effects of public debt on growth that do not depend either on unsustainability nor on default risk but, quite the contrary, *on the anticipation of the sustainable path of fiscal policy*. Finally, sustainable debt is not synonymous with efficient fiscal policy and optimal growth of the economy. As explained in the previous section, the threshold between efficient and inefficient level of debt is hard to draw in comparisons over time or across different countries.

4.4. Efficient but Unsustainable Debt: Again on Fiscal Consolidation

The third case we examine is one where public debt is ex-ante efficient and sustainable whilst it is not *ex-post*. We model this situation by means of an unanticipated shock that in period 2 of the t-th generation lowers total factor productivity. This simple device may capture different situations: from true recessions, to ex-ante overvaluation of public investment productivity, or misbehavior of the government that deviates a share of debt to unproductive uses. In any case, the consequence which we focus on is the necessity of fiscal consolidation in period 2, i.e., a fiscal adjustment that guarantees debt solvency.

The first period of the t-th generation is the same as in the base case, except that the coefficient A in the production function is now a (positive) random variable of unit expected value which in $t+1$ takes the value $A_{t+1} < 1$. Note that, by assumption, the stocks of private and public capital operational in t+1 have been installed in t and are irreversible (denoted by a bar) Consequently,

$$Y_{t+1} = A_{t+1}\bar{K}^{\alpha}_{t+1}\bar{K}^{\beta}_{Gt+1} = A_{t+1}Y^*_{t+1} \tag{17}$$

where Y^*_{t+1} denotes the ex-ante optimal GDP as in the base case. Therefore, the government budget as given by equations (7) and (8) and the optimal tax rate $\tau^* = 1 - \alpha$ can no longer be satisfied. A fiscal consolidation is necessary, and to this end the government changes the tax rate so that[12]:

$$\tau_{t+1}A_{t+1}Y^*_{t+1} = (1 - \tau_{t+1})D_t\bar{R}^d_{t+1} \tag{18}$$

[12] Unlike the equity-based private capital, the debt-based public capital is committed to paying the interest rate established ex ante.

From the base model, we know the optimal values of Y^*_{t+1} and $\bar{R}^d_{t+1}$. Upon substituting these values and $D_t = \bar{K}_{Gt+1}$ into (18), we find that the solvency tax rate is

$$\tau^s_{t+1} = \frac{1-\alpha}{1-\alpha(1-A_{t+1})} \tag{19}$$

which clearly shows that the new tax rate should be higher than τ^* the worse the productivity shock is.

What are the concomitant effects of fiscal consolidation on the economy? The first is that the growth rate is reduced, *yet this is the direct and exclusive effect of the productivity shock on the GDP path*, not of fiscal consolidation by itself. The second effect, directly due to fiscal consolidation, is on households' consumption which necessarily deviates from the optimal path given by (12). The increase in the tax rate, in addition to the productivity shock, affects the t+1 budget constraint as $C_{t+1} = (1 - \tau^s_{t+1})[(1 - \alpha)A_{t+1}Y^*_{t+1} + (K_t + I_t)R_{t+1} + D_t\bar{R}^d_{t+1}] - K_t$, where $(1-\alpha)A_{t+1}Y^*_{t+1}$ is the gross income share of labor. Likewise, we can write $(K_t + I_t)R_{t+1} = \alpha A_{t+1}Y^*_{t+1}$, and therefore

$$C_{t+1} = (1 - \tau^s_{t+1})[A_{t+1}Y^*_{t+1} + D_t\bar{R}^d_{t+1}] - K_t \tag{20}$$

As can be seen, households suffer from lower gross income from the private sector, and higher tax rate. Moreover, their consumption is fully constrained by current disposable incomes, so that the economy also displays this "Keynesian" feature.

4.5. Inefficient and Unsustainable Debt

Debt-financed public expenditure may be *ex-ante* inefficient for a number reasons, ultimately because the government spends and taxes too much (beyond the optimal level identified in the first scenario) or because the projects are in fact less productive. To simplify our analysis of the fourth scenario, we can note that when the economy is hit by an adverse shock as in the third scenario, public debt observationally results both inefficient and unsustainable *ex post*. Drawing on the political economy literature on the default choice mentioned in section 3, we now examine the point that, since fiscal consolidation is a costly decision for the government, it may consider the option of default. Yet also default is a costly decision.

To address this problem various specifications of the government's decision are available. In our context, it is natural to assume the representative consumer's utility as the welfare function of the government.[13] Consequently, let us consider the post-shock consumption level in $t + 1$:

$$C_{t+1} = (1 - \tau_{t+1})[A_{t+1}Y^*_{t+1} + (1-\phi)D_t\bar{R}^d_{t+1}] - K_t \tag{21}$$

where the government has two policy variables, the tax rate τ_{t+1} and the rate of "haircut" of the debt repayment ϕ. Note that the former variable affects consumption via after-tax income, whereas the latter affects consumption via pre-tax income. The point is that the two variables are inversely related: to the extent that the government lowers τ_{t+1} below the solvency level $\tau^S{}_{t+1}$ given by (19), it should raise ϕ. In fact, on the basis of the government's budget, we obtain that

$$\phi = (\tau^s{}_{t+1} - \tau_{t+1})\frac{(A_{t+1}Y^*{}_{t+1} + D_t\bar{R}^d_{t+1})}{D_t\bar{R}^d_{t+1}} \tag{22}$$

[13] This treatment simplifies the scenario in that taxation and haircut hit the same subject. This is not always (often it is not) the case. For instance, part of debt may be held by foreign subjects whose well-being is not relevant to the government. On the other hand, defaulting on foreign obligations may generate other kinds of costs (reputation, market access, etc.) that may be relevant.

where $\tau^s{}_{t+1} = D_t \bar{R}^d_{t+1} / (A_{t+1} Y^*{}_{t+1} + D_t \bar{R}^d_{t+1})$. Hence, $\phi = 0$ if $\tau_{t+1} = \tau^s{}_{t+1}$, and $\phi = 1$ if $\tau_{t+1} = 0$.

Upon substituting ϕ into (21), C_{t+1} results a concave quadratic function of τ_{t+1}. The optimal debt policy is the $(\tau^d{}_{t+1}, \phi)$ combination that maximizes the post-shock consumer utility, i.e.,

$$\tau^d{}_{t+1} = \tau^s{}_{t+1}/2, \ \phi = 0.5 \tag{23}$$

where (d) denotes that the tax rate implies default.

Interestingly, the optimal debt policy is independent of any other variable except the solvency tax rate $\tau^s{}_{t+1}$, but of course this is due to the utility function that we have assumed. It is however generally true that post-shock consumption is concave in τ_{t+1}, i.e., it reaches a maximum for a specific combination $(\tau^d{}_{t+1}, \phi)$. This result prompts two remarks. First, (partial) default is always a policy option for a government facing (unexpectedly) unsustainable debt. Second, the effect of debt on the economy cannot be gauged independently of whether debt is inefficient/unsustainable and the government chooses the default option.

CONCLUSION

Research on the relationship between public debt and growth has a long history. Interest has been revived by the fiscal consequences of the Great Recession of 2008-09. This new wave of research has been mostly empirical, and largely dominated by the pursuit of "the" debt-to-GDP ratio beyond which debt depresses growth; yet no univocal conclusion has been reached either about the quantification of the critical ratio or even about its existence.

Foundational work is however lacking: why should we expect a negative public debt-growth relationship in the first place? If such a relationship exists, why should it take the specific form of a threshold of the debt-GDP ratio, and why should we expect this threshold to be equally valid across time and space?

In an attempt to address these questions, we have examined a wide range of different literatures concerning public debt and its impact on economic activity. One main problem is that different analytical approaches are intertwined: static, single-period *vs.* dynamic, intertemporal setup; flow (budget deficits) vs. stock (outstanding debt) analysis; expected solvency vs. expected default. In each of them, or combination of them, debt has distinct effects on the economy. Some agreement has emerged in recent years around the idea that high debt may eventually impair growth through the default risk channel or through the consequences of large, unanticipated consolidation under market pressure after a debt shock or other unforeseen contingencies. The possibility of "expansionary consolidations" has lost force over time both theoretically and empirically. This consensus view, somewhat paradoxically, hinges more on the existence of Keynesian "large" fiscal multipliers, than on the neoclassical opposite presumption.

Our methodological conclusion is that no meaningful assessment of debt and its effect on growth at any point in time is possible without reference to the entire debt trajectory and the specific state of the economy along the trajectory. In this perspective, we have shown that an orderly and consistent analysis may be developed along two coordinates of debt assessment: sustainability/unsustainability, and efficiency/inefficiency. If, for instance, debt is on a sustainable and efficient trajectory, the debt level, the debt-to-GDP ratio and the growth rate at any point in time may be whatever is consistent with the fundamentals of the economy; the mere comparison between different countries has no informative value. Specific analyses, leading to different predictions, are necessary when public debt is either inefficient or unsustainable, and whether the government wishes to consolidate or not.

If a comprehensive conclusion may be drawn is that each country's debt history and specific characteristics, circumstances, and events have an overwhelming importance that cannot be encapsulated in a single general law. Research should concentrate on the former and abandon the pursuit of the latter.

References

Aizenman, Joshua. & Michael M. Hutchison. (2012). "What is The Risk of European Sovereign Debt Defaults. Fiscal Space, CDS Spreads and Market Pricing of Risk", Paper presented at the conference: "The European Sovereign Debt Crisis: Background and Perspectives", *Danmarks Nationalbank/JMF*, April 13-14, 2012.

Aizenman, Joshua, Kenneth Kletzer. & Pinto Brian. (2007). "Economic Growth with Constraints on Tax Revenues and Public Debt: Implications for Fiscal Policy and Cross-Country Differences", *NBER Working Paper* no. 12750.

Alcidi, Cinzia. & Daniel Gros. (2011a). "Adjustment Difficulties and Debt Overhang in the Euro- Zone Periphery", *LLEE Working Paper Series*, LUISS, Rome, n. 97.

Alcidi, Cinzia. & Daniel Gros. (2011b). "Adjustment Difficulties and Debt Overhangs in The Eurozone Periphery", *CEPS Working Documents*.

Alesina, Alberto. & Silvia Ardagna. (2010). "Large Changes in Fiscal Policy: Taxes Versus Spending", *Tax Policy and the Economy*, *24*, 35-68.

Alesina, Alberto. & Silvia Ardagna. (2013). "The design of fiscal adjustments", *Tax Policy and the Economy*, *27*, 19-67.

Alesina, Alberto. & Roberto Perotti. (1995). "Fiscal Expansions and Fiscal Adjustments in OECD Economies", *Economic Policy*, *10*, 207-247.

Alesina, Alberto, Alessandro Prati. & Guido Tabellini. (1989). "Public Confidence and Debt Management: A Model and a Case Study of Italy", *NBER Working Papers*, n. w3135.

Arghyrou, Michael G. & Alexandros Kontonikas. (2012). "The EMU Sovereign-Debt Crisis: Fundamentals, Expectations and Contagion", *Journal of International Financial Markets, Institutions and Money*, *22*, 658-677.

Arnone, Marco. & Andrea F. Presbitero. (2007). “External Debt Sustainability and Domestic Debt in Heavily Indebted Poor Countries”, *Rivista Internazionale di Scienze Sociali, 2.*

Attinasi, Maria-Grazia, Cristina Checherita-Westphal. & Christiane Nickel. (2009). “What Explains the Surge in Euro Area Sovereign Spreads During the Financial Crisis of 2007-09?”, *ECB Working Paper*, n. 1131.

Barro, Robert J. (1974). “Are Government Bonds Net Wealth?”, *Journal of Political Economy, 82*, 1095-1117.

Barro, Robert J. (1979). “On the Determination of The Public Debt”, *Journal of Political Economy. 87*, 940-971.

Barro, Robert J. (1989a). “The Neoclassical Approach to Fiscal Policy”, in Barro, Robert J. (ed.), *Modern Business Cycle Theory*, Cambridge Mass.: HarvardUniversity Press.

Barro, Robert. J. (1989b). “The Ricardian Approach to Budget Deficits”, *Journal of Political Economy, 97*, 940-971.

Barro, Robert J. (1990). “Government Spending in a Simple Model of Endogenous Growth”, *Journal of Political Economy, 98*, S103-S125.

Barro, Robert J. & Xavier Sala-I-Martin. (1998). *Economic Growth*, Cambridge Mass.: MIT Press.

Baum, Anja, Cristina Checherita-Westphal. & Philipp Rother. (2012). “Debt and Growth: New Evidence for the Euro Area”, *Journal of International Money and Finance, 32*, 809-821.

Beetsma, Roel, Jacopo Cimadomo, Oana Furtuna. & Massimo Giuliodori. (2015). “The Confidence Effects of Fiscal Consolidations”, *Economic Policy, 30*, 439-489.

Bernheim, Douglas B. (1989). “A Neoclassical Perspective on Budget Deficits”, *Journal of Economic Perspectives. 3*, 55-72.

Berti, Katia, Francisco de Castro. & Matteo Salto. (2013). “Effects of Fiscal Consolidation Envisaged in the 2013 Stability and Convergence Programmes on Public Debt Dynamics in EU Member States”, *European Economy*, Economic Papers, n. 504.

Blyth, Mark. (2013). *Austerity. History of a Dangerous Idea*, Oxford: Oxford University Press.

Bohn, Henning. (1995). "The Sustainability of Budget Deficits in a Stochastic Economy", *Journal of Money Credit and Banking, 27*, 257-271.

Bohn, Henning. (1998). "The Behavior of US Public Debt and Deficits", *Quarterly Journal of Economics, 113*, 949-963.

Born, Benjamin., Gernot J. Müller, Johannes Pfeffer. & Susanne Wellmann. (2018). "Market Discipline? Sovereign Spreads, Fiscal Adjustments, and Political Turnover", paper presented at the "Fiscal Policy Seminar 2018", *Federal Ministry of Finance*, Berlin, December 13-14.

Bowdler, Christopher. & Rui Pedro Esteves. (2013). "Sovereign Debt: the Assessment", *Oxford Review of Economic Policy*, Vol. *29*, No. 3, 463-477.

Bowen, William G., Richard G. Davis. & Davis H. Kopf. (1960). "The Public Debt: A Burden on Future Generations?", *American Economic Review*, *50*, 701-706.

Buiter, Willem H. & Ebrahim Rahbari. (2013). "Why Do Governments Default, And Why Don't They Default More Often?", *CEPR Discussion Paper* n. 9492.

Buti, Marco. & Nicolas Carnot. (2013). "The Debate on Fiscal Policy in Europe: Beyond the Austerity Myth", *ECFIN Economic Brief*, n. 20.

Buti, Marco. & Nicolas Carnot. (2016). "Fiscal Space and Low Interest Rates: A Eurozone Perspective", *Vox-EU*, November.

Buti, Marco. & Daniele Franco. (2005). *Fiscal Policy in the Economic and Monetary Union*. Cheltenham: Edward Elgar.

Buti, Marco. & Lucio Pench. (2012). "Fiscal Austerity and Policy Credibility" in Corsetti, Giancarlo (ed.) *Austerity: Too Much of a Good Thing?*. London. CEPR.

Caceres, Carlos, Vincenzo Guzzo. & Miguel A. Segoviano. (2010). "Sovereign Spreads: Global Risk Aversion, Contagion or Fundamentals?", *IMF Working Paper*, n. 120.

Calvo, Guillermo A. (1988). "Servicing the Public Debt: The Role of Expectations", *American Economic Review*, *78*, 647-661.

Cadsby, Charles B. & Frank Murray. (1991). "Experimental Tests of Ricardian Equivalence", *Economic Inquiry*. *29*, 645-664.

Carnot, Nicolas. (2013). "The Composition of Fiscal Adjustments: Some Principles", *ECFIN Economic Brief*, n. 23.

Checherita-Westpahl, Cristina. & Philipp Rother. (2012). "The Impact of High Government Debt on Economic Growth and its Channels: An empirical Investigation for the Euro Area", *European Economic Review*, *56*, 1392-1405.

Collignon, Stefan. & Susanne Mundschenk. (1999). "The Sustainability of Public Debt in Europe", *Economia internazionale*, *52*, 101-160.

Constancio, Vito. (2012). "Contagion and the European Debt Crisis", *Financial Stability Review*, *16*, 109-119.

Corsetti, Giancarlo. (ed.). (2012). *Austerity: Too Much of a Good Thing?*", London: CEPR.

Corsetti, Giancarlo, Keith Kuester, André Meier. & Gernot Mueller. (2010). "Debt Consolidation and Fiscal Stabilization in Deep Recessions", *American Economic Review*, *100*, 41- 45.

Corsetti, Giancarlo, Keith Kuester, André Meier. & Gernot Mueller. (2013). "Sovereign Risk, Fiscal Policy, and Macroeconomic Stability", *Economic Journal*, *123*, F99-F132.

Cunningham, Rosemary T. (1993). "The Effect of Debt Burden on Economic Growth in Heavily Indebted Developing Nations", *Journal of Economic Development*,*18*, 1.

De Grauwe, Paul. (2012). "The Governance of a Fragile Eurozone", *Australian Economic Review*, *45*, 255-268.

De Grauwe, Paul. & Yuemei Ji. (2012). "Mispricing of Sovereign Risk and Macroeconomic Stability in the Eurozone", *Journal of Common Market Studies*, *50*, 866-880.

De Grauwe, Paul. & Yuemei Ji. (2013). "Self-Fulfilling Crises in the Eurozone: An Empirical Test", *Journal of International Money and Finance*, *34*, 15-36.

DeLong, Bradford. & Lawrence Summers. (2012). "Fiscal Policy in a Depressed Economy", *Mimeo*.

Diamond, Peter A. (1965). "National Debt in a Neoclassical Growth Model", *American Economic Review*, *5*, 1125-1150.

Dotsey, Michael. & Ching Sheng Mao. (1994). "The Effects of Fiscal Policy in a Neoclassical Growth Model", *Working paper* n. 94-3. Federal Reserve Bank of Richmond, Richmond, VA.

Draghi, Mario. (2012). "Transcript of the Introductory Statement to the press conference", *Frankfurt*, September 6, 2012, www.ecb.org.

Eberhardt, Markus. & Andrea F. Presbitero. (2015). "Public Debt and Growth: Heterogeneity and Non-Linearity", *Journal of International Economics*, *97*, 45-58.

European Commission. (2014). "Assessing Public Debt Sustainability in EU Member States: A Guide", *Directorate-General for Economic and Financial Affairs, Occasional Paper*, n. 200.

Farmer, Roger A. E. (1993). *The Macroeconomics of Self-Fulfilling Prophecies*, Cambridge Mass.: MIT Press.

Fatàs, Andre. & Lawrence Summers. (2018). "The Permanent Effects of Fiscal Consolidations", *Journal of International Economics*, *112*, 238-250.

Favero, Carlo A., Francesco Giavazzi. & Jacopo Perego. (2011). "Country Heterogeneity and the International Evidence on the Effects of Fiscal Policy", *CEPR Discussion Paper*, n. 8517.

Fincke, Bettina. & Alfred Greiner. (2012). "How to Assess Debt Sustainability? Some Theory and Empirical Evidence for Selected Euro Area Countries", *Applied Economics*, *44*, 3717-3724.

Fragetta, Matteo. & Roberto Tamborini. (2019). "It's not austerity. Or is it? Assessing the Effect of Austerity on Growth in the European Union, 2010-15", *International Review of Economics and Finance*, *62*, 196-212

Foresti, Paolo. & Ugo Marani. (2014). "Expansionary Fiscal Consolidations: Theoretical Underpinnings and Their Implications for the Eurozone", *Contributions to Political Economy*, 1-15.

Gechert, Sebastian, Hallet A. Hughes. & Ansgar Rannenberg. (2015). "Fiscal Multipliers in Downturns and the Effects of Eurozone Consolidation", *CEPR Policy Insight*, n. 79.

Ghosh, Atish R., Jun I. Kim, Enrique G. Mendoza, Jonathan D. Ostry. & Mahvash S. Qureshi. (2013). "Fiscal Fatigue, Fiscal Space and Debt Sustainability in Advanced Economies", *Economic Journal*, *123*, F4-F30.

Giavazzi, Francesco. & Marco Pagano. (1990). "Can Severe Fiscal Contractions Be Expansionary? Tales of Two Small European Countries", in *NBER Macroeconomics Annual 1990*, *5*, 75-122.

Giavazzi, Francesco. & Marco Pagano. (1995). "Non Keynesian Effects of Fiscal Policy Changes: International Evidence and Swedish Experience", *Swedish Economic Policy Review*, *3*, 67-103.

Greiner, Alfred, Uwe Koeller. & Willi Semmler. (2007). "Debt Sustainability in the European Monetary Union: Theory and Empirical Evidence for Selected Countries", *Oxford Economic Papers*, *59.2.*, 194-218.

Gros, Daniel. (2012). "A simple model of multiple equilibria and default", *CEPS Working Document*, n. 366.

Gros, Daniel. (2013). "Foreign Debt Versus Domestic Debt in the Euro Area", *Oxford Review of Economic Policy*, *29*, 502-17.

Guajardo, Jaime, Daniel Leigh. & Andrea Pescatori. (2014). "Expansionary Austerity? International Evidence", *Journal of the European Economic Association*, *12*, 949-968.

Hebous, Shafik. (2011). "The Effects of Discretionary Fiscal Policy on Macroeconomic Aggregates: A Reappraisal", *Journal of Economic Surveys*, *25*, 647-707.

Herndon, Thomas, Michael Ash. & Robert Pollin. (2013). "Does High Public Debt Consistently Stifle Economic Growth? A Critique of Reinhart and Rogoff", Amherst, MA: Political Economy Research Institute, *University of Massachusetts Amherst Working Paper* No. 322.

IMF. (2010). "Will it Hurt? Macroeconomic Effects of Fiscal Consolidations", Chapter 3 of *The World Economic Outlook*, Washington, October.

IMF. (2012). "A Toolkit to Assessing Fiscal Vulnerabilities and Risks in Advanced Economies", *Working Paper*, n.11.

in't Veld, Jan. (2013). "Fiscal Consolidations and Spillovers in the Euro Area Periphery and Core", *European Economy*. Economic Papers. n. 1506.

Irons, John. & Josh Bivens. (2010). "Government Debt and Economic Growth", *Epi Brieng Paper*, n. 271.

Jordà, Oscar. & Mark A. Taylor. (2016). "The Time for Austerity: Estimating the Average Treatment Effect of Fiscal Policy". *Economic Journal*, *126*, 219-255.

Kamin, Steven B., Robert B. Khan. & Ross Levine. (1989). "External Debt and Developing Country Growth", *International finance discussion papers*, n. 352.

Karagol, Erdal. (2002). "The Causality Analysis of External Debt Service and GNP: The Case of Turkey", *Central Bank Review*. *1*, 39-64.

Krugman, Paul R. (1988). "Financing vs. Forgiving a Debt Overhang", *Journal of Development Economics*, *29*, 253-268.

Lin, Shuanglin. (2000). "Government Debt and Economic Growth in an Overlapping Generations Model", *Southern Economic Journal*., *66*, 754-763.

Liviatan, Oded. (1984). "A Macro-Absorption Approach for Estimating the Foreign Debt Burden", *Economic Development and Cultural Change*, *32*, 803-818.

Ludvigson, Sydney. (1996). "The Macroeconomic Effects of Government Debt in a Stochastic Growth Model", *Journal of Monetary Economics*, *38*, 25-45.

Manganelli, Simone. & Wolswijk Guido. (2009). "What Drives Spreads in the Euro Area Government Bond Market? ", *Economic Policy*, *24*, 191-240.

Minea, Alexandru. & Antoine Parent. (2012). "Is High Public Debt Always Harmful to Economic Growth. Reinhart and Rogoff and Some Complex Nonlinearities", Association Franaise de Cliomtrie. AFC. *Working Paper*, 12-08.

Meade, James E. (1958). "Is the National Debt a Burden?", *Oxford Economic Papers*, New Series, *10*, 163-183.

Mittone, Luigi. & Matteo Tomaselli. (2017). "Economic Growth and Public Debt: An Experimental Approach in Search of a Confidence Channel", University of Trento, Department of Economics and Management, *Mimeo*.

Modigliani, Franco. (1961). "Long-Run Implications of Alternative Fiscal Policies and the Burden of the National Debt", *Economic Journal*, *71*, 730-755.

Musgrave, Richard A. (1959). *The Theory of Public Finance*, New York: McGraw Hill.

Musgrave, Richard A. (1964). *Internal Debt in the Classical System*, in Ferguson James, M. (ed.) *Public Debt and Future Generations*, Chapel Hill.

Nuti, Mario D. (2013). "Perverse Consolidation", *paper presented at the international conference "Economic and political crises in Europe and the United States"*, University of Trento (Italy), November 7-8.

Panizza, Ugo. & Andrea F. Presbitero. (2014). "Public Debt and Economic Growth: Is There a Causal Effect?", *Journal of Macroeconomics*, *41*, 21-41.

Pattillo, Catherine, Hélène Poirson. & Luca Antonio Ricci. (2011). "External Debt and Growth", *Review of Economics and Institutions*, *2*, 30-55.

Passamani, Giuliana, Roberto Tamborini. & Matteo Tomaselli. (2015). "Sustainability vs Credibility of Fiscal Consolidation: A Principal Components Factor Analysis for the Euro Zone", *The Journal of Risk Finance*, *16*, 321-343.

Perotti, Roberto. (2012). "The "Austerity Myth": Gain Without Pain? ", in *Fiscal Policy After the Financial Crisis*, Chicago: Chicago University Press.

Pescatori, Andrea, Damiano Sandri. & John Simon. (2014). "Debt and Growth: Is There a Magic Threshold?", *International Monetary Fund*, n. 14-34.

Reihnart, Carmen M. & Kenneth S. Rogoff. (2009). *This Time is Different. Eight Centuries of Financial Folly*. Princeton: Princeton University Press.

Reihnart, Carmen M. & Kenneth S. Rogoff. (2010). “Growth in Time of Debt”, *American Economic Review*, Papers and Proceedings, *100*.

Ricciuti, Roberto. & Davide Di Laurea. (2003). “An Experimental Analysis of Two Departures from Ricardian Equivalence”, *Economics Bulletin*, *8*, 1-11.

Saint-Paul, Gilles. (1992). “Fiscal Policy in an Endogenous Growth Model”, *Quarterly Journal of Economics*, *107*, 1243-1259.

Slate, Stephen, Michael McKee, William Beck. & James Alm. (1995). “Testing Ricardian Equivalence under Uncertainty”, *Public Choice*, *85*, 11-29.

Stähler, Nikolai. (2013). “Recent Developments in Quantitative Models of Sovereign Default”, *Journal of Economic Surveys*, *27*, 605-633.

Sun, Norman. (1954). “An Economic Analysis of the Burden of Public Debt”, *The Journal of Finance*, *9*, 64-65.

Tamborini, Roberto. (2013). “The New Fiscal Rules for the EMU. Threats from Heterogeneity and Interdependence”, *The European Journal of Comparative Economics*, *10*, 315-336.

Tamborini, Roberto. (2015a). “Heterogeneous Market Beliefs, Fundamentals and the Sovereign Debt Crisis in the Eurozone”, *Economica*, *82*, 1153-1176.

Tamborini, Roberto. (2015b). “Transatlantic Austerity, 2010-13. A Comparative Assessment”, in Paganetto, Luigi (ed.), *Anaemic Europe - How to Achieve Dynamism and Mass Flourishing*, Wien: Springer, 123-161.

Tamborini, Roberto. & Matteo Tomaselli. (2019). “The Determinants of Austerity in the European Union 2010-16”, *North American Journal of Economics and Finance*, *51*, 101069.

Teles, Vladimir. K. & Caio Cesar Mussolini. (2014). “Public Debt and the Limits of Fiscal Policy to Increase Economic Growth”, *European Economic Review*, *66*, 1-15.

Tomz, Michael. & Mark L. J. Wright. (2013). “Empirical Research on Foreign Debt and Default”, *NBER Working Paper*, n. 18855.

Zagler, Martin. & Georg Dürnecker. (2003). “Fiscal Policy and Economic Growth”, *Journal of Economic Surveys*, *17*, 397-418.

Biographical Sketch

Matteo Tomaselli

Education: BA in Economics and Management, University of Trento (Italy), 2012. MA in Finance, University of Trento (Italy), 2014. PhD in Economics and Management, University of Trento (Italy), 2018.

Research and Professional Experience: My main research fields are Macroeconomics and Macroeconometrics. My Doctoral Thesis focused on the study of the relationship between economic growth and public debt in the Eurozone.

Publications from the Last 3 Years:

Passamani, G. & Tomaselli, M. (2018). "Air pollution and health risks: a statistical analysis aiming at improving air quality in an alpine Italian province", in *Demography and Health Issues – Population Ageing. Mortality and Data Analysis* (ISBN: 978-3-319-76001-8).

Tamborini, R. & Tomaselli, M. (2020). "The determinants of austerity in the European Union 2010-16", *North American Journal of Economics and Finance*, vol. *51*.

Roberto Tamborini

Affiliation: Department of Economics and Management, University of Trento, Trento (Italy)

Education: MPhil in Economics, University of Cambridge (UK), 1984. PhD in Economics at the European University Institute, Florence (Italy), 1991.

Research and Professional Experience: My main research fields are Macroeconomic theories and policies, Monetary and Financial economics. On the grounds of Economic policy, I have mainly focused on issues concerning the European Monetary Union, in particular monetary and fiscal policies and problems of the reform of the Union's governance. My researches have mainly been realized within reserach groups with Italian and foreign scholars, funded by academic institutions, the Italian National Research Council, the Italian Ministery of Research, the European Union, the German-Italian Research Programme (DAAD-CRUI, "Programma Vigoni"), the German Ministery of Finance (EconPol Programme)

Professional Appointments:

- Full Professor, Faculty of Economics, University of Trento, from 2001.
- Head of the Department of Economics, University of Trento, 2001-2007.
- Director of the Doctoral Programme in Economics and Management, University of Trento from 2010-16.
- Fellow of the School of European Political Economy, LUISS 'Guido Carli', Rome.
- Member of the Board of Experts of the "Monetary Dialogues" of the European Parliament

Publications from the Last 3 Years:

Andreozzi, L. & Tamborini, R. (2019). "Models of supranational policymaking and the reform of the EMU", *Journal of Policy Modelling*, vol. *41*, pp. 819-844.

Bonatti, L., Fracasso, A. & Tamborini, R. (2020). "COVID-19 and the Future of Quantitative Easing in the Euro Area: Three Scenarios with a Trilemma", *European Parliament, Monetary Dialogue Papers*, Brussels, September 2020.

Bonatti, L., Fracasso, A. & Tamborini, R. (2020). Rethinking Monetary and Fiscal Policy in the Post-COVID Euro Area, European Parliament, ECON Committee, *Monetary Dialogue Papers*, Brussels, November 2020.

Fragetta, M. & Tamborini, R. (2019). "It's not austerity. Or is it? Assessing the effect of austerity on growth in the European Union, 2010-15", *International Review of Economics and Finance*, vol. *62*.

Gobbi, L., Mazzocchi, R. & Tamborini, R. (2019). "Monetary policy, de-anchoring of inflation expectations, and the "new normal", *Journal of Macroeconomics*, vol. *61*, Special Issue "Macroeconomics, Rationality and Institutions" pp. 1-15.

Saraceno, F. & Tamborini, R. (2020). "How does quantitative easing work in a monetary union?" *Oxford Economic Papers*, vol. *72*, pp. 124-48,

Tamborini, R. & Tomaselli, M. (2020). "The determinants of austerity in the European Union 2010-16", *North American Journal of Economics and Finance*, vol. *51*.

Tamborini, R. (2018). "The reform of the EMU governance. Where do we stand?" *Law and Economics Yearly Review*, vol. *7*, pp. 29-48.

In: Public Debt
Editor: Antoine Bélanger
ISBN: 978-1-53619-326-8

Chapter 3

ARE THERE LIMITS TO PUBLIC DEBT IN NEO-CLASSICAL GROWTH MODELS WITH INVOLUNTARY UNEMPLOYMENT?

Karl Farmer*
University of Graz, Graz, Austria
University Cluj-Napoca, Cluj-Napoca, Romania

ABSTRACT

Governments in advanced countries are currently striving to combat the disastrous economic effects of SARS-CoV-2 related lockdowns by providing generous public expenditure programs. Simultaneously, tax revenues are collapsing due to the dramatic rise in unemployment, failing business earnings and tax deferrals. As a result, the deficits of federal and state governments are exploding. Unemployment rates in all advanced countries have risen to heights not seen since the Great Depression. Thus, the question arises as to whether, in the face of huge unemployment, limits to public debt can and/or ought to be respected, or simply

* Corresponding Author's E-mail: karl.farmer@uni-graz.at.

disregarded. Limits to public debt are a standard feature of neo-classical growth models. To the best of the present author's knowledge, Rankin and Roffia (2003) were the first to detect such limits to government debt in their Diamond-type overlapping-generations (OLG) model with internal public debt. However, as their model assumes full employment, it contrasts starkly with current lockdown-conditions involving high levels of involuntary unemployment. Thus, use is made here of a neo-classical growth model with involuntary unemployment, à la Farmer and Kuplen (2018), in order to investigate whether limits to public debt exist under involuntary unemployment and under full employment. The basic model version with exogenous growth reveals that absolute limits to public debt do exist and that they occur where the unemployment rate becomes zero. While this may be of some theoretical interest, from an empirical perspective it has become more important to investigate the possible connection between public debt and output growth. Does rising debt lead to diminished growth? By extending the basic model version so as to incorporate human capital accumulation and the crowding out of aggregate investment by private and public savings, a debt threshold can indeed be detected. In fact, the numerical values and the growth impact revealed by the extended model, are found to be close to World Bank estimates.

JEL classification: H63, E24, D91

Keywords: limits to public debt, neo-classical growth model, involuntary unemployment, closed economy

INTRODUCTION

It seems that the policy approach expressed in former ECB president Draghi's "Whatever it takes," as stated during the Euro crisis in 2012, is now being emulated by government representatives around the world when attempting to combat the disastrous economic effects of SARS-CoV-2 related lockdowns. Extremely generous public expenditure programs have been initiated to support ailing market economies, even in the face of collapsing public revenues as a result of dramatically rising unemployment, failing business earnings and tax deferrals. Consequently, the deficits of federal and state governments are exploding. Concomitantly, unemployment rates in all advanced countries have risen to heights not seen since the Great Depression. Thus, the question arises as to whether, in the face of huge unemployment, limits to public debt can and/or ought to be respected or disregarded.

Neo-classical growth models characteristically feature limits to public debt. To the best of this author's knowledge, Rankin and Roffia (2003) were the first to detect these limits to government debt in a Diamond-type overlapping-generations (OLG) economy with internal public (= government) debt. Rankin and Roffia (2003, p. 218) claim that "even with a constant stock of government debt, fiscal policy may be unsustainable because a steady state of the economy with non-degenerate values of the variables *may not exist*" (Italics in original). The private sector capital labor ratio (= aggregate capital intensity) associated with this unsustainable government debt level represents an 'interior maximum', in contrast to a position of 'degeneracy', in which, owing to the excessively high level of government debt, capital intensity approaches zero. Rankin and Roffia (2003) found in their version of Diamond's (1965) OLG model with a log-linear intertemporal utility function and a Cobb-Douglas production function that "maximum sustainable debt is generally reached at an interior maximum rather than at a degeneracy." (Rankin and Roffia 2003, p. 220). At this interior maximum the intertemporal equilibrium dynamics of the perfectly competitive market economy experience a saddle-note bifurcation (Azariadis 1993, p.152), eliciting a process of explosive capital decumulation and ending in a sudden implosion of the world economy.

Although invaluable, Rankin and Roffia's (2003) contribution is, however, restricted to an economy in which the labor supply is always fully employed. This precludes the investigation of limits to government debt in a world economy with involuntary unemployment. As is well-known, involuntary unemployment is usually associated with Keynesian macroeconomics (Keynes 1936; Hicks 1937), with involuntary unemployment being traced back to a lack of aggregate demand (so-called aggregate demand failures). To date, there is still no consensus among macroeconomists on why aggregate demand falls short of that needed for full employment. The majority adheres to the New-Keynesian approach in which prices and wages adapt sluggishly to market imbalances due to imperfect competition and other market failures (for a survey see Dixon 2000). In contrast, a minority of macroeconomists follow the lead of Morishima (1977) who attributes aggregate demand failures to inflexible aggregate investment demand, the latter being governed by the pessimistic "animal spirits" of investors (Keynes 1936) and acting independently of aggregate household savings. In contrast to the imperfectly flexible price approach of the majority view Morishima (1977) assumes perfectly flexible and perfectly competitive output prices, wage rates and interest rates. Despite these strong assumptions concerning the efficacy of the market system, involuntary unemployment is still said to occur because under an aggregate investment demand function acting independently of aggregate savings the system of temporal general equilibrium equations becomes over-determinate. Over-determinacy disappears only if at least one market clearing condition can be cancelled, and in this case, it is the labor market-clearing condition which is dropped.

More recently, Magnani (2015) – with no reference to Morishima (1977) – integrated this static macro-economic reasoning into Solow's (1956) neo-classical growth model with no public debt. The present author closely follows Magnani's lead in specifying the aggregate investment demand function. Since the subject of this chapter is limits to public debt given involuntary unemployment, use is made of Diamond's (1965) OLG model with non-neutral internal public debt. Farmer and Kuplen (2018) were the first to introduce Magnani's (2015) independent aggregate demand function into Diamond's neo-classic growth model. In their basic model, with exogenous growth of GDP (= gross domestic product), they show, as derived from household and firm optimization problems, from a government budget constraint and from the temporal market-clearing conditions, how the structure of the intertemporal equilibrium dynamics changes when aggregate investment is determined by an independent macroeconomic investment function, and how the unemployment rate becomes endogenous, as in Magnani (2015).

However, Farmer and Kuplen (2018) do not investigate the existence of limits to government debt in the modified OLG model with involuntary unemployment. This chapter addresses this gap in the published literature. To this end, Farmer and Kuplen's (2018) basic model is changed such that, instead of the public debt to capital and the capital to efficient labor ratio, the public debt to GDP ratio and the capital output ratio appear as the main dynamic variables. Due to aggregate investment being completely or moderately inflexible, it turns out that limits to the public debt to GDP ratio do exist, and that these arise since beyond the debt limit the unemployment rate would be inadmissibly less than zero. In contrast to the main insight of Rankin and Roffia (2003), that at the interior maximum of sustainable debt the model economy experiences catastrophe, in the basic OLG model presented here, there is no sudden implosion of the economy. Beyond the debt limit, one simply finds that a feasible steady-state solution does not exist.

In the more recent empirical literature concerning how public debt affects GDP growth (for an overview see Hayati et al. 2019), absolute limits to the public debt to GDP ratio do not feature prominently. However, and in line with the somewhat disputed study by Reinhart et al. (2015), the existence of a threshold to the debt to GDP ratio, beyond which GDP growth declines, is now attracting considerable attention. As this question was neither addressed in Farmer and Kuplen's (2018), nor in the present chapter's basic model, the second objective of the present discussion is to extend the basic model by introducing human capital accumulation à la Glomm and Ravikumar (1992), and thus shift attention from exogenous to endogenous GPD growth. The author can then investigate the existence and the numerical value of a debt threshold beyond which GDP growth decreases. The extended model reveals that in the absence of further modifications of the aggregate investment function employed thus far, no evidence of such a debt threshold appears. It is again Magnani (2015, pp. 18-20) who indicates why this may be the case by pointing out that, empirically, private and public consumption and private and public savings crowd out aggregate investment. Thus, by introducing a crowding-out effect for private and public savings on aggregate investment, it is shown below, given appropriate values for the crowding-out parameter and the interest-factor elasticity of aggregate investment, that a debt threshold can exist beyond which GDP growth declines. It is also revealed that, in a numerically specified version of the extended model, the numerical values found for the threshold and the growth detracting effect of larger public debt are in fact quite close to the empirical estimations provided by the World Bank.

The chapter is structured as follows: The next section outlines the basic model: a log-linear, Cobb-Douglas OLG model with internal public debt, exogenous GDP growth, and involuntary unemployment. The optimization problems of households and firms are first presented and the first-order conditions for intertemporal utility and atemporal profit maxima are then derived. From these conditions, together with the government budget constraint and the temporal market-clearing conditions, the intertemporal equilibrium dynamics of the capital-output ratio and the unemployment rate are then deduced. Thereafter, the existence of a steady-state solution and its local dynamic stability are analyzed. Following this, several structural parameters of the basic model are calibrated with respect to time-average figures for the global GDP growth rate, the global real interest rate, the global saving and investment ratios, all for the period 1995 to pre-pandemic 2020. Together with time averages for the same period of the policy parameters, the absolute limits for the public debt to GDP ratio are then numerically derived. In the subsequent section the basic model is extended by introducing human capital accumulation in line with Glomm and Ravikumar (1992). Again, the intertemporal equilibrium dynamics is derived from household and firm first-order optimization conditions, the government budget constraint, and market-clearing conditions. After proving the existence and dynamic stability of a steady-state solution the model's parameters are again numerically specified and the question of determining a numerical value for an absolute limit to the debt to GDP ratio is investigated. Then, in line with Magnani (2015), the crowding out of private and public savings on aggregate investment is introduced, and questions concerning the existence and numerical value of a debt ratio threshold, beyond which GDP growth declines, are explored. The last section concludes by summarizing the main results and providing some hints for future research.

The Basic Model: The Log-Linear Cobb-Douglas OLG Model with Internal Public Debt, Exogenous Growth, and Involuntary Unemployment

As in Farmer and Kuplen (2018), an infinite-horizon economy composed of perfectly competitive firms, finitely lived households, and a non-optimizing government is considered. A new generation, called generation t, enters the economy in each period $t = 0,1,2,...$. Generation t is composed of a continuum of $L_t > 0$ units of identical agents. It is assumed that the growth rate of the population is $g^L > -1$, which implies that $L_{t+1} = G^L L_t$, $G^L = 1 + g^L$.

Households, each consisting of one agent, are non-altruistic: The old do not take care of the young and the young do not take care of the old. They live a maximum of two periods, youth (adult) and old age. In youth, each agent is endowed with one unit of labor, which is supplied inelastically to firms. In exchange for the labor supply, each employed agent of generation t obtains the real wage rate w_t, which denotes the units of the produced good per unit of labor. In contrast to the original Diamond (1965) OLG model, not the whole labor supply is employed but only $(1-u_t)L_t$, where $0 \leq u_t < 1$ denotes the unemployment rate. The number of unemployed people is thus $u_t L_t$. The government collects taxes on wages, quoted as a fixed proportion of wage income, $\tau_t w_t$, $0 < \tau_t < 1$. The unemployed do not pay any taxes. Young, employed agents, denoted by superscript E, split the net wage income $(1-\tau_t)w_t$ each period between current consumption $c_t^{1,E}$ and savings s_t^E. Savings of the employed are invested in real capital in period t per employed capita, $I_t^D / L_t(1-u_t)$, demanded by employed households in youth, and in real government bonds per employed capita, $B_{t+1}^D / L_t(1-u_t)$, also demanded by employed households in youth. For simplicity, we assume a depreciation rate of one with respect to real capital. Any unemployed young-age household, denoted by superscript U, consumes $c_t^{1,U}$, saves s_t^U and receives from the government an unemployment benefit $\varsigma_t > 0$ in order to be able to finance its consumption and savings: $c_t^{1,U} + s_t^U = \varsigma_t$.

In old age, the employed household supplies inelastically $K_{t+1}^S / L_t(1-u_t) = I_t^D / L_t(1-u_t)$ to firms, and $B_{t+1}^S / L_t(1-u_t) = B_{t+1}^D / L_t(1-u_t)$ to young households in period $t+1$. Thus, the per capita savings of employed people are invested as follows: $s_t^E = K_{t+1}^S / L_t(1-u_t) + B_{t+1}^S / L_t(1-u_t)$. Similarly, the per capita savings of the unemployed household are invested as follows: $s_t^U = K_{t+1}^S / L_t u_t + B_{t+1}^S / L_t u_t$. In old age, both employed and unemployed households consume their gross return on assets: $c_{t+1}^{2,E} = q_{t+1} K_{t+1}^S / L_t(1-u_t) + (1+i_{t+1}) B_{t+1}^S / L_t(1-u_t)$, respectively $c_{t+1}^{2,U}$ = $q_{t+1} K_{t+1}^S / L_t u_t + (1+i_{t+1}) B_{t+1}^S / L_t u_t$, where $c_{t+1}^{2,E}$, and $c_{t+1}^{2,U}$, represent consumption of the employed, respectively unemployed, in old age, q_{t+1} denotes the gross rental rate on real capital, and i_{t+1} denotes the real interest rate on government bonds in period $t+1$. For simplicity, there are no taxes on rental and interest income.

The intertemporal preferences of the typical two-period lived household are represented by a log-linear intertemporal utility function slightly generalized in comparison to Diamond's (1965, p. 1134) leading example. As usual, this simple specification aims at closed form solutions for the intertemporal equilibrium dynamics (see e.g., de la Croix and Michel 2002, pp. 181-184).

The typical younger, employed household maximizes the following intertemporal utility function subject to the budget constraints of the active period (i) and the retirement period (ii):

$$\text{Max} \rightarrow \varepsilon \ln c_t^{1,E} + \beta \ln c_{t+1}^{2,E}$$

subject to:

$$(i)\ c_t^{1,E} + I_t^{D,E} / L_t(1-u_t) + B_{t+1}^{D,E} / L_t(1-u_t) = (1-\tau_t)w_t,$$
$$(ii)\ c_{t+1}^{2,E} = q_{t+1}K_{t+1}^{S,E} / L_t(1-u_t) + (1+i_{t+1})B_{t+1}^{S,E} / L_t(1-u_t),$$
$$K_{t+1}^{S,E} = I_t^{D,E},\ B_{t+1}^{S,E} = B_{t+1}^{D,E}.$$

$0<\varepsilon\leq 1$ denotes the utility elasticity of consumption in youth, while $0<\beta<1$ depicts the subjective future utility discount factor. As is well-known, the log-linear intertemporal utility function ensures the existence of a unique, interior solution of the above optimization problem. Hence, one may solve the old-age budget constraint for $B_{t+1}^{S,E} / L_t(1-u_t)$ and insert the result into the young-age, employed budget constraint of (i), and thus obtain:

$$c_t^{1,E} + c_{t+1}^{2,E} / (1+i_{t+1}) + [1-q_{t+1} / (1+i_{t+1})]K_{t+1}^{S,E} / L_t(1-u_t) = (1-\tau_t)w_t. \quad (1)$$

Obviously, a strictly positive and finite solution to maximizing the intertemporal utility function subject to constraint (1) requires that the following no-arbitrage condition holds:

$$q_{t+1} = 1 + i_{t+1} \quad (2)$$

The no-arbitrage condition (2) implies that $K_{t+1}^{S,E} / L_t(1-u_t)$ is optimally indeterminate, and the first-order conditions for a maximum solution read as follows:

$$c_t^{1,E} + c_{t+1}^{2,E} / (1+i_{t+1}) = (1-\tau_t)w_t, \quad (3)$$

$$(\beta / \varepsilon)c_t^{1,E} = c_{t+1}^{2,E} / (1+i_{t+1}). \quad (4)$$

Solving equations (3) and (4) for $c_t^{1,E}$ and $c_{t+1}^{2,E}$ yields the following optimal consumption for employed people in youth and old age:

$$c_t^{1,E} = [\varepsilon / (\varepsilon + \beta)](1 - \tau_t)w_t \; , \tag{5}$$

$$c_{t+1}^{2,E} = [\beta / (\varepsilon + \beta)](1 + i_{t+1})(1 - \tau_t)w_t . \tag{6}$$

Since $s_t^E = K_{t+1}^{S,E} / L_t(1-u_t) + B_{t+1}^{S,E} / L_t(1-u_t)$, we find for the utility maximizing savings:

$$s_t^E = [\beta / (\varepsilon + \beta)](1 - \tau_t)w_t \, . \tag{7}$$

The typical younger, unemployed household maximizes the following intertemporal utility function subject to the budget constraints of the active period (i) and the retirement period (ii):

$$\text{Max} \rightarrow \varepsilon \ln c_t^{1,U} + \beta \ln c_{t+1}^{2,U}$$

subject to:

$$(i)\ c_t^{1,U} + I_t^{D,U} / L_t u_t + B_{t+1}^{D,U} / L_t u_t = \varsigma_t ,$$
$$(ii)\ c_{t+1}^{2,U} = q_{t+1} K_{t+1}^{S,U} / L_t u_t + (1 + i_{t+1}) B_{t+1}^{S,U} / L_t u_t ,$$
$$K_{t+1}^{S,U} = I_t^{D,U} ,\ B_{t+1}^{S,U} = B_{t+1}^{D,U} .$$

Again, $0 < \varepsilon \leq 1$ denotes the utility elasticity of consumption in unemployed youth, while $0 < \beta < 1$ depicts the subjective future utility discount factor and ς_t denotes the unemployment benefit per capita unemployed. As above, the log-linear intertemporal utility function ensures the existence of a unique, interior solution for the above optimization problem. Hence, one may again solve the old-age budget constraint for $B_{t+1}^{S,U} / L_t u_t$ and insert the result into the young-age, unemployed budget constraint of (i), and thus obtain:

$$c_t^{1,U} + c_{t+1}^{2,U} / (1 + i_{t+1}) + [1 - q_{t+1} / (1 + i_{t+1})] K_{t+1}^{S,U} / L_t u_t = \varsigma_t \, . \tag{8}$$

The no-arbitrage condition (2) implies that $K_{t+1}^{S,U} / L_t u_t$ is optimally indeterminate, and the first-order conditions for a maximum solution read as follows:

$$c_t^{1,U} + c_{t+1}^{2,U} / (1 + i_{t+1}) = \varsigma_t \,, \tag{9}$$

$$(\beta / \varepsilon) c_t^{1,U} = c_{t+1}^{2,U} / (1 + i_{t+1}). \tag{10}$$

Solving equations (9) and (10) for $c_t^{1,U}$ and $c_{t+1}^{2,U}$ yields the following optimal consumption in youth and old age:

$$c_t^{1,U} = [\varepsilon / (\varepsilon + \beta)] \varsigma_t \,, \tag{11}$$

$$c_{t+1}^{2,U} = [\beta / (\varepsilon + \beta)](1 + i_{t+1}) \varsigma_t . \tag{12}$$

Since $s_t^U = K_{t+1}^{S,U} / L_t u_t + B_{t+1}^{S,U} / L_t u_t$, we find for the utility maximizing savings:

$$s_t^U = [\beta / (\varepsilon + \beta)] \varsigma_t \,. \tag{13}$$

All firms are endowed with an identical (linear-homogeneous) Cobb-Douglas production function: $Y_t = M(a_t N_t)^{1-\alpha} (K_t)^{\alpha}$, $0 < \alpha < 1$. Here, Y_t denotes aggregate output or GDP, $M > 0$ stands for total factor productivity, a_t features the efficiency level of employed laborers N_t, while K_t denotes the input of capital services, all in period t, and $1 - \alpha$ (α) depicts the production elasticity (= production share) of labor (capital services). The profit of the production sector (in terms of the single output) is $Y_t - w_t N_t - q_t K_t$. In addition, it is assumed that labor efficiency grows at the exogenously given rate $g^a \geq 0$ such that $a_{t+1} = G^a a_t$ with $G^a = 1 + g^a$ and $a_0 = a_- > 0$. Following normal practice in growth theory, $G^n \equiv G^L G^a$ is called the natural growth factor.

Maximization of $Y_t - w_t N_t - q_t K_t$ subject to the Cobb-Douglas production implies the following first-order conditions:

$$M(1-\alpha)a_t[K_t/(a_t N_t)]^{\alpha} = w_t, \tag{14}$$

$$M\alpha[K_t/(a_t N_t)]^{(\alpha-1)} = q_t. \tag{15}$$

However, since the number of employed workers is $N_t = L_t(1-u_t)$, we can rewrite the profit-maximization conditions (14) and (15) as follows:

$$M(1-\alpha)a_t[K_t/(a_t L_t(1-u_t))]^{\alpha} = w_t, \tag{16}$$

$$M\alpha[K_t/(a_t L_t(1-u_t))]^{(\alpha-1)} = q_t. \tag{17}$$

Finally, the GDP function can be rewritten as follows:

$$Y_t = M(a_t L_t(1-u_t))^{1-\alpha}(K_t)^{\alpha}. \tag{18}$$

The government does not optimize, but is subject to the following constraint period by period:

$$B_{t+1} = (1+i_t)B_t + \Gamma_t + L_t u_t \varsigma_t - \tau_t(1-u_t)w_t L_t, \tag{19}$$

where B_t denotes the aggregate stock of real public debt at the beginning of period t, and Γ_t indicates real government consumption expenditures exclusive of government's unemployment benefits $L_t u_t \varsigma_t$ during period t.

Magnani (2015, pp. 13-14) rightly claims that in Solow's (1956) neoclassical growth model investment in real capital is not micro- but macro-founded since aggregate investment is determined by aggregate savings. This is also true in Diamond's (1965) OLG model of neoclassical growth in which perfectly flexible aggregate investment is determined by aggregate savings of households in youth. In contrast to these neoclassical growth models, Morishima (1977) in "Walras' Economics" and more recently Magnani (2015, p. 14) assume that "investments are determined by an independent investment function." This function is specified in discrete time as follows:

$$I_t^D = \phi L_o (G^L)^t a_o (G^a)^t (1+i_t)^{-\theta}, \ \phi > 0, \theta \geq 0 \text{ ,} \tag{20}$$

The positive parameter ϕ reflects "Keynesian investors' animal spirits" (Magnani 2015, p. 14) while θ denotes the interest-factor elasticity of aggregate investment demand.

In addition to the restrictions imposed by household and firm optimizations and the above government budget constraint, markets for labor, capital services and assets, have to clear in all periods (the market for the output of production is cleared by means of Walras' Law[1]).

---

[1] The proof of Walras' law proceeds as follows: Denote by $P_t > 0$ the nominal price (level) of production output (GDP). Then, the current period budget constraint of employed households in youth can be rewritten as follows: $P_t L_t (1-u_t) c_t^{1,E} + P_t I_t^{D,E} + P_t B_{t+1}^{D,E} = (1-\tau_t) P_t w_t (1-u_t) L_t$. (F.1) The budget constraint of households in old age employed in youth reads as follows: $P_t L_{t-1} (1-u_{t-1}) c_t^{2,E} = P_t q_t K_t^{S,E} + P_t (1+i_t) B_t^{S,E}$. (F.2) The budget constraint of young unemployed households in period t is as follows: $P_t L_t u_t c_t^{1,U} + P_t I_t^{D,U} + P_t B_{t+1}^{D,U} = L_t u_t \varsigma_t$. (F.3) Moreover, the budget constraint of the household in old age in period t, which was unemployed in youth, reads as follows: $P_t L_{t-1} u_{t-1} c_t^{2,U} = P_t q_t K_t^{S,U} + P_t (1+i_t) B_t^{S,U}$. (F.4) In addition, maximum profits are zero, which implies: $P_t Y_t = P_t w_t N_t + P_t q_t K_t$. (F.5) Finally, the government's budget constraint is rewritten as follows: $P_t B_{t+1} = P_t (1+i_t) B_t + P_t \Gamma_t + P_t L_t u_t \varsigma_t - P_t \tau_t w_t L_t (1-u_t)$. (F.6) Adding up the left- and right-hand side of equations (F.1), (F.2), (F.3) and (F.4) yields: $P_t L_t (1-u_t) c_t^{1,E} + P_t I_t^{D,E} + P_t L_t u_t c_t^{1,U} + P_t I_t^{D,U} + P_t L_{t-1} (1-u_{t-1}) c_t^{2,E} + P_t L_{t-1} u_{t-1} c_t^{2,U} = (1-\tau_t) P_t w_t (1-u_t) L_t - P_t B_{t+1}^{D,E} - P_t B_{t+1}^{D,U} + L_t u_t \varsigma_t + P_t q_t K_t^{S,E} + P_t (1+i_t) B_t^{S,E} + P_t q_t K_t^{S,U} + P_t (1+i_t) B_t^{S,U}$. (F.7) Considering (21), (22) and (23) in (F.7), gives: $P_t L_t (1-u_t) c_t^{1,E} + P_t L_{t-1} (1-u_{t-1}) c_t^{2,E} + P_t I_t^{D,E} + P_t L_t u_t c_t^{1,U} + P_t L_{t-1} u_{t-1} c_t^{2,U} + P_t I_t^{D,U} = P_t w_t N_t - \tau_t P_t w_t N_t - P_t B_{t+1} + P_t q_t K_t + P_t (1+i_t) B_t$. (F.8) Considering labor market clearing condition (21) when inserting (F.6) into (F.8), and taking account of (F.5) in (F.8) yields: $P_t L_t (1-u_t) c_t^{1,E} + P_t L_{t-1} (1-u_{t-1}) c_t^{2,E} + P_t L_t u_t c_t^{1,U} + P_t L_{t-1} u_{t-1} c_t^{2,U} + P_t I_t^{D,E} + P_t I_t^{D,U} + P_t \Gamma_t$

$$L_t(1-u_t) = N_t, \forall t, \tag{21}$$

$$K_t^{S,E} + K_t^{S,U} = K_t, \forall t, \tag{22}$$

$$B_t^{D.E} + B_t^{D,U} = B_t^{S,E} + B_t^{S,U} = B_t, \forall t. \tag{23}$$

As a next step, the unemployment rate in period t (= temporary unemployment rate) is derived. To this end, we use the output market clearing identity:

$$\begin{aligned} &P_tL_t(1-u_t)c_t^{1,E} + P_tL_{t-1}(1-u_{t-1})c_t^{2,E} + P_tL_tu_tc_t^{1,U} + P_tL_{t-1}u_{t-1}c_t^{2,U} \\ &+P_tI_t^{D,E} + P_tI_t^{D,U} + P_t\Gamma_t = P_tY_t. \end{aligned} \tag{24}$$

Starting with identity (24), we insert equations (18), (11), and (ii) for period t, for the employed and/or unemployed. In addition, we also insert equation (20), with $I_t^D = I_t^{D,E} + I_t^{D,U}$ and add the market clearing conditions (22) and (23). In this way, the following equation for $P_t = 1, \forall t$ is obtained:

$$\begin{aligned} M(a_tL_t(1-u_t))^{1-\alpha}(K_t)^{\alpha} &= \varepsilon/(\varepsilon+\beta)(1-\tau_t)w_tL_t(1-u_t) + \varepsilon/(\varepsilon+\beta)\varsigma_tL_tu_t \\ &+ q_tK_t + (1+i_t)B_t + \phi a_tL_t(1+i_t)^{-\theta} + \Gamma_t, \end{aligned} \tag{25}$$

with $a_tL_t \equiv A_t$ as potential effective labor. Dividing equation (25) on both sides by Y_t, the following equation is arrived at:

$$\begin{aligned} 1 &= [\varepsilon/(\varepsilon+\beta)](1-\tau_t)w_tL_t(1-u_t)/Y(t) + [\varepsilon/(\varepsilon+\beta)]\varsigma_tL_tu_t/Y(t) \\ &+ q_t[K_t/Y(t)] + (1+i_t)[B_t/Y(t)] + \phi A_t(1+i_t)^{-\theta}/Y(t) + \Gamma_t/Y(t). \end{aligned}$$
(26)

$= P_tY_t$, which is production-output market clearing. Since this equation is always true, P_t is indeterminate and can be fixed as $P_t = 1$.

Due to the linear-homogeneity of the production function the profit-maximizing conditions (14) and (15) can be rewritten as follows:

$$w_t / a_t = M(1-\alpha)(K_t / A_t)^{\alpha}(1-u_t)^{-\alpha}, \tag{27}$$

$$q_t = M\alpha(K_t / A_t)^{\alpha-1}(1-u_t)^{1-\alpha}. \tag{28}$$

Upon considering the no-arbitrage condition (2) and equation (18), which can equivalently be written as $Y_t = M\,A_t(K_t / A_t)^{\alpha}(1-u_t)^{1-\alpha}$, defining $v_t \equiv K_t / Y_t$ as the capital-output ratio, $\gamma_t \equiv \Gamma_t / Y_t$ as the ratio of government consumption expenditures to GDP, $\xi_t \equiv (\varsigma_t u_t L_t)/Y_t$ as the unemployment benefit to GDP ratio, $b_t \equiv B_t / Y_t$ as the public debt to GDP ratio, rewriting (28) as $q_t = \alpha / v_t$ and inserting (27) and (28) into (26) then yields the following equation:

$$\begin{aligned} 1 &= (\varepsilon / (\varepsilon+\beta)(1-\tau_t)(1-\alpha) + (\varepsilon / (\varepsilon+\beta)\xi_t + \alpha[1 + b_t / v_t] \\ &\quad + \phi A_t(\alpha / v_t)^{-\theta} / Y_t + \gamma_t. \end{aligned} \tag{29}$$

Due to equation (28) and $q_t = \alpha / v_t$, K_t / A_t is related to v_t as follows:

$$K_t / A_t = v_t^{1/(1-\alpha)} M^{1/(1-\alpha)}(1-u_t). \tag{30}$$

Using equation (30), equation (29) can be rewritten as follows:

$$\begin{aligned} 1 &= (\varepsilon / (\varepsilon+\beta)(1-\tau_t)(1-\alpha) + (\varepsilon / (\varepsilon+\beta)\xi_t + \alpha[1 + b_t / v_t] \\ &\quad + \phi(\alpha / v_t)^{-\theta} M^{-1/(1-\alpha)}(1-u_t)^{-1} v_t^{-\alpha/(1-\alpha)} + \gamma_t. \end{aligned} \tag{31}$$

Next, it is apt to specify how the government determines its intertemporal policy profile. To this end, the author first assumes that both government consumption expenditures per GDP, γ_t, and unemployment benefits per GDP, ξ_t, are time-stationary, i.e., $\gamma_t = \gamma_{t+1} = \gamma, \forall t$ and $\xi_t = \xi_{t+1} = \xi, \forall t$. Before investigating the implications of these assumptions for equation (31), one needs to recall the governmental budget constraint (19) and divide it on both sides by Y_t. This then results in:

$$(B_{t+1} / Y_{t+1})(Y_{t+1} / Y_t) \equiv (1 + i_t)(B_t / Y_t) + \Gamma_t / Y_t + (\varsigma_t u_t L_t) / Y_t \\ - \tau_t (1 - u_t) w_t L_t / Y_t. \tag{32}$$

Upon acknowledging the stationarity of $\gamma_t = \gamma > 0$ and $\xi_t = \xi > 0, \forall t$, as well as equation (27), equation (32) then becomes:

$$b_{t+1}(Y_{t+1} / Y_t) = (1 + i_t)b_t + \gamma + \xi - \tau_t(1 - \alpha). \tag{33}$$

Taking account of the GDP definition and of equation (30), for the GDP growth factor $G_t^Y \equiv Y_{t+1} / Y_t$ the author then obtains:

$$G_t^Y = G^n (v_{t+1} / v_t)^{\alpha/(1-\alpha)} (1 - u_{t+1}) / (1 - u_t) \tag{34}$$

As in Diamond (1965, p. 1137) the author furthermore assumes that the government runs a 'constant-stock' fiscal policy: $b_{t+1} = b_t = b, \forall t$. Equation (31) implies that the wage-tax rate ought to become endogenous and is determined by the following equation:

$$\tau_t = [(\alpha / v_t - G_t^Y)b + \gamma + \xi] / (1 - \alpha). \tag{35}$$

Inserting τ_t from equation (35) into equation (31), leads to the following result:

$$1 = (\varepsilon / (\varepsilon + \beta)[1 - \alpha(1 + b / v_t) - \gamma - \xi + bG_t^Y] + (\varepsilon / (\varepsilon + \beta)\xi \\ + \alpha[1 + b_t / v_t] + \gamma + \phi(\alpha / v_t)^{-\theta} M^{-1/(1-\alpha)} (1 - u_t)^{-1} v_t^{-\alpha/(1-\alpha)}. \tag{36}$$

Collecting terms and simplifying the resulting expression yields the following equation for $(1-u_t)$:

$$(1-u_t) = \{(\varepsilon+\beta)\phi\alpha^{-\theta}M^{-1/(1-\alpha)}v_t^{[\theta(1-\alpha)-\alpha]/(1-\alpha)}\} \\ /\{\beta[1-\gamma-\alpha(1+b/v_t)]-\varepsilon b G_t^Y\}. \tag{37}$$

Equation (37) shows that the temporary equilibrium unemployment rate is determined by structural and policy parameters, by the historically given capital-output ratio and by the GDP growth factor. Obviously, $1-u_t>0 \Leftrightarrow u_t<1$ if the denominator in the fraction on the right-hand side of equation (37) is larger than zero, or $\beta[1-\gamma-\alpha(1+b/v_t)]>\varepsilon b G_t^Y$, $\forall t$.

To derive the intertemporal equilibrium dynamics, we use $K_{t+1}^S = I_t^D$, and by applying the market clearing condition (22) and equation (20), and dividing the resulting equation on both sides by Y_t, we thus obtain:

$$K_{t+1}/Y_{t+1}(Y_{t+1}/Y_t) \equiv v_{t+1}G_t^Y = I_t^D/Y_t = \phi\alpha^{-\theta}M^{-1/(1-\alpha)}v_t^{[\theta(1-\alpha)-\alpha]/(1-\alpha)}(1-u_t)^{-1}, \\ v_0 = v_- > 0. \tag{38}$$

As usual, the steady states of the intertemporal equilibrium dynamics (37) and (38) are defined as $\lim_{t->\infty} v_t = v$ and $\lim_{t->\infty} u_t = u$. It is obvious that a trivial steady state does not exist. Thus, one is entitled to focus on non-trivial steady-state solutions with $0<u<1$ and $v>0$. While there is an explicit solution for $1-u$, an explicit solution for v is impossible. We thus resort here to an intermediate value theorem to prove the existence of at least one feasible steady-state solution $0<v<\infty$ and $0<u<1$.

To this end, we thus first need to define, for given structural and policy parameters (with the exception of b), the government debt to GDP parameter denoted as $b^{\max}>0$ and the minimal capital-output ratio, $v_{\min}$, which ensure full employment, that is $u=0$. Using the steady state version of equation (38) with $u=0$, $v_{\min}$ can then be determined as follows:

$$v_{\min}=[\phi(G^{n})^{-1}\alpha^{-\theta}M^{-1/(1-\alpha)}]^{(1-\alpha)/[1-\theta(1-\alpha)]}>0\,. \tag{39}$$

Using the steady state version of equation (37) with $u=0$, $b=b^{\max}$ can also be determined as:

$$\begin{aligned} b^{\max}=&[\beta(1-\alpha-\gamma)-(\beta+\varepsilon)\phi\alpha^{-\theta}M^{-1/(1-\alpha)}v_{\min}{}^{[\theta(1-\alpha)-\alpha]/(1-\alpha)}] \\ &/(\varepsilon G^{n}+\beta/v_{\min}), \end{aligned} \tag{40}$$

whereby it is assumed that $\beta(1-\alpha-\gamma)>(\beta+\varepsilon)\phi\alpha^{-\theta}M^{-1/(1-\alpha)}\times$ $\times v_{\min}{}^{[\theta(1-\alpha)-\alpha]/(1-\alpha)}$, in order to ensure that $b^{\max}>0$.

For the proof of the existence of at least one $0<u<1$ and $v_{\min}<v<\infty$ we once more make use of the steady-state versions of equations (37) and (38) and define the following continuous, real-valued function $LHS(v)\equiv[\phi(G^{n})^{-1}\alpha^{-\theta}M^{-1/(1-\alpha)}]v^{[\theta(1-\alpha)-1]/(1-\alpha)}\{\beta[1-\alpha(1+b/v)\quad-\gamma]-\varepsilon bG^{n}\}$ which is obtained by inserting $(1-u)$ from the steady-state version of equation (37) into the steady-state of version of equation (38), and $RHS(v)\equiv\phi\alpha^{-\theta}M^{-1/(1-\alpha)}v^{[\theta(1-\alpha)-\alpha]/(1-\alpha)}$.

Proposition 1. Suppose that $\omega\equiv(\alpha,\beta,\varepsilon,\gamma,M,\phi,\theta)\in\Omega\equiv(0,1)^{4}\times\mathbb{R}_{+}^{3}$, $\alpha<(1-\alpha)\theta<1$, $\beta(1-\alpha-\gamma)>(\beta+\varepsilon)\phi\alpha^{-\theta}M^{-1/(1-\alpha)}v_{\min}{}^{[\theta(1-\alpha)-\alpha]/(1-\alpha)}$ and $\beta(1-\alpha)>\beta(b/v_{\min}+\gamma)+\varepsilon bG^{n}$. Then, exactly one steady-state solution $0<u<1$ and $0<v_{\min}<v<\infty$ exists.

Proof. For $b=b^{\max}$ it is known that $u=0$ and $v=v_{\min}$. Thus, let $b<b^{\max}$. Under this asumption, we need to show that $v_{\min}<v<\infty$ and $0<u<1$. From the last parameter restriction in Proposition 1 and $b<b^{\max}$, it is obvious that $0<u<1$. To show that $v_{\min}<v<\infty$, whereby v is the solution of $LHS(v)=RHS(v)$, we apply an intermediate value theorem. To this end, one must show that $LHS(v_{\min})>RHS(v_{\min})$ and

$\lim_{v\to\infty} LHS(v) < \lim_{v\to\infty} RHS(v)$. Note first that for $b = b^{\max}$ and $v = v_{\min}$ $LHS(v_{\min}) = RHS(v_{\min})$. Under $b < b^{\max}$ and with $dLHS(v)/db < 0$ it is clear that $LHS(v_{\min})(b) > LHS(v_{\min})(b^{\max})$. Since $RHS(v_{\min})$ does not depend on b, it follows that $RHS(v_{\min})(b) = RHS(v_{\min})(b^{\max})$ for all feasible b. Hence, $LHS(v_{\min})(b) > RHS(v_{\min})(b), \forall b < b^{\max}$. To show that $\lim_{v\to\infty} LHS(v)$ $< \lim_{v\to\infty} RHS(v)$ note that $\lim_{v\to\infty} LHS(v) = 0$ while $\lim_{v\to\infty} RHS(v) = \infty$ on account of the parameter restrictions in Proposition 1. Moreover, the solution is unique since $\alpha < (1-\alpha)\theta < 1$ $LHS(v)$ is monotonically decreasing, while $RHS(v)$ is monotonically increasing in v for $v_{\min} < v < \infty$.

The next step is to investigate the local dynamic stability of steady-state solutions $\{(v,u)\}$. To this end, we totally differentiate the intertemporal equilibrium equations (34), (37) and (38), with respect to all endogenous variables $v_{t+1}, v_t, u_{t+1}, u_t, G_t^Y$. We then form the Jacobian matrix of partial differentials evaluated at the steady state solution (v,u) as follows:

$$J(v,u) \equiv \begin{bmatrix} \frac{\partial v_{t+1}}{\partial v_t}(v,u) & \frac{\partial v_{t+1}}{\partial w_t}(v,u) \\ \frac{\partial w_{t+1}}{\partial v_t}(v,u) & \frac{\partial w_{t+1}}{\partial w_t}(v,u) \end{bmatrix}, \tag{41}$$

with

$$\frac{\partial v_{t+1}}{\partial v_t}(v,u) \equiv j_{11} = \frac{[(1-\alpha)\theta - \alpha]G^n[\varepsilon b + (\beta+\varepsilon)v] - \alpha(1-\alpha)\beta b / v}{(1-\alpha)b\,\varepsilon\, G^n},$$

$$\frac{\partial v_{t+1}}{\partial u_t}(v,u) \equiv j_{12} = \frac{\beta[1-\gamma-\alpha(1+b/v)]v}{b\varepsilon\, G^n(1-u)} > 0,$$

$$\frac{\partial u_{t+1}}{\partial v_t}(v,u) \equiv j_{21}$$

$$= \frac{(1-u)\{[(1-\alpha)\theta-\alpha]G^n(\beta+\varepsilon+\alpha\varepsilon b/v)-\alpha(1-\alpha)(\beta b/v^2+\varepsilon bG^n/v)\}}{(1-\alpha)^2 b\varepsilon G^n},$$

$$\frac{\partial u_{t+1}}{\partial u_t}(v,u) \equiv j_{22} = \frac{\beta[1-\gamma-\alpha(1+b/v)]}{(1-\alpha)\varepsilon bG^n} > 0.$$

Due to the condition $\beta[1-\gamma-\alpha(1+b/v_t)] > \varepsilon bG_t^Y, \forall t$ which ensures $u_t < 1, \forall t$, it is obvious that in general $j_{12} > 0$ and $j_{22} > 0$. The signs of j_{11} and j_{21} are in general unknown since it was assumed in Proposition 1 that $(1-\alpha)\theta-\alpha > 0$. To investigate the dynamic stability of steady-state solutions following from $LHS(v) = RHS(v)$, the signs and the magnitudes of the eigenvalues of the Jacobian (41) are needed. As is well-known, the eigenvalues of the 2x2 Jacobian matrix (41) are defined as follows: $\lambda_{1,2} \equiv [\mathrm{Tr}J(v,u) \pm \sqrt{\Delta(v,u)}]/2$, with $\mathrm{Tr}J(v,u)$ denoting the trace of the Jacobian matrix (41), $\Delta(v,u)$ being the discriminant of the matrix, defined as $\Delta(v,u) \equiv \mathrm{Tr}J(v,u)^2 - 4\mathrm{Det}\,J(v,u)$, and $\mathrm{Det}\,J(v,u)$ denoting the respective Jacobian determinant.

The algebraic calculation of the trace and of the determinant of the Jacobian matrix (41) yields the following results:

$$\begin{aligned}\mathrm{Tr}J(v,u) = \{&\beta[1-\gamma-\alpha(1+b/v)]+[(1-\alpha)\theta-\alpha]G^n[\varepsilon b+(\beta+\varepsilon)v] \\ &-\alpha(1-\alpha)\beta b/v\}/[(1-\alpha)\varepsilon bG^n],\end{aligned} \tag{42}$$

$$\mathrm{Det}\,J(v,u) = \{\beta\theta[1-\gamma-\alpha(1+b/v)]\}/[(1-\alpha)\varepsilon bG^n] > 0. \tag{43}$$

While, in general, the determinant of the Jacobian (41) is larger than zero, the sign of the trace of the Jacobian cannot unambiguously be determined. In addition, for a broad set of feasible parameters, the trace of the Jacobian (41) is larger than zero. The sign of the discriminant of the Jacobian (41) cannot unambiguously be determined but, again, for a broad set of feasible parameters it is larger than zero which implies that the eigenvalues of the Jacobian are real. It is also clear that both eigenvalues are larger than zero for a broad set of feasible parameters. To obtain information on the magnitudes of the eigenvalues use is made here of Lemma A1 from the Appendix in Galor (1992, p. 1383) which says inter alia: $\lambda_1 > 1$ and $0 < \lambda_2 > 1$ if and only if $\text{Tr}J(v,u) \geq 2$ $\vee\ 1 - \text{Tr}J(v,u) + \text{Det}\,J(v,u) < 0$ and $\text{Tr}J(v,u) > 0 \wedge \text{Det}J(v,u) > 0$ $\text{Tr}J(v,u) > 0 \wedge \text{Det}J(v,u) > 0$ and either $\text{Tr}J(v,u) \leq 2 \vee 1 - \text{Tr}J(v,u) + \text{Det}J(v,u) < 0$. For a broad set of feasible parameters $\text{Tr}J(v,u) > 2 > 0$ and $\text{Det}J(v,u) > 0$. Moreover, $1 - \text{Tr}J(v,u) +$ $\text{Det}J(v,u) < 0$.

Proposition 2. Suppose the assumptions of Proposition 1 hold. Then, the algebraic calculation of the eigenvalues λ_1 and λ_2 of the Jacobian at a steady state solution $v_{\min} < v < \infty$ and $0 < u < 1$ reveals that, for a broad set of feasible parameters, $\lambda_1 > 1$ and $0 < \lambda_2 < 1$.

In other words: steady-state solutions represent non-oscillating, monotone saddle points with v_t as a slowly moving variable and u_t as a jump variable. With $v_0 = v_{\_} > 0$ historically given, u_0 jumps onto the saddle-path, along which both variables then converge monotonically towards the steady-state solution.

Being now assured that steady-state solutions of the equilibrium dynamics (37) and (38) exist and are saddle-point stable, we may proceed to investigate the limits of government debt under involuntary unemployment. It is immediately apparent that the natural candidate for a limit to government debt is $b^{\max}$. Inserting $v_{\min}$ from equation (39) into equation (40) the reader can see that all structural parameters and the policy parameter γ determine the magnitude of the limit to public debt.

To derive a numerical value for $b^{\max}$, one needs to resort to a numerical specification of all structural parameters and of the policy parameter γ. To this end, we focus on the empirical development of the following: the growth rate of global real GDP, the long-term global real interest rate, the global personal saving rate and the global investment to GDP ratio, and then derive the respective time averages for the period 1995-2020. Taking the data from the World Economic Outlook reports (IMF 2008, 2014, 2020) the time-average of the global real GDP growth rate is found to amount to about 3% yearly, which is equal to a growth factor of 2 over a period of 25 years (= basic model period), the time-average of the (long-term) real interest rate is 2.3% yearly, which is equivalent to a growth factor of 1.79 for 25 years, the time-average of personal saving rates (= ratio of personal savings to disposable income) results in a factor of 0.24, and the time-average of investment ratios, a factor of 0.18. While the personal saving rate arrived at here seems to be rather high compared to the personal saving rates of most advanced countries, this is mainly due to the impact of the extremely high Chinese personal saving rate of about 40%. On the other hand, the assumed investment ratio of 0.18 is lower than the values found in the IMF database (World Economic Outlook). However, there is no necessary inconsistency between the published data and the values for the saving rates and the investment ratios used here in calibration of the basic model parameters. Remember that the difference between the saving rate of 0.24 and the investment ratio of 0.18 is filled by $G^n b$. We assume here, in line with the empirical time-average of global public debt to GDP ratios between 1995 and 2020, that $b = 0.03$. This is equivalent to an annual public debt to GDP ratio of 75%. For the other policy parameter γ, the ratio of government consumption expenditures to GDP, a value of 0.3 is assumed. This is significantly higher than the value usually found in macroeconomic textbooks, e.g., in Burda and Wyplosz (2017). However, this numerical specification makes sense given that in the model economy all social-policy expenditures by government (except unemployment benefits) are zero, while in reality, social policy expenditures make up a significant part of government consumption expenditures. The time-average for the median of national unemployment rates over the past 25 years was found to be 6% (ILO 2020). Thus, $u = 0.06$. Finally, the level parameter M, was set at 4, in accordance with Auerbach and Kotlikoff (1998).

The calibration exercise consists of feeding the numerical values of G^n, $1+i$, b, γ, u, together with the assumed saving rate and the investment ratio into the following simultaneous equation system:

$$\begin{aligned}&1.8 = \alpha / v,\ \ 0.18(1 - 0.06) = \phi\alpha^{-\theta} 4^{-1/(1-\alpha)} v^{[\theta(1-\alpha)-\alpha]/(1-\alpha)},\\ &0.24 = [\beta/(\beta + \varepsilon)][1 - b(\alpha/v\text{-}2)\text{-}\alpha\text{-}\gamma,\ (1 - 0.06)2v = \\ &\phi\alpha^{-\theta} 4^{-1/(1-\alpha)} v^{[\theta(1-\alpha)-\alpha]/(1-\alpha)},\ (1 - 0.06)\{\beta[1 - \alpha(1 + b/v)\text{-}\gamma)\text{-}\varepsilon b2\}= \\ &(\beta+\varepsilon)\ \phi\alpha^{-\theta} 4^{-1/(1-\alpha)} v^{[\theta(1-\alpha)-\alpha]/(1-\alpha)}.\end{aligned} \tag{44}$$

Solving the equation system numerically, produces the following values for the main structural parameters: $\alpha = 0.162, \beta = 0.397$, $\varepsilon = 0.5, \theta = 0.8, \phi = 0.89$. Both, the capital share of output, α, and the future discount factor, β, are significantly lower than those found in standard econometric studies. However, these lower parameter values accord well with the calibration results for the intertemporal equilibrium models described in Farmer and Schelnast (2021) and in Farmer and Ban (2017). The challenge in such models lies in aligning the rather simple model structure with the reality of low real interest rates and enormous international divergencies in saving rates. As claimed by Farmer and Mihaiescu (2016), and in line with Coeurdacier et al. (2015) and Farmer and Ban (2017), such a challenge can only be met successfully by introducing international divergencies in growth rates, financial constraints, and house price dynamics.

Given the numerical values of structural and policy parameters stated above, the question of the existence of limits to public debt can now be addressed numerically. To obtain a numerical value for $b^{\max}$ and $v_{\min}$, the parameter values specified above are introduced into equations (39) and (40). This procedure provides the following results: $b^{\max} = 0.041,\ v_{\min} = 0.077$. These results for the basic period of 25 calendar years may be transformed into the respective yearly values of $b^{\max} = 100\%$ and $v_{\min} \approx 2$. These results are worth stating in the form of the following proposition:

Proposition 3. Suppose that the structural and policy parameters (expect the public debt to GDP ratio b) are specified as follows: $\alpha = 0.162$, $\beta = 0.397$, $\varepsilon = 0.5, \theta = 0.8$, $\phi = 0.89, M = 4$, $G^n = 2$, $\gamma = 0.3$. This parameter set, which roughly mimics the actual evolution of the world economy between 1995 and 2020 (ahead of the outbreak of the Corona pandemic) implies a limit to public debt with involuntary unemployment of approximately 100%.

Remark 1. It goes without saying that Proposition 3 cannot claim immediate policy relevance. However, this key result remains significant in that it substantiates the claim that there are limits to government debt even under involuntary unemployment. In other words: Large involuntary unemployment does not justify limitless government debt. To the best of the current author's knowledge this result is new and has never appeared in the relevant economic literature. Hitherto, limits to government debt have only been shown in intertemporal equilibrium models with full employment (as first in Rankin and Roffia 2003).

Remark 2. Rankin and Roffia's (2003) limits to public debt were derived in a neoclassical growth model à la Diamond (1965). Full employment in this model type does not represent an assumption but is a consequence of perfectly flexible real wage and interest rates, and of perfectly flexible aggregate investment. It is the latter assumption which critically ensures full employment. Aggregate savings govern perfectly flexible aggregate investment which actuates capital accumulation. Rankin and Roffia (2003) use the intertemporal equilibrium condition that aggregate savings equal private capital accumulation and next-period public debt stock in order to derive a maximum sustainable debt stock. Using the notation employed in the model described in the present paper, this equilibrium relation reads as follows: $G_t^Y v_{t+1} + G_t^Y b_{t+1} = L_t s_t^E$ or in a steady state: $v = [\beta / (\beta + \varepsilon) G^n][1 - \alpha \quad - \gamma - b(\alpha / v - G^n)] - b$. Solving this equation for b, differentiating the resulting equation with respect to v, and setting the result equal to zero, yields the following equation for $b^{\max}$: $b^{\max} = [\varepsilon^2 (G^n)^2]^{-1} \{\beta[\alpha(2\beta + \varepsilon) \; + \varepsilon(1-\gamma)]G^n - 2\{\alpha\beta^2(\beta + \varepsilon)[\alpha\beta + \varepsilon(1-\gamma)]$ $(G^n)^2\}^{1/2}\}$. Using the same parameters for calculating this $b^{\max}$ as above in

Proposition 3, we obtain the following b^{max} value: $b^{max} = 0.055$ or 137% yearly, a value significantly higher than in the case with inflexible investment. If the public debt to GDP ratio approaches this limit, the dynamic system of the market economy with perfectly flexible investment undergoes a 'fold' bifurcation (Azariadis 1993, Appendix A5) which means that the market economy suddenly implodes, and the positive level of activity collapses.

Remark 3. As stated above, the maximally sustainable debt to GDP ratio under inflexible investment is lower than under perfectly flexible investment. In addition to this, no 'fold' bifurcation occurs as b approaches b^{max}. With b larger than b^{max} a steady state solution of the dynamic system (37) and (38) simply does not exist. The reason for the non-occurrence of economic catastrophe is that unlike the case with inflexible investment, where the feasible steady-state solution is unique (Proposition 1), in a situation of perfectly flexible investment two feasible steady state solutions occur which under $b = b^{max}$ collapse to a single steady state which is asymptotically unstable for any initial value v_0 smaller than the unique steady state value.

The Basic Model Extended by Human Capital Accumulation: The Log-Linear Cobb-Douglas OLG Model with Endogenous growth and Involuntary Unemployment

In the basic OLG model described above, growth was exogenous. Fiscal policy was therefore unable to affect the GDP growth rate in steady state. In addition, steady state limits for the public debt to GDP ratio could only be detected for the case of zero unemployment. What could not be addressed, and this has become a frequent subject of discussion in recent empirical literature (for an overview see Hayati et al. 2019), was whether there is a threshold for the public debt to GDP ratio beyond which the GDP growth starts to decline. Economists at the World Bank believe that such a threshold lies at a government debt to GDP ratio of 77%. Every percentage point beyond this debt threshold has been found to lead to a detraction in annual growth of 0.017 percentage points. Reinhart et al. (2015) claimed that, at most, the ratio should be 90%. Below such a threshold the GDP growth rate was found to respond positively to more public debt, and beyond it the growth rate declined. Thus, the question investigated in the present section is whether similar thresholds for the debt to GDP ratio can be detected in the following OLG model, now with endogenous growth and involuntary unemployment, and how strongly a debt ratio beyond the threshold (if existent) detracts from GDP growth in the long run.

To be able to address this question we now extend the basic OLG model by introducing human capital accumulation. In order to point out the growth enhancing effects of human capital accumulation most clearly, it is assumed here that there is no population growth ($g^L = 0 \Leftrightarrow G^L = 1$), and no exogenous growth in labor efficiency, i.e., $G^a = 1$. As a result of the first assumption, the number of households remains constant over time: $L_t = L_{t-1} = L$.

The optimization problem of the two-period lived household, which enters the economy in period t, is essentially the same as in the basic model above, but now with the addition of human capital h_t, accumulated by the household in period $t-1$, and which enters household labor supply and wage income.

Thus, the typical younger household[2] maximizes the following intertemporal utility function subject to the budget constraints for the active period (i) and the retirement period (ii):

$$\text{Max} \rightarrow \varepsilon \ln c_t^1 + \beta \ln c_{t+1}^2$$

subject to:

[2] Since, ultimately, the consumption of the unemployed household does not affect the intertemporal equilibrium solution, only the optimization problem of the employed household, and this without the superscript E, is presented here.

$$(i)\ c_t^1 + I_t^D / [L_t(1-u_t)] + B_{t+1}^D / [L_t(1-u_t)] = w_t h_t (1-\tau_t),$$
$$(ii)\ c_{t+1}^2 = q_{t+1} K_{t+1}^S / [L_t(1-u_t)] + (1+i_{t+1}) B_{t+1}^S / [L_t(1-u_t)]_t,$$
$$K_{t+1}^S = I_t^D,\ B_{t+1}^S = B_{t+1}^D.$$

Obviously, the utility maximizing consumption and savings function read as follows:

$$c_t^1 = [\varepsilon / (\varepsilon + \beta)](1-\tau_t) w_t h_t, \quad (45)$$

$$c_{t+1}^2 = [\beta / (\varepsilon + \beta)](1+i_{t+1})(1-\tau_t) w_t h_t, \quad (46)$$

$$s_t = [\beta / (\varepsilon + \beta)](1-\tau_t) w_t h_t. \quad (47)$$

All firms are again endowed with an identical (linear-homogeneous) Cobb-Douglas production function which now reads as follows: $Y_t = M(h_t N_t)^{1-\alpha}(K_t)^{\alpha}$, $0 < \alpha < 1, M > 0$. Maximization of $Y_t - w_t h_t N_t - q_t K_t$ subject to this Cobb-Douglas production implies the following first-order conditions:

$$(1-\alpha) M [K_t / (h_t N_t)]^{\alpha} = w_t, \quad (48)$$

$$\alpha M [K_t / (h_t N_t)]^{(\alpha-1)} = q_t. \quad (49)$$

However, since the number of employed workers is $N_t = L(1-u_t)$, we can rewrite the profit maximization conditions (48) and (49) as follows:

$$(1-\alpha) M [K_t / (h_t L(1-u_t))]^{\alpha} = w_t, \quad (50)$$

$$\alpha M [K_t / (h_t L(1-u_t))]^{(\alpha-1)} = q_t. \quad (51)$$

Finally, the GDP function can be rewritten as follows:

$$Y_t = M(h_t L(1-u_t))^{1-\alpha}(K_t)^{\alpha}. \tag{52}$$

As in the basic model, the government does not optimize, but is subject to the following constraint period by period:

$$B_{t+1} = (1+i_t)B_t + \Delta_t + \Gamma_t - \tau_t(1-u_t)w_t h_t L, \tag{53}$$

whereby Γ_t now denotes human capital investment (HCI) expenditures, and Δ_t denotes all non-HCI expenditures of the government during period t.

In line with Glomm and Ravikumar (1992) human capital in period t is determined by the human capital of the generation entering the economy in period $t-1$, and by government HCI spending in period $t-1$, Γ_{t-1}:

$$h_t = H_0(h_{t-1})^{\mu}(\Gamma_{t-1}/L)^{1-\mu}, H_0 = \bar{H} > 0,\ 0 < \mu < 1, \tag{54}$$

where H_0 represents a level parameter, μ denotes the production elasticity of human capital, and $1-\mu$ features the production elasticity of public HCI spending. Multiplying equation (54) on both sides by L, we thus obtain the aggregate version of (54):

$$Lh_t \equiv H_t = H_0(Lh_{t-1})^{1-\mu}(\Gamma_{t-1})^{\mu} \equiv H_0(H_{t-1})^{1-\mu}(\Gamma_{t-1})^{\mu}. \tag{55}$$

The economy grows, even in the absence of population growth and exogenous progress in labor efficiency. Using the GDP growth factor $G_t^Y \equiv Y_{t+1}/Y_t$ as well as equations (52) and (55), the former can be written as follows:

$$G_{t+1}^Y = \frac{H_{t+1}}{H_t}\frac{(1-u_{t+1})^{1-\alpha}}{(1-u_t)^{1-\alpha}}\frac{(k_{t+1})^{\alpha}}{(k_t)^{\alpha}}, k_t \equiv \frac{K_t}{H_t}. \tag{56}$$

It is not difficult to see that Magnani's (2015) macro-founded investment function reads in our new model context as follows:

$$I_t^D = \phi H_t (1+i_t)^{-\theta}, \; \phi > 0, \theta \geq 0 . \tag{57}$$

Since the market clearing conditions remain as in the basic model, they are not explicitly stated again.

To be able to calibrate the present model with respect to empirical data, the main endogenous variables are again transformed into GDP ratios.

To start with, the government budget constraint (53) is rewritten as follows:

$$\begin{aligned}\frac{B_{t+1}}{Y_{t+1}}\frac{Y_{t+1}}{Y_t} \equiv b_{t+1}G_{t+1}^Y &= (1+i_t)\frac{B_t}{Y_t} + \frac{\Gamma_t}{Y_t} + \frac{\Delta_t}{Y_t} - \frac{\tau_t(1-u_t)w_t h_t L}{Y_t} \\ &\equiv (1+i_t)b_t + \gamma_t + \delta_t - \frac{\tau_t(1-u_t)w_t h_t L}{Y_t},\end{aligned} \tag{58}$$

with $\delta_t \equiv \Delta_t / Y_t$ and b_t and γ_t as in the basic model.

Since the profit maximizing condition (50) can be rewritten as

$$w_t h_t L(1-u_t) = (1-\alpha)(K_t)^\alpha (h_t L(1-u_t))^{1-\alpha} = (1-\alpha)Y_t, \tag{59}$$

the government budget constraint can be written as follows:

$$b_{t+1}G_{t+1}^Y = (1+i_t)b_t + \delta_t + \gamma_t - \tau_t(1-\alpha). \tag{60}$$

As in the basic model, the wage-tax rate is assumed to be endogenous while both the non-HCI expenditure and the HCI-expenditure ratios remain time-stationary and are exogenously given, i.e.: $\delta_{t+1} = \delta_t = \delta$, $\gamma_{t+1} = \gamma_t = \gamma$. Moreover, since – as in the basic model – it is the limit to the government debt to the GDP ratio, which is being scrutinized, the government debt to

GDP ratios are also assumed to be time-stationary: $b_{t+1} = b_t = b$. Given these assumptions, the budget constraint of the government then reads as follows:

$$\tau_t = \{b[(1+i_t) - G^Y_{t+1}] + \gamma + \delta\} / (1-\alpha) \,. \tag{61}$$

The capital output ratio v_t is related to the real-capital to human-capital ratio as follows:

$$v_t = \frac{K_t}{M(H_t)^{1-\alpha}(1-u_t)^{1-\alpha}(K_t)^{\alpha}} = \frac{(K_t)^{1-\alpha}}{M(H_t)^{1-\alpha}(1-u_t)^{1-\alpha}} = \frac{(k_t)^{1-\alpha}}{M(1-u_t)^{1-\alpha}} \,, \tag{62}$$

which implies as above: $q_t = \alpha / v_t$.

In terms of the transformed variables, the growth factor of human capital reads as follows:

$$\begin{aligned} &\frac{H_{t+1}}{H_t} = H_0 (H_t)^{\mu-1} (\gamma)^{1-\mu} (Y_t)^{1-\mu} = \\ &H_0 (H_t)^{\mu-1} (\gamma)^{1-\mu} M^{(1-\mu)} (K_t)^{\alpha(1-\mu)} (H_t)^{(1-\alpha)(1-\mu)} (1-u_t)^{(1-\alpha)(1-\mu)} \\ &= H_0 M^{(1-\mu)/(1-\alpha)} (\gamma)^{1-\mu} (v_t)^{\alpha(1-\mu)/(1-\alpha)} (1-u_t)^{(1-\mu)}. \end{aligned} \tag{63}$$

The GDP growth factor in terms of the capital output ratio can be rewritten as follows:

$$\begin{aligned} G^Y_t &= \frac{H_{t+1}}{H_t} \left(\frac{v_{t+1}}{v_t} \right)^{\alpha/(1-\alpha)} \frac{(1-u_{t+1})}{(1-u_t)} \\ &= H_0 M^{(1-\mu)/(1-\alpha)} (\gamma)^{1-\mu} (v_{t+1})^{\alpha/(1-\alpha)} (v_t)^{-\alpha\mu/(1-\alpha)} (1-u_{t+1})(1-u_t)^{-\mu}. \end{aligned} \tag{64}$$

By using again $K^S_{t+1} = I^D_t$, one obtains the following equation for the dynamics of the capital output ratio:

$$v_{t+1}G_t^Y = \phi\frac{H_t}{K_t}\frac{K_t}{Y_t}q_t^{-\theta} = \phi\frac{1}{k_t}v_t q_t^{-\theta} = \alpha^{-\theta}\phi M^{\frac{-1}{(1-\alpha)}}(v_t)^{\frac{\theta(1-\alpha)-\alpha}{(1-\alpha)}}(1-u_t)^{-1}. \quad (65)$$

The temporary equilibrium unemployment rate can be derived analogously to the derivation employed in the basic model by using the output market equilibrium equation and inserting the optimal consumption of youth- and old-age consumers, the investment function and government consumption expenditures as a proportion of GDP. This then yields:

$$Y_t = \varepsilon/(\beta+\varepsilon)(1-\alpha)(1-\tau_t)Y_t + (\alpha/v_t)(K_t+B_t) + (\delta+\gamma)Y_t + \phi H_t. \quad (66)$$

On dividing equation (66) on both sides by Y_t, and after introducing the capital-output and the debt to GDP ratio, one obtains the following intertemporal equilibrium unemployment rate:

$$1-u_t = \frac{\alpha^{-\theta}\phi M^{\frac{-1}{(1-\alpha)}}(v_t)^{\frac{\theta(1-\alpha)-\alpha}{(1-\alpha)}}}{[1-\frac{\varepsilon}{(\beta+\varepsilon)}(1-\alpha)(1-\tau_t)-\alpha(1+b/v_t)-\gamma-\delta]}. \quad (67)$$

The final steps needed to arrive at the equation of motion for the capital-output ratio entail, first, inserting the GDP growth factor equation (64) into equation (65). This procedure yields:

$$v_{t+1}^{1/(1-\alpha)}(1-u_{t+1}) = [\phi/(\alpha^{\theta}H_0)]\gamma^{\mu-1}M^{(\mu-2)/(1-\alpha)}v_t^{[\theta(1-\alpha)-\alpha(1-\mu)]/(1-\alpha)}(1-u_t)^{\mu-1}. \quad (68)$$

Then, the growth factor equation (64) is inserted into equation (61) which yields, after rearranging:

$$\begin{aligned} 1-\tau_t = {} & (1-\alpha)^{-1}\{1-\alpha(1+b/v_t)-\gamma-\delta \\ & + bH_0 M^{(1-\mu)/(1-\alpha)}\gamma^{1-\mu}(v_{t+1})^{\alpha/(1-\alpha)}(v_t)^{-\alpha\mu/(1-\alpha)}(1-u_{t+1})(1-u_t)^{-\mu}\}. \end{aligned} \quad (69)$$

Next, after inserting $1-\tau_t$ from equation (69) into equation (67) and rearranging, we arrive at the following intermediate result:

$$v_{t+1}{}^{\alpha/(1-\alpha)}(1-u_{t+1}) = (\varepsilon b H_0)^{-1}\gamma^{\mu-1}M^{(1-\mu)/(\alpha-1)}(1-u_t)^{\mu-1}v_t{}^{(\alpha\mu)/(1-\alpha)} \times$$
$$\times\{\beta(1-u_t)[1-\alpha(1+b/v_t)-\gamma-\delta]-(\beta+\varepsilon)\phi M^{-1/(1-\alpha)}v_t{}^{[\theta(1-\alpha)-\alpha]/(1-\alpha)}\}. \quad (70)$$

Solving equation (68) for $1-u_{t+1}$ and inserting the result into equation (70) then yields, after re-arranging the first equation of motion:

$$v_{t+1} = \frac{\varepsilon b}{\beta\phi^{-1}\alpha^{\theta}M^{1/(1-\alpha)}[1-\alpha(1+b/v_t)-\gamma-\delta](1-u_t)v_t{}^{[\alpha-\theta(1-\alpha)]/(1-\alpha)}-\beta-\varepsilon}.$$

(71)

Reinserting the dynamic equation (71) into equation (68) and solving for $1-u_{t+1}$ generate the second equation of motion:

$$u_{t+1} = 1-\phi(\alpha^{\theta}H_0)^{-1}\gamma^{\mu-1}(\varepsilon b)^{-1/(1-\alpha)}M^{(2-\mu)/(\alpha-1)}v_t{}^{[\theta(1-\alpha)-\alpha(1-\mu)]/(1-\alpha)}(1-u_t)^{\mu-1}$$
$$\times\{\alpha^{\theta}\beta\phi^{-1}M^{1/(1-\alpha)}(1-u_t)[1-\alpha(1+b/v_t)-\gamma-\delta]v_t{}^{[\alpha-\theta(1-\alpha)]/(1-\alpha)}-(\beta+\varepsilon)\}^{1/(1-\alpha)}.$$

(72)

As above, the steady states of the equilibrium dynamics depicted by the difference equations (71) and (72) are defined as $\lim_{t->\infty} v_t = v$ and $\lim_{t->\infty} u_t = u$. As in the basic model, explicit steady state solutions are not possible. Thus, once again, we need to resort to an intermediate value theorem to prove the existence of at least one feasible steady state solution $v_{\min} < v < \infty$ and $0<u<1$.

To this end, for given structural and policy parameters (except b), the maximal sustainable debt to GDP parameter is defined as $b^{\max}$, and the minimal capital output ratio as $v_{\min}$. This ensures full employment. On inserting G^Y from the steady-state version of equation (64) into the steady-state version of equation (65) with $u=0$, $v_{\min}$ can then be explicitly determined as follows:

$$v_{\min} = [\alpha^{-\theta}\gamma^{\mu-1}\phi(H_0)^{-1} M^{(\mu-2)/(1-\alpha)}]^{(1-\alpha)/[1+\alpha(1-\mu)-\theta(1-\alpha)]} . \tag{73}$$

Using the steady-state version of equation (67) with $u=0$, $b=b^{\max}$ can be determined as follows:

$$\begin{aligned} b^{\max} &= [\beta(1-\alpha-\gamma-\delta)-\alpha^{-\theta}(\beta+\varepsilon)\phi M^{-1/(1-\alpha)} v_{\min}{}^{[\theta(1-\alpha)-\alpha]/(1-\alpha)}] \\ &\quad /[\alpha\beta(v_{\min})^{-1}+\varepsilon H_0 M^{(1-\mu)/(1-\alpha)}\gamma^{1-\mu}(v_{\min})^{\alpha(1-\mu)/(1-\alpha)}], \end{aligned} \tag{74}$$

Whereby, to ensure a strictly larger than zero $b^{\max}$, it is assumed that: $\beta(1-\alpha-\gamma-\delta) > \alpha^{-\theta}(\beta+\varepsilon)\phi M^{-1/(1-\alpha)} \times \times v_{\min}{}^{[\theta(1-\alpha)-\alpha]/(1-\alpha)}$.

For the proof of the existence of at least one $0<u<1$ and $v_{\min}<v<\infty$ the steady-state versions of equations (71) and (72) are used. This results in:

$$v = \frac{\varepsilon b}{\alpha^{\theta}\beta\phi^{-1}M^{1/(1-\alpha)}[1-\alpha(1+b/v)-\gamma-\delta](1-u)v^{[\alpha-\theta(1-\alpha)]/(1-\alpha)}-\beta-\varepsilon}. \tag{75}$$

$$\begin{aligned} 1-u &= \phi(\alpha^{\theta}H_0)^{-1}\gamma^{\mu-1}(\varepsilon b)^{-1/(1-\alpha)}M^{(2-\mu)/(\alpha-1)}v^{[\theta(1-\alpha)-\alpha(1-\mu)]/(1-\alpha)}(1-u)^{\mu-1} \\ &\quad \times\{\alpha^{\theta}\beta\phi^{-1}M^{1/(1-\alpha)}(1-u)[1-\alpha(1+b/v)-\gamma-\delta]v^{[\alpha-\theta(1-\alpha)]/(1-\alpha)} \\ &\qquad -(\beta+\varepsilon)\}^{1/(1-\alpha)}. \end{aligned} \tag{76}$$

By substituting $\alpha^{\theta}\beta\phi^{-1}M^{1/(1-\alpha)}(1-u)[1-\alpha(1+b/v_t)-\gamma-\delta]v^{\alpha/(1-\alpha)}-\beta$ $-\varepsilon$ in (76) for $\varepsilon b/v$, equation (76) can be reduced to the following simpler equation:

$$1-u = \alpha^{-\theta}\gamma^{\mu-1}\phi H_0{}^{-1}M^{(\mu-2)/(1-\alpha)}(1-u)^{\mu-1}v^{[\theta(1-\alpha)-\alpha(1-\mu)-1]/(1-\alpha)} \tag{77}$$

Using the short cut $1-u \equiv w$, the two equations (75) and (77) can be explicitly solved for w as follows:

$$w_1 = \frac{\alpha^{-\theta}\phi M^{-1/(1-\alpha)} v^{[\theta(1-\alpha)-\alpha]/(1-\alpha)}[\beta+\varepsilon(1+b/v)]}{\beta[1-\alpha(1+b/v)-\gamma-\delta]},, \tag{78}$$

$$w_2 = [\alpha^{-\theta}\gamma^{\mu-1}\phi H_0^{-1} M^{(\mu-2)/(1-\alpha)} v^{[\theta(1-\alpha)-\alpha(\mu-1)-1]/(1-\alpha)}]^{1/(2-\mu)}. \tag{79}$$

Hereby, w_1 represents the solution of equation (75) for w, while w_2 gives the solution of equation (77) for w. A steady state solution exists if $w_1(v) = w_2(v)$ for at least one $v_{min} < v < \infty$.

Proposition 4. Suppose there exist $\eta > 0$ and $v^{max} > 0$ such that $w_1(v^{max}) = w_2(v^{max}) + \eta$. Then, the solution of $w_1(v) = w_2(v)$ for at least one $v_{min} < v < v^{max}$ exists and represents a steady state of the equilibrium dynamics (71) and (72) with $0<u<1$.

Proof. For $b = b^{max}$ it is known from above that $v = v_{min}$ and $u = 0$. Thus, let $b < b^{max}$. Using this assumption, we may then show that $0<u<1$ and $v_{min} < v < v^{max}$. From both $b < b^{max}$, $dw_1/db = \{[\varepsilon(1-\gamma-\delta)+\alpha\beta]\times$ $\times\alpha^{-\theta}\phi M^{-1/(1-\alpha)} v^{[1-2\alpha+\theta(1-\alpha)]/(1-\alpha)} / \{\beta[\alpha b-(1-\alpha-\gamma-\delta)]v\}^2 > 0$ and from equations (78) and (79), it follows that $0<u<1$. As in the proof of Proposition 1, an intermediate value theorem is applied to demonstrate that $w_1(v) = w_2(v)$ for $v_{min} < v < v^{max}$. To this end, notice first that for $b = b^{max}$, $w_1(v_{min}) =$ $w_2(v_{min})$. Under $b < b^{max}$ and $dw_1/db > 0$ it is clear that $w_1(v_{min};b) < w_1(v_{min};b^{max})$. Since $w_2(v)$ does not depend on b, it follows that $w_2(v_{min};b) = w_2(v_{min};b^{max})$ for all feasible b. Hence, $< w_2(v_{min};b), \forall b < b^{max}$ $w_1(v_{min};b)$. At the upper boundary of feasible values for v, at $v = v^{max}$, the assumption employed in Proposition 4 ensures that $w_1(v^{max};b) > w_2(v^{max};b)$. Since the two functions $w_1(v;b)$ and $w_2(v;b)$ are continuous on $v_{min} < v < v^{max}$, the intermediate value theorem implies at least one $v_{\min} < v < v_{\max}$ such that $w_1(v) = w_2(v)$. Moreover, for a broad set of feasible parameters the solution is unique.

As above, the next step is to investigate the local dynamic stability of the unique steady-state solution. To this end, the intertemporal equilibrium equations (64), (65), (67) and (69) are totally differentiated with respect to $v_{t+1}, u_{t+1}, G_t^Y, \tau_t, v_t, u_t$. Then, the Jacobian matrix $J(v,u)$ of all partial differentials with respect to v_t and u_t is formed as follows:

$$J(v,u) \equiv \begin{bmatrix} \frac{\partial v_{t+1}}{\partial v_t}(v,u) & \frac{\partial v_{t+1}}{\partial w_t}(v,u) \\ \frac{\partial w_{t+1}}{\partial v_t}(v,u) & \frac{\partial w_{t+1}}{\partial w_t}(v,u) \end{bmatrix}, \tag{80}$$

with

$$\frac{\partial v_{t+1}}{\partial v_t} \equiv j_{11} = -\frac{b\{[\alpha - \theta(1-\alpha]\varepsilon G^Y + (1-\alpha)\beta q\}(1-u) + [\alpha - \theta(1-\alpha](\beta+\varepsilon)G^Y v}{(1-\alpha)\varepsilon b G^Y (1-u)},$$

$$\frac{\partial v_{t+1}}{\partial u_t} \equiv j_{12} = \frac{v[\varepsilon b + (\beta+\varepsilon)v]}{\varepsilon b(1-u)} > 0,$$

$$\frac{\partial u_{t+1}}{\partial v_t} \equiv j_{21} =$$

$$-\frac{[\alpha - \theta(1-\alpha)](\beta+\varepsilon)G^Y v + bq(1-u)\{\beta(1-\alpha) + \varepsilon G^Y v[\alpha + \mu(1-\alpha) - \theta(1-\alpha)]\}}{(1-\alpha)^2 \varepsilon b G^Y v},$$

$$\frac{\partial u_{t+1}}{\partial u_t} \equiv j_{22} = \frac{\varepsilon b[\alpha + \mu(1-\alpha)] + (\beta+\varepsilon)v}{\varepsilon b(1-\alpha)} > 0.$$

The signs of j_{12} and j_{22} are unambiguously larger than zero. The signs of j_{11} and j_{21} depend on whether $\theta \le \alpha/(1-a)$ or $\theta > \alpha/(1-a)$. In the former case both j_{11} and j_{21} are less than zero. In the latter case, the signs of these entries of the Jacobian (80) are in general ambiguous, while for a broad set of feasible parameters both entries are larger than zero. To evaluate the dynamic stability of the equilibrium dynamics in the neighborhood of the steady-state solution, again, the eigenvalues of the Jacobian matrix (80) are needed. As in the basic model, the trace $\mathrm{Tr}J(v,u)$, the determinant $\mathrm{Det}J(v,u)$ and $1-$ $\mathrm{Tr}J(v,u)+\mathrm{Det}J(v,u)$ need to be calculated.

$$\mathrm{Tr}J(v,u) = v + \mu - \frac{\alpha\beta}{\varepsilon G^Y v} - \frac{(\beta+\varepsilon)v[u-(1+\theta)(1-\alpha)]}{(1-\alpha)\varepsilon b(1-u)}, \tag{81}$$

$$\mathrm{Det}J(v,u) = \theta\mu + \frac{\alpha\beta(1-\mu)}{\varepsilon G^Y v} + \frac{(\beta+\varepsilon)[(1-\alpha)\theta(\mu-u)+\alpha(1-\mu)u]v}{(1-\alpha)\varepsilon b(1-u)} > 0, \tag{82}$$

$$\begin{aligned} 1-\mathrm{Tr}J(v,u)+\mathrm{Det}J(v,u) &= (1-\theta)(1-\mu) + \frac{\alpha\beta(2-\mu)}{\varepsilon G^Y v} \\ &+ \frac{(\beta+\varepsilon)v\{\theta(\mu-u)+u[1+\alpha(1-\mu)]+\alpha[1+\theta u+\theta(1-\mu)]-(1+\theta)\}}{(1-\alpha)\varepsilon b(1-u)}. \end{aligned} \tag{83}$$

The sign of the trace turns out to be, in general, indeterminate, while the determinant of the Jacobian (80) is larger than zero. Moreover, the sign of$1-\mathrm{Tr}J(v,u)+\mathrm{Det}J(v,u)$ is in general ambiguous. However, for a broad set of feasible parameters, all of which are in accordance with the assumptions used thus far, the trace is larger than zero (larger than 2) and $1-TrJ(v,u)\ \ +DetJ(v,u)<0$.

Proposition 5. Suppose the assumptions of Proposition 4 hold. Then, the calculation of the eigenvalues λ_1 and λ_2 of Jacobian (80) at the steady-state solution $0<u<1$ and $v_{\min}<v<v^{\max}$ shows that for a broad set of feasible parameter combinations with $b<b^{\max}$, $\lambda_1>1$ and $0<\lambda_2<1$.

In other words: as in the basic model with exogenous growth, steady state solutions in the present endogenous growth model with involuntary unemployment represent non-oscillating, monotone saddle points with v_t as a slowly moving variable and u_t as a jump variable. With $v_0 = v_- > 0$ historically given, u_0 jumps onto the saddle-path along which both variables converge monotonically towards the steady-state solution.

Being thus assured that steady-state solutions of the equilibrium dynamics (71) and (72) both exist, and are saddle-point stable, one may proceed to investigate limits for government debt under endogenous growth and involuntary unemployment. It is immediate that the natural candidate for a limit to government debt is – as in the basic model – b^{max}. Inserting v_{min} from equation (73) into equation (74) the reader can again see that all structural parameters, together with the policy parameters γ and δ, determine the magnitude of the limit to the debt to GDP ratio. As in the basic model, the author resorts to a numerical specification of all structural and policy parameters in line with 25 years of relevant time-average data. Such data cover the empirical development of the growth rate of global real GDP, the long-term real interest rate, the global average of national saving rates and the global average of investment to GDP ratios. Differing slightly to the time-averages used in the basic model, the time-average of the global real GDP growth rate is now set equal to a growth factor of 2.3 for 25 years (= basic model period), the time-average of the (long-term) real interest rate is assumed to be 1.64 for the basic model period, the time-average of national saving rates (= ratio of GDP minus aggregate private and government consumption expenditures to GDP) is 0.22, and that of investment ratios is also 0.22 (IMF 2008, 2014, 2020). As in the basic model, it is assumed, in line with the empirical time average for global public debt to GDP ratios between 1995 and 2020, that $b = 0.03$ which is equivalent to an annual public debt ratio of 75%. For the human capital investment ratio γ, a value of 0.05 is assumed, and the non-HCI public expenditure ratio is set at $\delta = 0.2$. The time-average of the median of national unemployment rates over the past 25 years was found to be 6% (ILO 2020). Thus, $u = 0.06$. Finally, the level parameter M, is set at 5, in accordance with Auerbach and Kotlikoff (1998), and $\mu = 0.5$, as in Glomm and Ravikumar (1997).

To perform the calibration exercise, first the budget constraint (61) is needed. This is reproduced here for the convenience of the reader:

$$\tau = [b(q - G^Y) + \gamma + \delta] / (1 - \alpha). \tag{84}$$

Equilibrium equation (66) divided by Y_t on both sides is substituted for the following equilibrium equation in steady state:

$$1 = \frac{\varepsilon}{\beta + \varepsilon}(1-\alpha)(1-\tau) + \alpha(1 + b/v) + \gamma + \delta + \alpha^{-\theta}\phi M^{-1/(1-\alpha)} v^{[\theta(1-\alpha)-\alpha]/(1-\alpha)}(1-u)^{-1}. \tag{85}$$

To be able to calibrate the remaining parameters with respect to the empirical data for the past 25 years, two additional equations are needed. The first one represents the steady state version of the growth factor equation which reads as follows:

$$G^Y = H_0 M^{(1-\mu)/(1-\alpha)} (\gamma)^{1-\mu} (v)^{[\alpha(1-\mu)]/(1-\alpha)} (1-u)^{1-\mu}. \tag{86}$$

Inserting G^Y from equation (86) into the steady state version of dynamic equation (38) yields the required second equation as follows:

$$H_0 M^{(1-\mu)/(1-\alpha)} (\gamma)^{1-\mu} (v)^{[\alpha(1-\mu)]/(1-\alpha)} (1-u)^{1-\mu} = \alpha^{-\theta}\phi M^{\frac{-1}{(1-\alpha)}} (v)^{\frac{\theta(1-\alpha)-1}{(1-\alpha)}} (1-u_t)^{-1}. \tag{87}$$

Equations (84)-(87) together with $\alpha / v = 1.64$, $G^Y = 2.3$, $0.22 = \phi\alpha^{-\theta} \times \times M^{-1/(1-\alpha)} v^{[\theta(1-\alpha)-\alpha]/(1-\alpha)}(1-u)^{-1}$, and $0.22 = \beta / (\beta + \varepsilon)[1 - \alpha(1 + b/v) - \gamma - \delta] \quad -\beta / (\beta + \varepsilon) b G^Y$, thus form six equations which may be used to calibrate the parameters α, β, ϕ, H_0 and the endogenous variables v and G^Y to the data. The result of this calculation exercise, together with $\varepsilon = 0.5$, reads as follows: $\alpha = 0.15687, \beta = 0.44608,$ $\phi = 0.9014, H_0 = 5.08152, v = 0.09565,\ G^Y = 2.3.$ In attempting to determine the value of the remaining parameter, the interest-factor elasticity of aggregate investment, three different scenarios are considered: (1) The vulgar-Keynesian Scenario under $\theta = 0$, (2) the moderately interest-elastic

Keynesian scenario $\theta < \alpha/(1-\alpha)$, and (3) the highly interest-elastic, "neo-classical" scenario $\theta = 1$. The latter is based on the careful empirical study of Guiso et al. (2002), who, using Italian firm-level data, found that the elasticity of capital demand with respect to the user cost of capital equals -1.

Before the values for maximum sustainable debt ratios are presented, one needs to note that different values of the interest factor-elasticity of investment demand do not change the parameters calibrated, except the animal spirits parameter ϕ. It turns out from the calibration exercises that, as a rule, a higher ϕ is associated with a higher θ: For the vulgar-Keynesian scenario, ϕ is as reported above; in the moderately interest-elastic scenario, where $\theta = 0.186$, we find that $\phi = 0.98828$, and finally in the neo-classical scenario, $\phi = 1.47831$. Proposition 6 reports the values of maximum sustainable debt ratios and how the GDP growth factor responds to a higher sustainable government debt ratio below the maximum level.

Proposition 6. Suppose that the values of all structural and policy parameters except θ and ϕ are as reported above. Then, in the vulgar-Keynesian scenario $b^{\max} = 0.03379(\approx 84.33\% \text{ yearly})$, for the moderately interest-elastic scenario $b^{\max} = 0.03494(\approx 87.33\% \text{ yearly})$, and in the neo-classical scenario $b^{\max} = 0.0531(\approx 132.5\% \text{ yearly})$. Moreover, in all scenarios, both the capital-output ratio and the unemployment rate decrease with rising government debt ratios up to the maximum sustainable debt ratio. Finally, the GDP growth factor increases with rising public debt ratios up to the maxima, except in the neo-classical scenario, where the GDP growth factor does not respond at all to rising debt ratios.

Proposition 6 implies that in the OLG model of the global economy presented thus far, there does not exist a threshold for the public debt ratio beyond which the GDP growth factor decreases with rising debt ratios. Thus, it seems to be apt to look for a modification of the aggregate investment function in order to be able to investigate the research question elaborated in the introduction to this section. Fortunately, Magnani (2015, p. 17) also provides the requested modification of the aggregate investment function by noticing that in his base model (= the Vulgar-Keynesian model presented above) "an increase in the saving rate has a negative effect on employment and on real GDP, both in short and long run" a result "which is not consistent with the empirical evidence." To accord with the data, Magnani (2015, pp. 18-20) proposes a re-specification of the aggregate investment function which takes the crowding-out effects of private and public consumption, as well as those of private and public savings, on aggregate investment into account. In the present analysis, the focus is placed on the crowding-out effects of saving, and in compliance with the suggestion made by Magnani (2015, pp. 18-20), the aggregate investment ratio is rewritten as follows:

$$\begin{aligned} I_t^D / Y_t &= \alpha^{-\theta} \phi M^{-1/(1-\alpha)} (v_t)^{[\theta(1-\alpha)-\alpha]/(1-\alpha)} (1-u_t)^{-1} \\ &\quad + \nu(S_t / Y_t - S / Y + S_t^P / Y - S^P / Y), \text{ with} \\ S_t / Y_t &= [\beta / (\beta+\varepsilon)(1-\alpha)(1-\tau_t) + \beta / (\beta+\varepsilon)\xi][(1-u)/(1-u_t)]^{1-\alpha}, \\ S / Y &= \beta / (\beta+\varepsilon)(1-\alpha)(1-\tau) + \beta / (\beta+\varepsilon)\xi, \\ S_t^P / Y_t &= b^{new}(1-G_t^Y),\ S / Y = b(1-G^Y). \end{aligned} \tag{88}$$

Here, the endogenous variables without a time subscript denote the steady state values associated with the initial public debt ratio b, while the endogenous variables with a time subscript feature the values associated with $b < b^{new} < b^{\max}$. Clearly, S_t represents aggregate private savings, while S_t^P is public savings and equals the difference between government's revenues and expenditures. Finally, $0 \leq \nu \leq 1$ features the crowding-out parameter with $\nu = 0$ signifying no crowding out at all, and $\nu = 1$ signifying complete crowding out, as in Diamond's (1965) neo-classical growth model. Magnani's (2015, pp. 29-30) econometric analysis using 1955-2012 data from six OECD countries results in a value of $0.6 \leq \nu \leq 0.8$.

Using the modified aggregate investment function (88) in equations (85) and (87), and sticking to $\nu = 0.8$ it first turns out that for $0 \leq \theta < \alpha / (1-\alpha)$ and the associated ϕ values, the maximum sustainable debt values increase, e.g., from $b^{\max}=84.33\%$ to $b^{\max}=110.5\%$ in the case of the vulgar Keynesian scenario, and from $b^{\max}=87.33\%$ to $b^{\max}=126.38\%$ for $\theta=0.186$, although, even with a rather large crowding-out parameter, a higher public debt ratio below the maximum level always raises the GDP growth factor. In other words: Under conditions of completely inelastic or moderately interest-elastic aggregate investment even rather strong crowding out of private and public savings with respect to investment does not seriously dampen the growth generating effect of a larger public debt ratio below the now higher debt limits. That the debt limits are higher makes sense, since with strong crowding out the unemployment-reducing effect of larger public debt is lower than with less or no crowding out.

This leads us to the scenarios with $\alpha/(1-\alpha)<\theta\leq 1$, in particular, to the neo-classical scenario with $\theta=1$ and $\phi=1.47831$. First, it is interesting to note that again the $b^{\max}$ values are in general larger than in the case of no investment crowding out. Secondly, and more interesting, for $0.3\leq\theta\leq 1$ and the associated ϕ values a threshold for the debt ratio appears beyond which more public debt reduces GDP growth. Taking, e. g. $\theta=0.3$ and, $\phi=1.04562$ we obtain a $b_{threshold}=0.0321(\approx 80.25\%)$, beyond which $dG^{Y}/db<0$. Moreover, it is interesting to ascertain the extent to which strong GDP growth is diminished when the debt ratio is raised by one percentage point. Experimenting with differing values of $0.3<\theta\leq 1$ reveals that the growth detracting effect of larger public debt is strongest when $\theta=1$. It is worth summarizing the results thus far in the following proposition.

Proposition 7. Suppose that the structural and policy parameters, except θ and ϕ, exhibit the values as in Proposition 6. Assume $\nu=0.8$. Then, for all $\alpha/(1-\alpha)<\theta\leq 1$, and the associated ϕ values, thresholds for the global public debt ratio exist beyond which larger debt reduces GDP growth. Moreover, the growth detracting effect is larger, the higher the value for θ. For $\theta=1,\phi=1.47831$, the debt ratio threshold

$b_{threshold} = 0.03 (\approx 75\%)$ and the growth detracting effect equals 0.013 percentage points where the debt ratio is raised from 75% to 76%.

It is comforting to see that these numerical values for larger debt, both for the debt threshold and the growth detracting effect, come close to the values estimated in the World Bank studies mentioned above.

CONCLUSION

Given the current enormous public deficits, and the unprecedently high unemployment rates, particularly in the advanced countries, it is surprising that macroeconomic theory has paid so little attention to the limits of public debt in the context of involuntary unemployment. It seems likely that even mainstream macroeconomists presume that in order to combat high unemployment, the limits to public debt may safely be disregarded, i.e., they are willing to go along with the commonly held view that public deficits ought to be expanded "whatever it takes."

The findings of the present paper, however, indicate that such a perspective should not go unchallenged. In fact, a minority of macroeconomists exist who hold that aggregate investment is not determined by aggregate savings but by an independent function based on Keynes' (1936) notion of investor "animal spirits." This additional function makes the system of general equilibrium equations, for a perfectly flexible and perfectly competitive market system, over-determinate, and results in an inconsistency which can only be resolved if one of the market-clearing conditions is dropped. The obvious candidate here is the labor market-clearing condition. Once this is done, the system of general equilibrium equations becomes determinate again. Moreover, the unemployment rate becomes endogenous through the identity that the unemployment rate equals 1 minus the number of employed people relative to the number of employment-seeking people. It is thus aggregate demand (including investment demand) which governs aggregate production, and not aggregate supply.

Following Magnani's (2015) lead, such atemporal macroeconomic reasoning has been integrated in the present chapter into two versions of Diamond's (1965) OLG model with internal public debt: into a basic model with exogenous growth, and into an extended model with endogenous growth based on human capital accumulation. Both model variants can be regarded as highly stylized, intertemporal macro-models of the world economy. From this perspective, they can be used to explore the limits of public debt for the global economy. Employment in both models is driven by aggregate demand, and since in both model variants public debt is non-neutral it is not surprising that more public debt increases employment and reduces unemployment. More public debt raises aggregate demand because the older household becomes wealthier, and therefore increases consumption demand. This also applies to the younger household since its tax burden declines due to the fact that under dynamic inefficiency (= the interest factor is smaller than the GDP growth factor) a higher debt to GDP ratio reduces the tax rate. On the other hand, aggregate investment demand remains initially unchanged since the initial capital-output ratio is historically given, and under the proviso that the unemployment rate remains unchanged. Under the pre-shock unemployment rate the ratio between the aggregate investment demand and aggregate private and public consumption is incompatible with product-market clearing (see equation (67)). The disequilibrium vanishes via a declining unemployment rate since less unemployment decreases the investment to GDP ratio, a decline necessary to create room for the larger, private consumption ratio. A limit to the public debt to GDP ratio arises when the unemployment rate approaches zero.

While it is one thing to make these relationships intuitively plausible, it is quite another to make the relationships precise, in particular, to attribute numerical values to the debt limits. To this end, in both the basic and the extended model, the sufficient conditions for the existence and the dynamic stability of steady states for the capital output ratio und the unemployment rate are stated first, as presented in Propositions 1 and 2, and in 4 and 5, respectively. Then, the structural parameters of the basic model are calibrated such that the base model reproduces the time-average values for the growth rate of global GDP, the global real interest rate, the global savings and investment ratios, all for the period 1995 to pre-Corona 2020, together with the time-averages of policy parameters for the same period. This procedure provides maximum sustainable debt to GDP ratios of about 100% yearly. This debt limit is significantly lower than the corresponding limit in a model where aggregate savings determine perfectly flexible aggregate investment. Furthermore, in the basic model with involuntary unemployment, as opposed to the model with full employment, the economy does not need to implode when the debt ratio approaches its limit.

In the basic model, public debt does not impact the GDP growth rate. In more recent discussions about limits to public debt, it is exactly the growth effects of public debt which feature prominently. Thus, as described above, in the model extension using human capital accumulation, variations of the debt to GDP ratio principally impact the GDP growth. As Proposition 6 makes clear, the magnitude of the interest factor elasticity of aggregate investment demand and the associated animal spirits parameter are decisive in determining the maximum sustainable debt ratios. Under interest factor inelastic or moderately interest factor elastic investment demand, the debt limits remain below 100%, In contrast, under a unit interest factor elasticity (neo-classical case) the debt limit is significantly higher than 100%. In addition, as the economy approaches the debt limits, except for the neo-classical case, it was found that higher debt to GDP ratios raise the GDP growth factor.

Using the above model, it not possible to ascertain whether there is a debt ratio threshold beyond which growth decreases. In order to investigate this question, the model was therefore extended to incorporate the impact of private and public savings on aggregate investment, in line with Magnani (2015). Under a rather high crowding out parameter, and unit interest factor elasticity of investment demand, the model produces a debt threshold. The value of such a threshold, as well as that of the associated growth detracting effect, are found to be only slightly lower than corresponding World Bank estimates.

The two-pronged model analysis described above allows us to answer the main research question as follows: Yes, there are limits to public debt in highly stylized intertemporal equilibrium models of the world economy, even in the face of involuntary unemployment. Such limits stem more from the efficacy of government debt to reduce unemployment than from its inability to do so. Under a unit interest-factor elasticity of aggregate investment demand, and rather strong crowding-out effects of private and government savings on investment, a debt threshold appears beyond which more debt reduces GDP growth. This form of debt limit exists even in a demand-driven macro-model.

The limitations of the present study are obvious. The most severe limitation is with respect to the international dimension. Savings ratios and GDP growth rates diverge hugely among advanced and newly developing countries. To cope with these differences, at least a two-country version of the present models à la Farmer and Zotti (2010) and Farmer and Schelnast (2021) would be necessary. However, this must remain the subject of future research.

ACKNOWLEDGMENTS

The author is very grateful to Laurie Conway for his excellent English editing of a preliminary version of the chapter.

REFERENCES

Auerbach, A. & L. Kotlikoff (1998) *Macroeconomics. An integrated approach*. 2nd ed. Cambridge (Mass.): MIT Press.

Azariadis, C. (1993) *Intertemporal macroeconomics*. Oxford: Blackwell.

Burda, M. & Ch. Wyplosz (2017) *Macroeconomics. A European text*. 7th ed. Oxford: Oxford University Press.

Coeurdacier, N., St. Guiband & K. Jin (2015) Credit constraints and growth in a global economy. *American Economic Review* 105 (9), 2838-2081.

De la Croix, D. & Ph. Michel (2002) *A theory of economic growth. Dynamics and policy in overlapping generations.* Cambridge: Cambridge University Press.

Diamond P. (1965). National debt in a neoclassical growth model. *American Economic Review* 55, 1126-1150.

Dixon H. (2000). New Keynesian economics: Theory and evidence, in: Backhouse R. & A. Salanti (eds.) *Theory and evidence in macroeconomics*, Oxford: O. U. P., 203-214.

Farmer, K. & M. Schelnast (2021) *Growth and international trade. An introduction to the overlapping generations approach*. 2nd ed., Berlin et al.: Springer.

Farmer, K. & St. Kuplen (2018) Involuntary unemployment in an OLG growth model with public debt and human capital. *Studia Universitatis Babes-Bolyai Oeconomica* 63 (2), 3-34.

Farmer, K. & I. Ban (2017), Modeling financial Integration and intra-EMU and Asian-US external imbalances, *International Advances in Economic Research*, 10.1007/s11294-017-9638-8 2017.

Farmer, K. & B. Mihaiescu (2016) Credit constraints and differential growth in equilibrium modeling of EMU and global imbalances. *GEP-Graz Economic Papers* 2016-05.

Farmer, K. & J. Zotti (2010) Sustainable government debt in a two-good, two-country overlapping generations model. *International Review of Economics* 57, 289-316.

Galor, O. (1992) A two-sector overlapping-generations model: A global characterization of the dynamical system. *Econometrica* 60 (6), 1351-1386.

Glomm G. & B. Ravikumar (1992) Public versus private investment in human capital: Endogenous growth and income inequality. *Journal of Political Economy* 100, 818-834.

Guiso, L., A. K. Kashyap, F. Panetta & D. Terlizzese (2002) *How Interest Sensitive is Investment? Very (when the data are well measured).* Working Paper: Federal Reserve Bank of Chicago.

Hayati A. R., I. Shafinar & A. R. Ridzuan (2019) How does public debt affect economic growth? A systematic review. *Cogent Business & Management* 6, 1-16.

Hicks, J. (1937). Mr. Keynes and the "Classics": A suggested interpretation. *Econometrica* 5 (2), 147-159.

ILO (2020) International Labor Organization, *ILOSTAT database*. Graph of unemployment rates downloaded on December 21, 2020.

IMF (2008, 2014, 2020) *World Economic Outlook*. Washington.

Keynes, J. M. (1936) *The general theory of employment, interest, and money*. London: Macmillan.

Magnani, R. (2015) *The Solow growth model revisited. Introducing Keynesian involuntary unemployment.* downloaded from https://hal.archives-ouvertes.fr/hal-01203393 on December 8, 2017.

Morishima, M. (1977) *Walras' economics: A pure theory of capital and money*. New York: Cambridge University Press.

Rankin, N. & B. Roffia (2003) Maximum sustainable government debt in the overlapping generations model. *Manchester School* 71 (3), 217-241.

Reinhart, C. M., V. Reinhart & K. Rogoff (2015) Declining with debt. *Journal of International Economics* 96, 543-555.

Solow R. M. (1956). A contribution to the theory of economic growth. *The Quartely Journal of Economics* 70, 65-94.

In: Public Debt
Editor: Antoine Bélanger
ISBN: 978-1-53619-326-8

Chapter 4

DO CENTRAL BANKS ENGAGE IN PUBLIC DEBT MANAGEMENT? THE CASE OF EMERGING MARKETS INFLATION TARGETERS WITH FLOATING EXCHANGE RATES

Joanna Mackiewicz-Łyziak*[*] *and Dagmara Mycielska
Faculty of Economic Sciences, University of Warsaw, Warsaw, Poland

ABSTRACT

In this chapter, we analyze the response of central banks in emerging inflation targeting countries with floating exchange rates to changes in public debt. Using panel data we estimate Taylor-rule type central banks' reaction functions including government debt as one of the determinants of the policy interest rates. We argue that, on the one hand, the central bank observing increasing public debt may try to discipline fiscal

* Corresponding Author's E-mail: jmackiewicz@wne.uw.edu.pl.

authorities by increasing interest rates. On the other hand, increasing public debt may threaten macroeconomic stability and high interest rates translate into higher interest payments that in turn increase public debt further. In this situation, the central bank, trying to prevent the accumulation of debt, may react by lowering interest rates. However, this dilemma is complicated further if a significant proportion of the public debt is denominated in foreign currency as it is often the case of emerging market economies. Our findings suggest that central banks in emerging economies tend to lower interest rates in response to increase in government debt denominated in domestic currency and to increase interest rates in response to an increase in government debt denominated in foreign currency. This reaction may suggest a fiscal dominance regime.

Keywords: inflation targeting, public debt management, Taylor rule

Introduction

According to the conventional view widely accepted in economic literature, the primary goal of monetary policy is to achieve price stability, while fiscal policy should be conducted in such a manner to assure the fulfillment of the intertemporal budget constraint, which is consistent with debt sustainability. To isolate monetary policy from governments' pressures to finance deficits or to ease the debt burden through inflation, many central banks were granted formal independence. A consensus occurred that monetary and fiscal policies should be conducted separately with a fiscal policy not threatening the ability of the central banks to achieve price stability.

The global financial crisis and most recently the Covid-19 crisis has renewed the debate about the interactions between monetary and fiscal policy. Many governments issue large deficits increasing public debts and central banks engage in different types of unconventional monetary policy actions raising questions about their mandates. In the face of increasing worldwide public debts, the conventional view of monetary policy starts to be questioned. If fiscal policy becomes unsustainable – it will no longer be conducted to satisfy the intertemporal government budget constraint – monetary policy could not be conducted independently. In this debate, an increasingly accepted view is that independent conduct of monetary and fiscal policy is one of possible policy mix regimes and in the face of growing public debts central banks will have to take fiscal sustainability concerns into account (Leeper and Walker 2013). The monetary-fiscal policy mix regime in which it is monetary policy that takes actions to stabilize debt is called fiscal dominance (or the non-Ricardian regime). The government sets primary balances regardless of the needs of fiscal sustainability. In this situation, the central bank loses control over inflation. Accordingly, monetary dominance (or the Ricardian regime) is a policy regime, in which the central bank controls inflation and the fiscal authorities stabilize public debt (Canzoneri et al. 2001). Monetary dominance corresponds to the conventional view of monetary policy while fiscal dominance is particularly stressed by the fiscal theory of the price level. In the current situation, it seems that fiscal dominance may become the prevailing regime in contemporary economies.

Although the problem of fiscal dominance is widely debated in the recent literature, it is not new. It goes back to the "unpleasant monetarist arithmetic" of Sargent and Wallace (1981) and was further discussed by the aforesaid fiscal theory of the price level (Woodford 1994, 1995, 1996, 1998, 2001; Sims 1994, 2001; Leeper 1991; Cochrane 2000, 2001). Results arising from this literature show that even if the central banks are independent, they may not be able to control inflation if irresponsible fiscal policy is conducted by governments. Therefore, forward-looking central banks, whose primary goal is price stability, may respond to the growing public debt as it may threaten the future inflation outlook. Moreover, if the central bank considers the overall macroeconomic stability it should also monitor and react to fiscal imbalances, as they are one of the main sources of economic instability.

These conclusions seem to contradict the standard approach to monetary policy analysis. Conventionally, monetary policymakers' behavior is described by a simple Taylor rule, relating the level of the policy interest rate to the inflation rate and output gap (Taylor 1993). This behavior is consistent with a flexible inflation targeting regime allowing the central bank to respond to output gap fluctuations. According to this standard approach, the monetary policymakers do not respond directly to the fiscal policy stance. The simple Taylor rule has been, however, subject to many modifications since it has been proposed in its original form. Ball (1999), Svensson (2000), and Taylor (1999) argued that the monetary policy rule for an open economy should include the exchange rate. Exchange rate changes influence aggregate demand and as such should cause interest rate adjustments. Another variable incorporated into the Taylor rule is the foreign interest rate. Bruno and Shin (2012) showed that low interest rates set by major central banks increase risk-taking in other countries, which may cause them to lower interest rates as well. Taylor (2013) explained several reasons why foreign interest rates may have an impact on the central banks' decisions. In the light of the presented discussion, it seems therefore justified to include in the Taylor rule variables representing fiscal stance. To the best of our knowledge, the first to notice it was Hallet and Lewis (2015).

Hallet and Lewis (2015) argue that the level of the public debt may affect the central banks interest rate-setting by for several reasons. Firstly, high debt levels create an incentive for the governments to reduce the real debt burden by generating higher inflation. If they can effectively pressure the central banks, the estimated coefficient on debt in the Taylor rule should be negative. On the other hand, if the central bank counteracts the effects of overly expansive (or restrictive) fiscal policy on inflation, the coefficient would be positive. Secondly, a governments' debt level, similarly to the output gap, conveys information about future threats to price stability – the primary objective of central banks. Growing debt levels may indicate future inflationary pressures, to which the central bank should respond by increasing interest rates. This means a positive coefficient on debt in the Taylor rule. Finally, the central bank may try to prevent the public debt from becoming unsustainable and the collapse of the bond market. This would happen if the government was not able to service its debt. We argue that in this case, the central bank might try to lower the debt servicing costs by lowering interest rates, which indicates a negative response of interest rate to growing public debt. In the empirical analysis of the ECB policy, Hallet and Lewis (2015) found a positive response of short-term nominal interest rate to the level of public debt in the euro area.

Another piece of empirical evidence on the impact of fiscal stance on the interest rate-setting by the central banks is provided by Ahmed et al. (2019). Like Hallet and Lewis (2015), they estimate Taylor rules directly incorporating public debt for several advanced and emerging economies. In addition, they control for a share of public debt denominated in a foreign currency. They analyse different groups of countries divided according to several characteristics (e.g., monetary policy regime, and the volatility of the exchange rate). In general, they find signs of fiscal dominance for both advanced and emerging economies. A slightly different approach was taken by Afonso et al. (2019), introducing the cyclically adjusted primary balance into the Taylor rule. In the study conducted for the 28 EU countries, they find that the central banks do not react to fiscal policy.

In this chapter, we analyze the response of the central banks to the growing public debts estimating the debt-augmented Taylor rules. Following the cited literature, we assume that on the one hand, the central bank observing increasing public debt may try to discipline fiscal authorities by increasing interest rates. This strategy could be identified as monetary dominance. On the other hand, increasing public debt may threaten macroeconomic stability and high interest rates translate into higher interest payments that in turn increase public debt further. In this situation, the central bank, trying to prevent the accumulation of debt, may react by lowering interest rates. We interpret this reaction of the central banks as fiscal dominance. However, this dilemma is complicated further if a significant proportion of the public debt is denominated in foreign currency as it is often the case of emerging market economies due to their inability to borrow abroad in their currencies (Eichengreen et al. 2007). Lowering interest rates will lead – according to the interest rate parity – to a depreciation of the domestic currency and will increase the burden of debt. On the other hand, increasing interest rates would strengthen the domestic currency and would help to reduce the level of foreign debt. Therefore, in this case, the positive response to debt denominated in foreign currency would not necessarily mean a monetary dominance regime. On the contrary, if the central bank aimed to reduce the debt burden, it would be a sign of fiscal dominance.

The contribution of this study is as follows. We analyze the central banks' reaction to the growing government debt. In particular, we test empirically the hypothesis that the currency structure of the government debt affects the policy interest rates-setting behavior of the central bank. We believe that such dependence will be especially visible in the case of emerging economies.

In times of a pandemic, the burden on the public sector increased, but the case of developing countries is particularly worrying. The threat of economic collapse and subsequent wave of unemployment menace the solvency and sustainability of debt of both the public and private sectors, and the risk of a debt crisis has increased significantly. Some economists suggested the introduction of a temporary moratorium on all external debt repayment of distressed developing countries (Reinhart and Rogoff, 2020). But the domestic debt of governments increased as well. The average public debt of developing and emerging economies increased from 33.7% in 2008 to 52.1% of GDP in 2019 and early projections point to further increases. Hence, increasing public debt might weaken long term economic growth.

This study focuses on inflation targeting emerging economies that operate within a floating exchange rate regime. Many emerging economies adopted an inflation targeting regime as the element of disinflation policy. In 2019 24 developing countries followed this monetary policy framework under floating exchange rate arrangements (IMF 2020a). At that time, the average inflation rate in these countries was 4.4%. But it was over 11% in 2000. The experience of high levels of inflation and costly disinflationary policies could make the monetary authorities in these countries more sensitive to different inflationary factors, including the level of the public debt. Moreover, given the limited ability of the emerging economies to borrow in the domestic currency and their higher dependence on the investors' sentiment as well as the fact that debt problems were the source of many recent crises in emerging countries (Byrne et al. 2011), the responsiveness of monetary policy to government debt may be higher in these countries in comparison with advanced economies.[1]

To the best of our knowledge, this is the first study that addresses the issue of central bank reaction to changes in government debt directly to the inflation targeting emerging countries pursuing monetary policy under floating exchange rate regime. Eliminating official focus on the exchange rate allows central banks' commitment to the inflation target and avoidance of target conflict.

We estimate the adjusted Taylor rules on a sample of emerging countries that reported following inflation targeting strategy using three estimation methods: fixed effects least squares, two-stage least squares and pooled mean group estimation. Our results show that central banks of emerging markets inflation targeters react differently to the increasing government debt depending on the currency structure of the debt.

The remainder of the chapter is organized as follows; the next section discusses the data sources and empirical methodology. Section 2 reports our empirical findings concerning central banks' response to the government debt burden. Section 3 concludes.

DATA AND METHODS

In our study, we use quarterly data on macroeconomic variables for 20 emerging economies. We focus on inflation targeters that adopted this monetary regime by 2012 Q1 (IMF 2012). Due to the gaps in data, some countries were excluded from the sample[2]. The detailed list of countries is provided in the Appendix (Table A.1). The sample covers the period 2008 Q1 –2020 Q1 which is determined by the data availability. The dependent variable is the policy interest rate and among the exogenous variables are:

---

[1] Moreover, we are able to estimate the Taylor rule for emerging economies since they did not reach the zero lower bound on nominal interest rates, as was the case in many advanced economies.

[2] We excluded Ghana, Serbia, Thailand, and Uruguay. We include Russia and Costa Rica as those countries were in the transition stage to full-fledged inflation targeting (IMF 2014, 2018).

inflation rate, output gap, and central government debt. As the data for public sector debt is unavailable for many small countries, we use the central government debt instead.

The complete description of the dataset and data sources used in our study is provided below:

- Central bank policy rates: data on the central banks' policy interest rates or monetary policy-related interest rates comes from the International Financial Statistics database, compiled by International Monetary Fund (IMF IFS) and from the central banks' websites.
- Inflation: data comes from the IMF IFS database. The variable was measured using quarter to the same quarter of the previous year changes in the CPI.
- Output gap: GDP data comes from different databases: IMF IFS, OECD Statistics, and national central bank statistics. The output gap was calculated as the percentage deviation from the potential output. The potential output was compiled using the one-sided Hodrick-Prescott filter with the smoothing parameter 1600.
- Central government debt: in nominal value, measured as % of GDP. Data comes from the Quarterly Public Sector Debt database compiled jointly by the International Monetary Fund and the World Bank.

Table 1 describes and summarizes the descriptive statistics for the variables of interest. To provide the context, the statistics for inflation targeting advanced countries are presented as well. The emerging markets have (on average) lower central government debts comparing to advanced economies (in terms of GDP), but also the debt dispersion is smaller. However, given the currency structure of government debt, the conclusions are not so straightforward. Emerging markets government debt denominated in foreign currencies account for nearly 40% of their total government debts (on average). For advanced countries, the debt in foreign currencies accounts for only 10% of their total government debt.

Table 1. Descriptive statistics for inflation targeting countries

Variable	Emerging countries (20)				Advanced countries (10)			
	Min	Max	Mean	St. dev.	Min	Max	Mean	St. dev.
Central gov. debt (% of GDP)	3,4	82,4	36,5	17,8	17,9	202,8	67,1	44,1
Central gov. debt in domestic currency (% of GDP)	0,5	70,3	21,4	15,5	17,9	89,4	53,1	18,7
Central gov. debt in foreign currency (% of GDP)	1,3	44,0	14,1	10,1	0	25,5	6,7	6,8

Source: Own calculations.

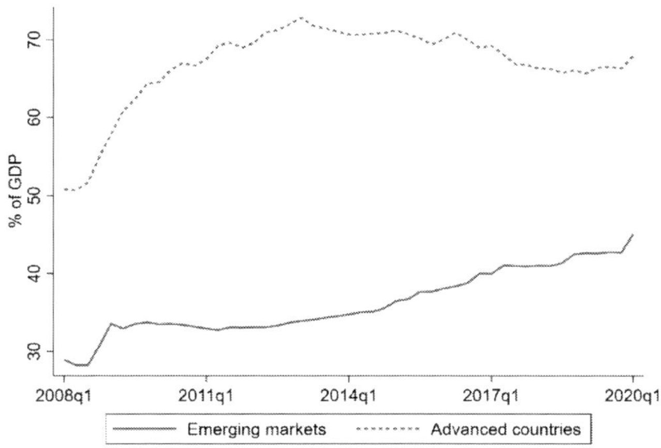

Source: Own calculations.

Figure 1. Central government debt in advanced and emerging economies (average, in % of GDP).

After a surge in the wake of the financial crisis, the advanced countries government debts stabilized at the level of about 70% of GDP. However, emerging markets debt was still gradually increasing (Figure 1). While in recent years the foreign currency debt of advanced countries had started to decline, in the case of emerging countries it had increased by almost 5 p.p. (Figure 2). Thus, if central banks in inflation targeting countries indeed engage in debt management, the banks' reaction might vary depending on the currency composition of government debt. Moreover, the inclination for fiscal dominance could be more pronounced in the case of emerging countries.

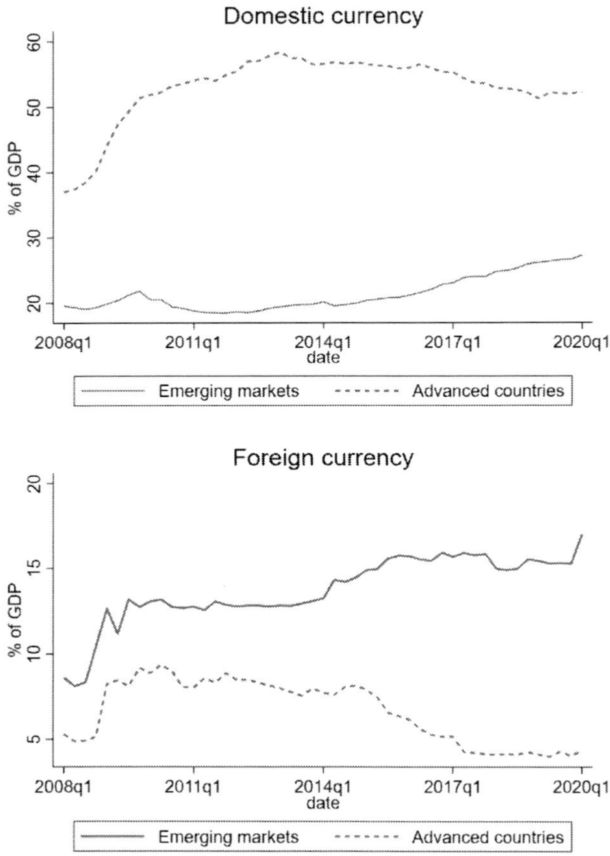

Note: the currency composition of central government debt is incomplete. The detailed information is provided in Appendix (Table A.1).
Source: Own calculations.

Figure 2. Central government debt in advanced and emerging economies, domestic and foreign currencies (average, in % of GDP).

To verify if the level of government debt affects the monetary policymaking of the central banks, we estimate monetary policy rule including debt as one of the interest rate determinants. The original interest rule, proposed by Taylor (1993) for Fed, was formulated as follows:

$$i_t = r^* + \pi_t + \alpha_1(\pi_t - \pi^*) + \alpha_2 y_t \quad (1)$$

where i_t is the nominal interest rate set by the central bank, r^* is the natural (equilibrium) real interest rate, π_t is the inflation rate, π^* is the inflation target and y_t denotes the output gap.

It follows from Eq. (1), that the original Taylor rule did not include other variables than the inflation rate and output gap (the natural interest rate and the inflation target were treated as constant). However, as discussed in the introduction, empirical studies over time added additional variables as potentially influencing the interest setting behavior by the central banks. A common assumption made in estimating Taylor's rules is that the central banks tend to smooth the interest rate path, a feature firstly noticed by Judd and Rudebusch (1998). Therefore, the estimated equation for the Taylor rule takes the following form:

$$i_t = \rho i_{t-1} + (1 - \rho)(\gamma + \beta_1 \pi_{t+k} + \beta_2 y_{t+l}) + \varepsilon_t \quad (2)$$

where ρ is a smoothing parameter, $\gamma = r^* + (1 - \beta_1)$, π_{t+k} is an actual or predicted inflation rate, y_{t+l} is an actual or predicted output gap and ε_t is an error term.

According to eq. (2), monetary policy may be forward-looking, reacting to forecasted rather than current values of macroeconomic variables, which seems to describe better the behavior of the inflation targeting central banks.

In our study we follow the approach proposed by Judd and Rudebusch (1998), assuming the interest rate smoothing. Moreover, similar to Hallet and Lewis (2015) and Ahmed et al. (2019), we add to the monetary policy rule an additional variable – the level of the government debt, to verify, if the central banks take it into account while deciding about the level of interest rates. We estimate the debt-augmented Taylor rule for a panel of countries, so the estimated equation reads as follows:

$$i_{j,t} = \delta_j + \tau_t + \delta_1 i_{j,t-1} + \delta_2 \pi_{j,t+1} + \delta_3 y_{j,t+1} + \delta_4 d_{j,t-1} + \varepsilon_{j,t} \quad (3)$$

where δ_j denotes country fixed effects including the natural real interest rate and inflation target, which are country-specific and assumed time-invariant; τ_t denotes period fixed effects, and $d_{j,t-1}$ is the central government debt-to-GDP ratio, lagged by one period.

Besides, distinguishing between possibly different effects of debt denominated in domestic and foreign currency, we estimate the following equation:

$$i_{j,t} = \delta_j + \tau_t + \delta_1 i_{j,t-1} + \delta_2 \pi_{j,t+1} + \delta_3 y_{j,t+1} + \delta_4 d_{j,t-1}^{DC} + \delta_5 d_{j,t-1}^{FC} + \varepsilon_{j,t} \quad (4)$$

where $d_{j,t-1}^{DC}$ denotes the central government debt denominated in domestic currency and $d_{j,t-1}^{FC}$ is the central government debt denominated in foreign currency, both expressed as a percent of GDP.

In both estimated equations we assume a forward-looking behavior of the central banks by taking one-period leads of the inflation rate and output gap. As Hallett and Lewis (2015) pointed out, the analysis of central bank policymakers' decisions should depend on real-time data instead of ex-post data. The best approach would be to use the projected values of the variables, but it seems impossible to collect all the data available to policymakers at the time the decision was being made for a large sample of countries. Therefore, we decided to use the known ex-post next period values as an approximation of today's forecast for the future[3]. To avoid a situation in which interest rate changes affect future inflation and output gap we use only one-quarter lead, because in this short-term horizon

[3] The use of the future inflation rate as the projected inflation rate is a common approach in empirical studies.

interest rate changes have little impact on these variables.[4] In the case of the governments' debt, we use values lagged by one quarter because the central banks are not likely to know the current or future levels of the public debt at the time of monetary policy decisions, since such data are revealed with a lag and the central banks do not have superior information on this matter.

We estimate equations (3) and (4) using fixed effects least squares. The results of tests indicating the need to use the country and period fixed effects are presented in the Appendix (Table A.3). Our panel is dynamic – it includes a lagged value of the dependent variable as we assume interest rate smoothing – which may raise questions about the problem of the Nickell bias (Nickell, 1981). This problem arises when the time dimension in a dynamic panel is small. The usual solution to this problem is the use of GMM estimators such as Arellano-Bond or system GMM estimators (Arellano and Bond, 1991; Arellano and Bover, 1995; Blundell and Bond, 1998). It seems, however, that these estimators would not be a proper choice for our study, since the time dimension of the panel is over two times larger than the number of cross-sections and it is close to 50, at which point the Nickell bias seems to be negligible.

In our panel, however, there may be another source of endogeneity. As the Taylor rule includes variables that may be interdependent and the problem of simultaneity may arise, to correct the potential bias in the OLS estimates we use a second estimation method – two stage least squares. We use up to two lags of explanatory variables as instruments. The validity of instruments is tested using the J-statistics (reported in the results tables).

Another problem that arises while estimating the debt-augmented Taylor rules is that, according to test, the debt-to-GDP time-series are non-stationary (the results of panel unit root tests for all variables are presented in the Appendix, Table A.2). We include these variables as levels in the estimated equations for two reasons. First, taking differences (which are

[4] In the Appendix (Table A.4 and A.5) we present results for the Taylor rules estimated with actual values of inflation and output gap. The results are very similar to those obtained with future values of inflation and the output gap.

stationary) instead of levels would lead to a significant loss of information. The discussion presented above suggests that it is the scope of the government indebtedness rather than its increases that may cause concerns of the central banks. Less indebted economies may be able to increase their debt at a higher pace than more indebted ones without severe threats to economic stability. Also, the debt servicing costs depend on the level of government debt. Therefore, according to our hypothesis, the central banks should react to levels of government debt rather than to its increases. Second, there is a large body of empirical literature analyzing the fiscal reaction functions, following the seminal paper of Bohn (1998), that uses in standard regressions debt-to-GDP ratio as an independent variable. In fact, in his paper Bohn (1998) proved that unit root tests are misleading and the debt-to-GDP ratio was stationary despite the results of these tests suggesting the opposite. Hallet and Lewis (2015) are also skeptical regarding the results of the unit root tests and they argue that the debt-to-GDP ratio in fact cannot be non-stationary.

However, taking into account the possible non-stationarity of the debt time series and the inconclusive unit root test results for the dependent variable[5], we use a third estimation method – a pooled mean group estimation. This estimation method has also this advantage over the fixed effects estimators that it allows for differences in the short-run dynamics between countries – all the coefficients in the short-run relationship are individual for each country – and only the long-run relationship is assumed to be common. In the case of the fixed effects estimators, we assume the differences between countries only in the intercepts while all the other coefficients are the same. Therefore, in the case of heterogeneity in the sample of countries, the pooled mean group estimator may be preferred to the fixed effects estimators.

For the robustness purposes, we present results for these three estimation methods.

---

[5] One of the panel unit root tests indicated non-stationarity of the interest rate time series (Appendix, Table A.2).

RESULTS

Table 2 presents estimated coefficients in the Taylor rule including government debt for the panel of 20 emerging countries, obtained with the use of three estimation methods.

The results obtained using two estimation methods suggest a negative coefficient on debt in the Taylor rule, however, in only one case – the panel two-stage least squares – it was statistically significant. This would suggest that the central banks lowered interest rates responding to growing public debt burdens. According to the discussion presented in the introduction, a negative reaction of policy interest rates to the level of public debt would be a sign of a fiscal dominance regime prevailing in these economies. In the case of the pooled mean group estimation, the coefficient on debt is positive and statistically significant, suggesting the tightening of monetary policy in response to fiscal expansion. The obtained results are therefore inconclusive.

Table 2. Taylor rules augmented with government debt

	I FE-LS	II FE-2SLS	III PMG
Lagged rate	0.817*** (0.023)	0.787*** (0.029)	--
Inflation	0.212*** (0.019)	0.149*** (0.029)	0.693*** (0.057)
Output gap	-0.003 (0.006)	-0.007 (0.009)	0.003 (0.035)
Gov. debt	-0.003 (0.007)	-0.016* (0.008)	0.033* (0.018)
Adj. R^2	0.934	0.930	--
Country FE	Yes	Yes	--
Period FE	Yes	Yes	--
Prob. J-stat	--	0.282	--

Note: Standard errors in parenthesis. *,**,*** denote significance at 10, 5, 1 percent level, respectively. In the case of 2SLS estimation, lagged values of independent variables were used as instruments (up to 2 lags). In the case of PMG estimation, ARDL(2,1,1,1) model was selected.

Source: Own calculations.

As far as other determinants of interest rates are concerned, we obtained similar results for the FE-LS and FE-2SLS estimators (columns I and II). Both suggest a high (and similar) degree of interest rate smoothing. The response of the central banks to the inflation rate is positive and statistically significant, while the central banks seem not to react to the output gap – the estimated coefficients are not statistically significant.

The results obtained for the pooled mean group estimation (column III) are qualitatively similar. This estimation method allows not only the intercepts but also short-run coefficients and cointegrating terms to differ across countries and assumes a common relationship only in the long run. The difference in coefficients is also because the estimated long-run relationship does not include the smoothing coefficient – lags of the dependent variable are included in the short-run dynamics. Table 2. presents only the common coefficients for the long-run equation. The findings confirm a positive and statistically significant reaction of the policy interest rates to inflation, and no reaction to the output gap.

The presented results are ambiguous regarding the impact of the government debt on the interest-rate setting behavior of the central banks. Moreover, as discussed above, in the case of emerging economies, having a significant share of government debt denominated in foreign currencies, the impact of the level of government debt on interest rates may be more complicated, since a decrease of interest rates may lead to depreciation of the domestic currency, increasing the value of government debt. Therefore, in the next step, we divide government debt into two components: outstanding debt denominated in domestic currency and denominated in foreign currency (both expressed as a percentage of GDP). These two components are included independently in the Taylor rule. The results are presented in Table 3.[6]

Considering the currency in which government debt is denominated we obtain more robust results. For all three estimation methods, the response of a central bank to debt denominated in domestic currency is negative and

[6] The sample includes smaller set of countries because of the lack of data for Armenia and Poland.

statistically significant. It seems that the central banks try to manage their governments' debt by lowering the debt servicing costs. These results confirm our weak conclusions based on the findings presented in Table 2. This evidence suggests fiscal dominance regime, according to the interpretation presented in Ahmed et al. (2019), since it shows accommodative behavior of the central banks as a reaction to increasing debt burden.

Table 3. Taylor rules augmented with the government debt denominated in domestic and foreign currency

	I FE-LS	II FE-2SLS	III PMG
Lagged rate	0.791*** (0.025)	0.760*** (0.032)	--
Inflation	0.227*** (0.022)	0.160*** (0.033)	0.549*** (0.055)
Output gap	-0.10 (0.012)	-0.010 (0.024)	0.152*** (0.057)
Gov.debt DC	-0.022* (0.012)	-0.038*** (0.014)	-0.055* (0.030)
Gov.debt FC	0.018** (0.008)	0.011 (0.009)	0.171*** (0.036)
Adj. R^2	0.932	0.928	--
Country FE	Yes	Yes	--
Period FE	Yes	Yes	--
Prob. J-stat	--	0.832	--

Note: Standard errors in parenthesis. *,**,*** denote significance at 10, 5, 1 percent level, respectively. In the case of 2SLS estimation, lagged values of independent variables were used as instruments (up to 2 lags). In the case of PMG estimation, ARDL(2,1,1,1,1) model was selected.

Source: Own calculations.

In line with our expectations, the response of the central banks to increase in the level of government debt denominated in foreign currency is the opposite. The findings suggest a positive response for all three estimation methods, but in one case (2SLS, column II) the result is statistically not significant. It seems, therefore, that the central banks tend to increase interest rates when the government debt denominated in foreign currencies increases. Strengthening domestic currency in this way would help to limit the value of the debt. Both these conclusions provide the evidence that the central banks in inflation targeting emerging economies actively try to limit the debt burdens of domestic governments, which is rather opposite to the conventional view of monetary policy conducted under inflation targeting and to results obtained in studies for advanced economies.

For the other independent variables, the results are very similar to those presented in Table 2. The monetary policy is characterized by a high degree of interest rate smoothing (columns I and II). The response of interest rates to inflation is positive and statistically significant, which is in line with assumptions about the Taylor rule. The output gap is again not statistically significant according to FE-LS and FE-2SLS estimation methods (columns I and II), but is significant with a positive coefficient in the long-run relationship according to the PMG estimator (column III). Therefore, dividing government debt into two components according to the currency denomination does not significantly change the results for the other determinants of the policy interest rates.

CONCLUSION

The recent decade saw a significant increase in the level of government debts in many countries – advanced and emerging – due to large shocks hitting the global economy. This increase in the debt burdens creates a real challenge not only for the fiscal authorities but also for monetary policy as well. This situation may be especially severe for emerging economies due to their lower ability to borrow on international markets and higher vulnerability to the investors' sentiment.

In this chapter, we argue that the central banks may take the fiscal situation into account while deciding about the level of policy interest rates. Their response may be twofold: they may try to counteract the fiscal expansion and the threats to macroeconomic stability by increasing interest rates or may try to lower the debt burdens by lowering the interest rates. Both reactions justify augmenting the standard monetary reaction function such as the Taylor rule with fiscal variables. Moreover, if the sign of the coefficient on government debt in the Taylor rule is negative, i.e., the central bank lowers interest rates in response to the growing debt, it suggests that the central bank acts to stabilize debt, which is a sign of the fiscal dominance regime.

However, debt stabilization is complicated further if a significant share of the government debt is denominated in foreign currency. In this case, lower interest rates would lead to domestic currency depreciation and an actual increase in the value of debt. Therefore, we argue that while verifying the response of the central banks to government debt, these two components – debt denominated in domestic and foreign currency – should be considered separately. This distinction may be particularly important in the case of emerging economies, because advanced economies sparsely issue debt denominated in foreign currency.

In this study, we analyze monetary policy reaction functions, with government debt as one of the interest rate determinants, for the panel of 20 emerging economies pursuing inflation targeting strategy. Our findings confirm our predictions: the response of the central banks to the government debt seems to be statistically significant and is different for the debt denominated in domestic and foreign currency. Moreover, the results suggest that monetary authorities in emerging economies lower interest rates when government debt in domestic currency increases and increase interest rates in response to an increase in the debt denominated in foreign currency. We interpret these results as a sign of fiscal dominance – monetary authorities try to accommodate fiscal expansion by lowering the debt burden.

Consequently, our study seems to confirm the findings of Ahmed et al. (2019) but it should be noted that there are very few studies analyzing these issues using a similar approach. Therefore, we treat our results as preliminary. Although it seems that the currency denomination of debt matters and it should be taken into account while analyzing the monetary–fiscal interactions, further studies are needed to deepen the understanding of this complicated relationship.

REFERENCES

Afonso, António, José Alves, and Raquel Balhote. 2019. "Interactions between monetary and fiscal policies." *Journal of Applied Economics* 22:131-50. doi:10.1080/15140326.2019.1583309.

Ahmed, Rashad, Joshua Aizenman, and Yothin Jinjarak. 2019. "Inflation and exchange rate targeting challenges under fiscal dominance." *NBER Working Paper* 25996. National Bureau of Economic Research, Cambridge, MA. doi: 10.3386/w25996.

Arellano, Manuel, and Stephen Bond. 1991. "Some Tests of Specification for Panel Data: Monte Carlo Evidence and an Application to Employment Equations." *Review of Economic Studies* 58(2):277-97. doi:10.2307/2297968.

Arellano, Manuel, and Olympia Bover. 1995. "Another look at the instrumental variable estimation of error-components models." *Journal of Econometrics* 68(1):29-51. doi:10.1016/0304-4076(94)01642-D.

Ball, Laurence. 1999. "Policy rules for open economies." In *Monetary Policy Rules*, edited by John B. Taylor, 127-56. Chicago: University of Chicago Press.

Blundell, Richard, and Stephen Bond. 1998. "Initial conditions and moment restrictions in dynamic panel data models." *Journal of Econometrics* 87(1):115-43. doi:10.1016/S0304-4076(98)00009-8.

Bohn, Henning. 1998. "The behavior of U.S. public debt and deficits." *Quarterly Journal of Economics* 113(3):949–63.

Bruno, Valentina, and Hyun Song Shin. 2015. "Capital flows and the risk-taking channel of monetary policy." *Journal of Monetary Economics*, 71(C):119-32. doi: 10.1016/j.jmoneco.2014.11.011.

Byrne, Joseph P., Norbert Fiess, and Ronald MacDonald. 2011. "The global dimension to fiscal sustainability." *Journal of Macroeconomics*, 33: 137-150. doi:10.1016/j.jmacro.2011.01.002.

Canzoneri, Matthew B., Robert E. Cumby, and Behzad T. Diba. 2001. "Is the price level determined by the needs of fiscal solvency?" *American Economic Review* 91(5):122-38. doi:10.1257/aer.91.5.1221.

Cochrane, John H. 2000. "Money as stock: Price level determination with no money demand." *NBER Working Paper* 7498. National Bureau of Economic Research, Cambridge, MA. doi:10.3386/w7498.

Cochrane, John H. 2001. "Long-term debt and optimal policy in the fiscal theory of the price level." *Econometrica* 69(1):69-116. doi:10.1111/1468-0262.00179.

Eichengreen, Barry, Ricardo Hausmann, and Ugo Panizza. 2007. "Currency Mismatches, Debt Intolerance, and the Original Sin: Why They Are Not the Same and Why It Matters." In *Capital Controls and Capital Flows in Emerging Economies: Policies, Practices, and Consequences*, edited by Sebastian Edwards, 121-70. National Bureau of Economic Research, Inc.

Hallett, Andrew H., and John Lewis. 2014. "Monetary policy and sovereign debt: Does the ECB take the eurozone's fiscal risks into account?" *Empirica* 42:499-520. doi:10.1007/s10663-014-9260-4.

International Monetary Fund (IMF). 2012. "Annual Report on Exchange Arrangements and Exchange Restrictions 2012." *International Monetary Fund*, Washington, DC.

International Monetary Fund (IMF). 2014. "Annual Report on Exchange Arrangements and Exchange Restrictions 2014." *International Monetary Fund*, Washington, DC.

International Monetary Fund (IMF). 2018. "Annual Report on Exchange Arrangements and Exchange Restrictions 2017." *International Monetary Fund*, Washington, DC.

International Monetary Fund (IMF). 2020a. "Annual Report on Exchange Arrangements and Exchange Restrictions 2019." *International Monetary Fund*, Washington, DC.

International Monetary Fund (IMF). 2020b. "World Economic Outlook: A Long and Difficult Ascent." *International Monetary Fund*, Washington, DC, October.

Judd, John P., and Glenn Rudebusch. 1998. "Taylor's rule and the Fed, 1970-1997." *Economic Review* 3:3-16.

Leeper, Eric M. 1991. "Equilibria under active and passive monetary policies." *Journal of Monetary Economics* 27:129-47. doi:10.1016/0304-3932(91)90007-B.

Leeper, Eric M., and Todd B. Walker. 2013. "Perceptions and misperceptions of fiscal inflation." In *Fiscal Policy after the Financial Crisis* edited by Alberto Alesina and Francesco Giavazzi, 255-29. Chicago: University of Chicago Press.

Nickell, Stephen. 1981. "Biases in Dynamic Models with Fixed Effects." *Econometrica* 49(6):1417-26. doi:10.2307/1911408.

Reinhart, Carmen M., and Kenneth Rogoff. 2020. "Suspend Emerging and Developing Economies' Debt Payments." *Project Syndicate*. Accessed December 18, 2020. https://www.project-syndicate.org/commentary/suspend-emerging-and-developing-economies-debt-payments-by-carmen-reinhart-and-kenneth-rogoff-2020-04.

Sargent, Thomas J., and Neil Wallace. 1981. "Some unpleasant monetarist arithmetic." *Quarterly Review* 5:1-17. Federal Reserve Bank of Minneapolis.

Sims, Christopher A. 1994. "A simple model for the determination of the price level and the interaction of monetary and fiscal policy." *Economic Theory* 4:381-99. doi:10.1007/BF01215378.

Sims, Christopher A. 2001. "Fiscal consequences for Mexico of adopting the dollar." *Journal of Money, Credit and Banking* 33(2):597-616. doi:10.2307/2673918.

Svensson, Lars E. O. 2000. "Open-economy inflation targeting." *Journal of International Economics* 50(1):155-83. doi:10.1016/S0022-1996(98)00078-6.

Taylor, John B. 1993. "Discretion versus policy rules in practice." Carnegie-Rochester Conference Series on Public Policy 39(1):195-214. doi:10.1016/0167-2231(93)90009-L.

Taylor, John B. 1999. "A historical analysis of monetary policy rules." In *Monetary Policy Rules*, edited by John B. Taylor, 319-48. Chicago: University of Chicago Press.

Taylor, John B. 2013. "International monetary coordination and the great deviation." *NBER Working Paper* 18716. National Bureau of Economic Research, Cambridge, MA. doi:10.3386/w18716.

Woodford, Michael. 1994. "Monetary policy and price level determinacy in a cash-in-advance economy." *Economic Theory* 4(3):345-89. doi:10.1007/BF01215377.

Woodford, Michael. 1995. "Price level determinacy without control of a monetary aggregate." *Carnegie-Rochester Conference Series on Public Policy* 43:1-46. doi:10.1016/0167-2231(95)90033-0.

Woodford, Michael. 1996. "Control of the public debt: A requirement for price stability?" *NBER Working Paper* 5684. National Bureau of Economic Research, Cambridge, MA. doi:10.3386/w5684.

Woodford, Michael. 1998. "Comment." In *NBER Macroeconomics Annual 1998* edited by Ben Bernanke, and Julio J. Rotemberg, 390-418. MIT Press.

Woodford, Michael. 2001. "Fiscal requirement for price stability," *Journal of Money, Credit and Banking* 33(3):669-728. doi:10.2307/2673890.

APPENDIX

Table A.1. Sample countries

Advanced economies	Australia (no FC data), Canada, Czechia (no DC and FC), Iceland, Israel, Japan (no DC and FC data), New Zealand (no DC and FC data), Norway (no DC and FC data), Sweden, United Kingdom
Emerging markets	Albania, Armenia (no DC and FC data), Brazil, Chile, Costa Rica, Colombia, Dominican Rep., Georgia, Guatemala, Hungary, Indonesia, Mexico, Moldova, Peru, Philippines, Poland (no DC and FC data), Romania (no DC and FC data), Russia, South Africa

Note: countries grouped according to IMF classification.
Source: IMF 2020b.

Table A.2. Results of panel unit root tests

		Method			
Variable		Levin, Lin and Chu	Im, Pesaran and Shin	ADF-Fisher	PP-Fisher
Interest rate	Stat.	-4.360	-6.230	127.017	48.605
	Prob.	0.000	0.000	0.000	0.165
Inflation	Stat.	-3.844	-7.170	137.715	69.262
	Prob.	0.000	0.000	0.000	0.002
Output gap	Stat.	2.655	-4.252	93.071	277.113
	Prob.	0.996	0.000	0.000	0.000
Debt	Stat.	0.785	2.327	43.458	41.136
	Prob.	0.784	0.990	0.326	0.421
Debt DC	Stat.	1.144	4.786	13.908	16.204
	Prob.	0.874	1.000	0.999	0.998
Debt FC	Stat.	1.098	3.957	21.893	29.028
	Prob.	0.864	1.000	0.969	0.789

Source: Own calculations.

Table A.3. Results of redundant fixed effects tests

Effects test	**Statistic**	**d.f.**	**Prob.**
	Equation (3)		
Cross-section F	2.917	(19,757)	0.000
Cross-section Chi-sq	58.443	19	0.000
Period F	2.489	(46,757)	0.000
Period Chi-sq	116.483	46	0.000
Cross-Section/Period F	2.801	(65,757)	0.000
Cross-Section/Period Chi-sq.	178.254	65	0.000
	Equation (4)		
Cross-section F	2.933	(17,650)	0.000
Cross-section Chi-sq	53.140	17	0.000
Period F	2.342	(46,650)	0.000
Period Chi-sq	110.285	46	0.000
Cross-Section/Period F	2.659	(63,650)	0.000
Cross-Section/Period Chi-sq.	164.849	63	0.000

Source: Own calculations.

Table A.4. Taylor rules augmented with government debt estimated with current values of inflation and output gap

	I **FE-LS**	II **FE-2SLS**	III **PMG**
Lagged rate	0.830*** (0.027)	0.778*** (0.032)	--
Inflation	0.134*** (0.021)	0.113*** (0.025)	0.589*** (0.066)
Output gap	-0.004 (0.006)	-0.005 (0.010)	0.423*** (0.088)
Gov. debt	-0.010 (0.008)	-0.022** (0.009)	-0.011 (0.022)
Adj. R^2	0.923	0.919	--
Country FE	Yes	Yes	--
Period FE	Yes	Yes	--
Prob. J-stat	--	0.136	--

Source: Own calculations.

Table A.5. Taylor rules augmented with the government debt denominated in domestic and foreign currency, estimated with current values of inflation and output gap

	I **FE-LS**	II **FE-2SLS**	III **PMG**
Lagged rate	0.811*** (0.030)	0.749*** (0.037)	--
Inflation	0.141*** (0.022)	0.129*** (0.029)	0.404*** (0.043)
Output gap	0.001 (0.014)	0.006 (0.027)	0.277*** (0.063)
Gov.debt DC	-0.030** (0.013)	-0.047*** (0.014)	-0.064** (0.032)
Gov.debt FC	0.012 (0.009)	0.005 (0.010)	0.098*** (0.033)
Adj. R^2	0.918	0.915	--
Country FE	Yes	Yes	--
Period FE	Yes	Yes	--
Prob. J-stat	--	0.191	--

Source: Own calculations.

INDEX

A

accommodation, vii, 1, 4, 5, 7, 9, 11, 15, 53
accumulation, ix, 6, 9, 12, 13, 23, 28, 33, 60, 95, 116, 119, 120, 138, 140, 157, 158, 164, 167
adjustment, 11, 13, 14, 97
age, 122, 123, 124, 127, 145
aggregate, ix, 9, 16, 74, 79, 82, 92, 116, 117, 118, 119, 120, 125, 126, 127, 138, 142, 151, 152, 153, 154, 156, 157, 158, 159, 166, 185
aggregate demand, 74, 82, 117, 118, 156, 157, 166
aggregate investment, ix, 116, 118, 119, 120, 127, 138, 152, 153, 154, 156, 157, 158, 159
aggregate output, 92, 125
aggregate supply, 156
animal, 118, 127, 153, 156, 158
animal spirits, 118, 127, 153, 156, 158
arbitrage, 17, 123, 125, 129
assessment, viii, 65, 81, 82, 101
authorities, ix, 10, 11, 12, 13, 14, 27, 32, 41, 42, 43, 164, 165, 167, 168, 180, 181

B

balance sheet, 15
balanced budget, 91
banks, ix, 33, 41, 42, 43, 163, 164, 165, 166, 167, 169, 170, 172, 173, 175, 176, 178, 179
benefits, 10, 42, 55, 68, 81, 84, 126, 130, 136
bias, 12, 16, 21, 48, 175
bifurcation, 139
bond market, 166
bonds, 3, 4, 6, 7, 9, 17, 18, 43, 82, 84, 121, 122
budget deficit, 66, 77, 101
business cycle, 88

C

calibration, 136, 137, 151, 153
capital, ix, 4, 7, 23, 28, 33, 74, 82, 83, 88, 89, 90, 92, 93, 94, 95, 96, 97, 116, 117, 119, 120, 121, 122, 125, 126, 127, 129,

131, 137, 138, 140, 142, 144, 145, 146, 151, 153, 157, 158, 160, 161, 182, 183
capital accumulation, 23, 28, 33, 95, 138, 140
capital goods, 82
capital markets, 4
capital mobility, 7
capital output ratio, 119, 144, 146, 157
causality, 67, 78, 79, 83, 86
central bank, vii, ix, 1, 3, 4, 5, 8, 9, 10, 11, 12, 13, 14, 15, 16, 32, 33, 34, 35, 37, 38, 39, 40, 41, 42, 43, 44, 47, 48, 49, 50, 51, 52, 53, 54, 85, 163, 164, 165, 166, 167, 168, 169, 170, 171, 173, 174, 176, 177, 178, 179, 180, 181
challenges, 85, 182
classification, 68, 116, 185
competition, 2, 23, 118
competitiveness, 14, 21, 29, 30, 82
composition, 77, 81, 82, 172
conference, 102, 106, 109
consensus, 101, 117, 164
consolidation, 11, 66, 73, 75, 76, 77, 78, 79, 81, 82, 85, 86, 97, 98, 99, 101
consumer price index, 21
consumers, 7, 29, 74, 89, 145
consumption, 3, 16, 17, 18, 19, 20, 21, 22, 28, 30, 34, 36, 37, 39, 40, 41, 49, 50, 51, 52, 74, 75, 82, 84, 89, 90, 94, 95, 98, 99, 100, 119, 121, 122, 123, 124, 125, 126, 129, 130, 136, 140, 141, 145, 151, 154, 157
controversial, 66, 77, 80, 81
coordination, 6, 8, 13, 32, 55, 61, 185
cost, 11, 12, 13, 14, 25, 26, 31, 33, 34, 39, 40, 70, 86, 89, 153
credit rating, 8
creditors, 7, 68, 70, 84, 86
crises, 7, 11, 66, 71, 72, 87, 109, 168
crisis management, 43
crowding-out, 7, 33, 74, 82, 90, 119, 154, 155, 159
crowding-out effect, 7, 33, 90, 119, 154, 159
crowding-out parameter, 119, 154, 155
currency, ix, 2, 9, 85, 164, 167, 168, 169, 170, 171, 172, 174, 178, 179, 180, 181, 187
current account, 72
current account deficit, 72

D

data availability, 169
database, 136, 161, 170
debt burden, 66, 68, 69, 70, 71, 72, 73, 74, 80, 81, 85, 92, 95, 105, 108, 164, 166, 168, 177, 179, 180, 181
debt service, 9, 12, 33, 69, 72, 75, 80, 89, 93
debt servicing, 166, 176, 179
debt sustainability, 4, 66, 69, 83, 84, 103, 106, 107, 164
debt to GDP ratio, vii, 1, 5, 27, 28, 31, 32, 33, 34, 35, 38, 39, 40, 44, 47, 48, 50, 52, 53, 54, 119, 120, 129, 136, 138, 139, 144, 145, 151, 157, 158
decision-making process, 47
decreasing returns, 23
deficit, 3, 6, 7, 8, 66, 71, 73, 75, 77, 90
degeneracy, 117
degenerate, 117
demand, vii, 1, 2, 5, 28, 29, 30, 31, 34, 35, 37, 38, 39, 40, 45, 46, 47, 48, 50, 51, 52, 53, 54, 55, 56, 74, 82, 117, 118, 127, 153, 156, 157, 158, 159, 166, 183
demand shocks, vii, 1, 2, 5, 34, 38, 45, 47, 48, 52, 54
dependent variable, 169, 175, 176, 178
depreciation, 9, 76, 82, 92, 121, 167, 178, 181
developing countries, 66, 85, 159, 168
deviation, 19, 24, 48, 78, 170, 185
disposable income, 98, 136

dominance, x, 3, 11, 164, 165, 167, 172, 177, 179, 181, 182
dynamics, 61, 63, 103, 118, 120, 131, 135, 137, 144, 146, 148, 149, 151, 160, 176, 178

E

earnings, viii, 115, 116
economic activity, viii, 2, 5, 30, 31, 33, 34, 35, 36, 37, 38, 40, 41, 44, 46, 48, 49, 50, 51, 53, 54, 55, 66, 68, 74, 75, 77, 79, 82, 83, 87, 101
economic consequences, 84
economic crisis, 53
economic cycle, 33, 38, 48, 54
economic development, 72
economic efficiency, 88
economic growth, v, vii, viii, 29, 30, 32, 53, 56, 57, 65, 66, 72, 73, 89, 91, 102, 103, 105, 107, 108, 109, 110, 111, 160, 161, 168
economic incentives, 70
economic performance, 72
economic policy, 43
economic resources, 74
economics, 112, 160, 161
economy, viii, 13, 16, 30, 65, 66, 68, 69, 70, 75, 81, 82, 84, 86, 88, 90, 92, 93, 94, 96, 98, 99, 100, 101, 102, 103, 104, 105, 106, 107, 108, 112, 116, 117, 119, 121, 136, 138, 139, 140, 142, 153, 157, 158, 159, 160, 166, 180, 184, 185
effect, viii, 6, 8, 9, 36, 38, 39, 46, 48, 50, 53, 54, 60, 65, 68, 71, 72, 74, 76, 77, 78, 79, 82, 83, 91, 95, 98, 100, 101, 105, 106, 108, 109, 113, 119, 154, 155, 156, 158
elasticity, 18, 30, 35, 36, 39, 40, 52, 123, 124, 125, 142, 153, 158
emerging markets, 169, 170, 171
empirical studies, 85, 173, 174
employment, ix, 116, 138, 154, 156, 157, 161
endogenous, 27, 66, 68, 74, 90, 91, 94, 103, 110, 118, 119, 130, 133, 139, 140, 143, 150, 151, 152, 154, 156, 157, 160
endogenous growth models, 66
equilibrium, 4, 12, 13, 19, 20, 23, 24, 26, 28, 29, 31, 32, 34, 35, 44, 58, 59, 85, 86, 90, 117, 118, 120, 122, 131, 133, 135, 137, 138, 140, 145, 146, 148, 149, 151, 152, 156, 158, 160, 173
equilibrium unemployment, 131, 145
European Commission, 80, 106
European Monetary Union, 107, 112
European Parliament, 112, 113
European System of Central Banks, 41
European Union, 7, 41, 106, 110, 111, 112, 113
evidence, 7, 32, 42, 75, 76, 77, 85, 87, 119, 154, 160, 167, 179, 180
evolution, 68, 76, 138
exchange rate, 2, 82, 166, 167, 168, 169, 182
exchange rate target, 182
exercise, 137, 151, 152
exogenous, ix, 28, 71, 85, 86, 90, 116, 118, 119, 120, 121, 139, 140, 142, 150, 157, 169
expenditures, 16, 68, 126, 129, 130, 136, 142, 145, 151, 154
experimental design, 76
externalities, vii, 1, 2, 3, 5, 6, 7, 9, 15, 32, 34, 40, 41, 47, 48, 53, 54, 55

F

financial, 2, 3, 6, 7, 9, 11, 17, 18, 41, 42, 43, 70, 71, 80, 81, 82, 84, 137, 160, 164, 171
financial crisis, 11, 43, 84, 164, 171
financial distress, 6
financial markets, 2, 6, 17

financial resources, 41
financial system, 43
fiscal deficit, 7, 13, 61
fiscal policy, 2, 4, 11, 12, 13, 14, 16, 61, 62, 70, 76, 77, 83, 88, 91, 96, 102, 103, 104, 105, 106, 107, 108, 109, 110, 113, 117, 130, 139, 164, 165, 166, 167, 184
fiscal surpluses, 77
flexible, 2, 118, 127, 138, 139, 156, 158, 165
floating exchange rates, vii, ix, 163
fluctuations, vii, 1, 5, 33, 35, 36, 44, 46, 47, 48, 52, 53, 54, 55, 165
full employment, ix, 116, 117, 132, 138, 146, 158
funding, 42, 43
funds, 42, 74, 82

G

global demand, 3, 28
global economy, 153, 157, 159, 180
government budget, 73, 93, 97, 118, 120, 127, 143, 164
government debt, ix, 6, 9, 11, 14, 27, 43, 62, 70, 89, 90, 91, 105, 108, 116, 117, 118, 131, 135, 138, 140, 143, 151, 153, 159, 160, 161, 163, 168, 169, 170, 171, 172, 173, 174, 176, 177, 178, 179, 180, 181, 187
government expenditure, 90
government spending, 12
governments, viii, 3, 5, 7, 8, 9, 10, 12, 13, 14, 15, 17, 32, 33, 36, 41, 42, 43, 71, 81, 115, 116, 164, 165, 166, 168, 175, 179, 180
growth, vii, viii, 7, 8, 29, 30, 32, 53, 56, 57, 65, 66, 67, 68, 69, 70, 71, 72, 73, 74, 75, 76, 77, 78, 79, 80, 83, 84, 85, 87, 88, 89, 90, 91, 94, 95, 96, 98, 100, 101, 103, 106, 108, 109, 110, 111, 113, 116, 117, 118, 119, 120, 121, 126, 130, 131, 135, 137, 138, 139, 140, 142, 144, 145, 150, 151, 152, 153, 154, 155, 156, 157, 158, 159, 160, 161, 168
growth factor, 126, 130, 131, 136, 142, 144, 145, 151, 152, 153, 155, 157, 158
growth models, 117
growth rate, 70, 74, 77, 85, 90, 91, 98, 101, 120, 121, 135, 137, 139, 151, 157, 158, 159
growth theory, 90, 126

H

health, 53, 92, 111
health care, 92
health risks, 111
human, ix, 90, 116, 119, 120, 139, 140, 142, 144, 151, 157, 158, 160
human capital, ix, 90, 116, 119, 120, 140, 142, 144, 151, 157, 158, 160
human capital accumulation, ix, 116, 119, 120, 139, 140, 157, 158
hypothesis, 76, 83, 93, 168, 176

I

imbalances, 66, 75, 82, 118, 160, 165
implosion, 117, 119
income, 17, 27, 33, 89, 90, 94, 95, 98, 99, 121, 122, 140, 160
income inequality, 160
income tax, 17, 27, 90
independence, 3, 5, 9, 33, 37, 40, 41, 42, 43, 48, 54, 164
independent variable, 176, 177, 179, 180
inefficiency, viii, 65, 69, 96, 101, 157
inflation, vii, ix, 3, 4, 10, 11, 12, 13, 14, 15, 16, 19, 21, 22, 25, 26, 30, 31, 32, 34, 42, 48, 83, 113, 163, 164, 165, 166, 168,

169, 170, 171, 173, 174, 175, 178, 180, 181, 184, 187
inflation target, vii, ix, 32, 163, 164, 165, 168, 169, 170, 171, 173, 174, 180, 181, 184
inflation targeting, vii, ix, 163, 164, 165, 168, 169, 170, 171, 173, 180, 181, 184
interest rate, vii, ix, 1, 2, 3, 4, 5, 6, 7, 8, 10, 11, 12, 13, 14, 15, 16, 17, 19, 26, 30, 31, 33, 34, 35, 37, 38, 39, 43, 45, 49, 51, 52, 53, 70, 74, 75, 78, 80, 82, 84, 86, 93, 94, 97, 104, 118, 120, 122, 136, 137, 138, 151, 157, 163, 165, 166, 167, 168, 169, 170, 173, 174, 175, 176, 177, 178, 179, 180, 181, 186
interest rates, ix, 3, 4, 6, 7, 11, 12, 13, 14, 15, 16, 35, 43, 45, 53, 84, 118, 137, 138, 163, 166, 167, 168, 169, 170, 174, 177, 178, 179, 180, 181
interest-factor elasticity, 119, 127, 152, 159
interior, 117, 119, 123, 124
interior maximum, 117, 119
internal, ix, 41, 88, 89, 109, 116, 117, 118, 120, 121, 156
intertemporal, 7, 13, 18, 22, 30, 34, 35, 36, 39, 40, 68, 75, 76, 81, 87, 91, 93, 101, 117, 118, 120, 122, 123, 124, 130, 131, 133, 137, 138, 140, 145, 149, 157, 158, 159, 164
intertemporal equilibrium dynamics, 117, 118, 120, 122, 131
investment, ix, 3, 7, 28, 38, 85, 89, 90, 92, 96, 97, 116, 118, 119, 120, 126, 127, 136, 137, 138, 139, 142, 143, 145, 151, 152, 153, 154, 155, 156, 157, 158, 159, 160
investment demand, 118, 153, 156, 157, 158
investors, 7, 81, 82, 84, 86, 118, 127, 168, 180
involuntary, v, ix, 115, 116, 117, 118, 120, 121, 135, 138, 139, 140, 150, 151, 156, 158, 160, 161
involuntary unemployment, v, ix, 115, 116, 117, 118, 119, 120, 121, 135, 138, 139, 140, 150, 151, 156, 158, 160, 161

K

Keynes, 117, 156, 161
Keynesian, 14, 30, 61, 62, 73, 74, 75, 76, 77, 78, 79, 81, 82, 84, 98, 101, 107, 117, 127, 152, 153, 154, 160, 161
Keynesian model, 14, 74, 84, 153

L

labor market, viii, 2, 5, 38, 41, 44, 54, 118, 128, 156
limits, v, vii, viii, 79, 110, 115, 116, 117, 118, 119, 120, 135, 137, 138, 139, 151, 155, 156, 157, 158
limits to public debt, vii, viii, 115, 116, 117, 118, 137, 138, 156, 158

M

macroeconomic models, 86
macroeconomics, 117, 159, 160
magnitude, 5, 135, 151, 158
management, 4, 43, 54, 68, 164, 172
marginal product, 23, 25, 26, 89, 93, 94, 95
market access, 99
market economy, 117, 139
market failure, 118
matrix, 133, 134, 149, 150
matter, iv, 73, 75, 77, 81, 175
maximum, 100, 117, 121, 123, 125, 127, 138, 153, 154, 158, 161
models, viii, 23, 66, 67, 73, 74, 75, 81, 82, 89, 91, 116, 127, 137, 138, 157, 158, 159, 182
monetary authority, 4, 10, 11, 12, 13, 34, 46

monetary policy, v, vii, 1, 2, 3, 4, 5, 8, 10, 11, 12, 13, 14, 15, 16, 26, 32, 33, 34, 35, 37, 38, 39, 40, 41, 43, 44, 45, 46, 47, 48, 49, 50, 51, 53, 54, 61, 62, 63, 76, 82, 83, 113, 164, 165, 167, 168, 169, 170, 173, 175, 177, 180, 181, 182, 183, 184, 185
monetary union, v, vii, 1, 2, 3, 4, 5, 6, 8, 9, 10, 11, 12, 13, 14, 15, 16, 19, 21, 22, 26, 29, 30, 31, 32, 33, 34, 35, 37, 38, 39, 40, 41, 46, 47, 48, 49, 50, 51, 52, 53, 54, 55, 56, 60, 61, 62, 104, 107, 112, 113
moratorium, 168
multiplier, 74, 78, 82

N

national debt, 6, 88
national income, 70, 88
national product, 72
negative consequences, 6, 7
negative effects, 75, 78, 80, 87, 89, 91
negative externality, 8
negative relation, 67
neo-classical growth, v, viii, 115, 116, 117, 118, 154
neo-classical growth model, v, viii, 115, 116, 117, 118, 154
net exports, 2, 38
net investment, 92
neutral, 75, 76, 79, 118, 157

O

old age, 121, 122, 123, 125, 127
open economy, 30, 166
operational independence, 42
optimization, 24, 45, 118, 120, 123, 124, 140
output gap, 31, 165, 166, 170, 173, 174, 175, 178, 180, 187
over-determinacy, 118
over-determinate, 118, 156
overlapping-generations, ix, 116, 117, 160

P

parameter, 30, 33, 119, 127, 131, 132, 135, 137, 138, 142, 146, 150, 151, 152, 153, 154, 155, 158, 170, 173
policy, vii, ix, 1, 2, 3, 5, 8, 11, 12, 13, 14, 16, 27, 34, 35, 36, 37, 38, 42, 43, 45, 46, 48, 53, 54, 62, 68, 73, 81, 83, 91, 96, 99, 100, 112, 113, 116, 120, 130, 131, 135, 137, 138, 139, 146, 151, 153, 155, 157, 160, 163, 164, 165, 166, 168, 169, 170, 173, 177, 178, 180, 183, 184, 185
policy choice, 68, 83
policy rate, 170
policy variables, 99
policymakers, 165, 174
population, 121, 140, 142
population growth, 140, 142
price stability, 3, 11, 12, 33, 42, 48, 164, 165, 166, 185
private good, 18, 29
private investment, 38, 160
private sector, 16, 77, 82, 92, 98, 117, 168
production costs, 26
production function, 23, 26, 92, 97, 117, 125, 129, 141
profit, 23, 24, 120, 125, 126, 129, 141, 143
public capital, 92, 93, 95, 96, 97
public debt, v, vii, viii, ix, 1, 2, 3, 5, 6, 7, 8, 9, 10, 11, 12, 13, 14, 15, 17, 27, 28, 31, 32, 33, 34, 35, 38, 39, 40, 42, 44, 45, 46, 47, 48, 50, 52, 53, 54, 57, 60, 65, 66, 67, 69, 70, 72, 73, 75, 83, 84, 85, 87, 89, 91, 92, 93, 95, 96, 97, 99, 100, 101, 102, 103, 104, 105, 106, 107, 108, 109, 110, 111, 115, 116, 117, 118, 119, 120, 121, 126, 129, 135, 136, 137, 138, 139, 151, 153, 154, 155, 156, 158, 160, 161, 163,

164, 165, 166, 167, 168, 175, 177, 182, 185
public debt management, v, 163, 164
public debt shocks, 2, 36, 40, 45, 47, 48, 50, 52, 53, 54
public finance, 15, 68, 69, 84, 87, 89, 95
public goods, 18, 23, 92
public investment, 96, 97
public sector, 42, 76, 93, 168, 170

R

rate, vii, ix, 1, 2, 3, 5, 6, 8, 10, 11, 12, 13, 14, 16, 17, 19, 24, 27, 30, 31, 32, 34, 35, 37, 38, 39, 40, 43, 45, 48, 49, 51, 52, 53, 57, 70, 72, 74, 75, 76, 77, 78, 80, 82, 84, 85, 86, 90, 91, 92, 93, 94, 95, 97, 98, 99, 100, 101, 116, 118, 119, 120, 121, 122, 125, 128, 130, 131, 135, 137, 139, 143, 145, 151, 153, 154, 156, 157, 158, 165, 166, 167, 168, 169, 170, 173, 174, 175, 176, 177, 178, 179, 180, 181, 182, 186, 187
rate of change, 72
real wage, 20, 37, 38, 50, 51, 55, 121, 138
response, vii, ix, 11, 13, 14, 90, 163, 166, 167, 169, 177, 178, 179, 180, 181
restrictions, 73, 74, 76, 127, 133, 182
retirement, 122, 124, 140
risk, 3, 4, 6, 8, 9, 10, 11, 13, 27, 46, 48, 60, 81, 82, 83, 85, 86, 87, 96, 101, 166, 168, 182
rules, 32, 42, 48, 62, 66, 71, 167, 169, 173, 175, 177, 179, 182, 184, 187

S

saddle-note bifurcation, 117
savings, ix, 74, 89, 90, 91, 116, 118, 119, 120, 121, 122, 124, 125, 127, 136, 138, 141, 154, 155, 156, 157, 158, 159
services, iv, 2, 18, 23, 125, 127
shock, viii, 2, 13, 14, 23, 26, 28, 29, 31, 35, 37, 38, 39, 46, 47, 49, 50, 51, 52, 53, 54, 76, 97, 98, 99, 100, 101, 157
smoothing, 33, 36, 37, 38, 39, 51, 52, 170, 173, 175, 178, 180
solution, 4, 32, 48, 54, 119, 120, 123, 124, 125, 131, 132, 133, 135, 139, 140, 146, 148, 149, 150, 175
spending, 14, 30, 35, 77, 142
spillovers, 7, 8, 9, 62
stability, ix, 4, 15, 38, 43, 54, 70, 71, 120, 133, 134, 149, 157, 164, 165, 167, 176, 180
stabilization, 13, 52, 55, 181
stock, 12, 73, 74, 75, 82, 88, 89, 92, 93, 94, 95, 101, 117, 126, 130, 138, 183
strategic position, 9, 10, 13
structure, 41, 118, 137, 168, 169, 170
substitution, 18, 20, 30, 31, 34, 35, 36, 39, 40, 52, 90
sustainability, viii, 4, 8, 65, 66, 69, 80, 81, 83, 84, 86, 87, 88, 89, 91, 96, 101, 164, 165, 168, 182

T

taxation, 4, 16, 27, 68, 69, 75, 83, 90, 92, 95, 96, 99
taxes, 10, 11, 70, 75, 77, 81, 82, 89, 90, 98, 121, 122
taxpayers, 75
Taylor rule, 32, 164, 165, 166, 167, 169, 173, 174, 175, 177, 178, 179, 180, 181, 187
threats, 66, 166, 176, 180
threshold, ix, 11, 66, 67, 69, 87, 96, 101, 109, 116, 119, 120, 140, 153, 155, 156, 158, 159
total factor productivity, 97, 125
trajectory, viii, 65, 68, 88, 101

transmission, 6, 8, 12, 53, 85

U

unemployment, vii, viii, 115, 116, 117, 118, 119, 120, 121, 124, 126, 128, 129, 130, 131, 135, 136, 138, 139, 145, 150, 151, 153, 155, 156, 157, 158, 161, 168
unemployment rate, ix, 116, 117, 118, 119, 120, 121, 128, 131, 136, 145, 151, 153, 156, 157, 161
unification, 2, 3, 6, 8, 9, 10, 12, 13, 60

V

variables, viii, 2, 15, 19, 23, 32, 50, 51, 52, 54, 58, 67, 81, 90, 91, 99, 117, 119, 133, 135, 143, 144, 150, 152, 154, 166, 169, 170, 173, 174, 175, 181
variations, 19, 20, 26, 28, 29, 33, 34, 35, 37, 39, 40, 49, 53, 158

W

wage rate, 118
wages, 4, 16, 118, 121
wealth, 10, 17, 18, 94
welfare, 7, 11, 12, 13, 14, 99

Y

yield, 6, 73, 78, 83, 96